THE TEARS OF OLIVE TREES

THE TEARS OF OLIVE TREES

ABDULKARIM AL MAKADMA

Edited by Wid Bastian

ISBN-13: 978-1514795811

Publisher: Genius Media, Inc.,

P.O. Box 4125, Logan, Utah 84323.

Illustrations by Rawya M. Wadi

Poetry courtesy of The Mahmoud Darwish Foundation

To Jewish people everywhere, including the Israelis, who have been the target of relentless persecution. The evils of racism, intolerance and blind hatred have been unjustly heaped upon them for 2000 years.

To Palestinian people who suffer from injustice, discrimination, occupation and oppression. We are being punished for a crime that we never committed. May God grant us relief from our suffering.

To my grandfather, AlShaikh, who was part of the last generation of historical Palestine. His vision was simple: peace, tolerance and basic human rights for everyone regardless of their race or religious affiliation.

To my father, Saeed, who in his great wisdom taught me infinite forgiveness, acceptance and resilience.

To the strongest woman ever, my beloved mother Miriam, who overcame every challenge in her life and taught me what it was to love someone with all your heart and soul.

To my wife, Sara, who has stood by me shoulder to shoulder, a beautiful lady whose heart is filled with unlimited kindness.

To my children; I tried my best to teach them the meaning of love and about the joy and rewards of living for others. I am proud and blessed to be the father of such wonderful people.

Table of Contents

All I Have xi

Author's Foreword xii

Chapter One: September 2011 1

Chapter Two: Mogadishu 9

Chapter Three: Hell on Earth 19

Chapter Four: Innocent Children 27

Chapter Five: Beit Daras, Palestine 1923-1947 37

Chapter Six: The Exile (Nakba) March 1948 45

Chapter Seven: Love in the Midst of Misery. 53

Chapter 8: 1965 Beach Boy 63

Chapter 9: Six-Day War (Naksat Huzeiran) June 5th, 1967 73

Chapter 10: Daily Life in Al Shati 1968-1971 81

Chapter 11: Night Terror 95

Chapter 12: The Soap Factory 1975. 105

Chapter 13: Leaving Gaza 1976. 119

Chapter 14: Tanta. 129

Chapter 15: Student Life and Sara 1979. 137

Chapter 16: Dr. Karim Returns to Gaza 1984. 147

Chapter 17: A Difficult Journey August 1984 155

Chapter 18: A New Life Begins 165

Chapter 19: A Most Welcome Addition 1987 173
Chapter 20: The Unthinkable Happens 181
Chapter 21: Battling a Greater Enemy 1993. 191
Chapter 22: An Innocent Victim 2001 205
Chapter 23: O' Canada July 2000. 217
Chapter 24: The Passport 229
Chapter 25: Dream House 2010 237
Chapter 26: Wedding Day 249
Chapter 27: 2011 A New Friend 259
Chapter 28: Gaza 2014. 279
Epilogue 283
Palestinian Terms and Vocabulary 289
Acknowledgments. 293
Social Media 295
A Short Biography of Dr. AbdulKarim S. Al Makadma 297

"O mankind, indeed we have created you from male and female and made you peoples and tribes that you may know one another. Indeed, the noblest of you in the sight of God is the most righteous of you."

Quran Verse (39:13)

All I Have

I never carried a rifle on my shoulder,
Nor did I pull a trigger.
All I have is a flute's melody.
A brush to paint my dreams,
A bottle of ink.
All I have is unshakeable faith,
And an infinite love for my people in pain.

Mahmoud Darwish

Author's Foreword

I AM A very fortunate person. Despite being born into the harshest of circumstances, my family and I are now prosperous and blessed. However, the vast majority of Palestinians remain an oppressed and suffering people. The great evil of the Nakba, the ethnic cleansing of Palestine that began in 1947, remains unaddressed and festers like an open sore in the Mid-East causing unending violence and strife. Millions of stateless Palestinians cry out for justice as do their parents and grandparents, the original refugees, now largely from the grave.

Over the decades, I have struggled to find an answer, a solution to this seemingly intractable problem. Destroying what has been built is not the answer. It was not the answer in 1948 either. Laying waste to one society to make room for another is a great evil. Palestine was not a barren land in 1948, awaiting a race of people to inhabit it and cultivate its treasures. Around a million Palestinians were forced from their homes in 1947-48 in a brutal, coordinated and systematic plan by an ethnic colonial movement to take the land they wanted for themselves. My father personally experienced the catastrophic displacement and dispossession of the Palestinian people. The chronic suffering and oppression that has followed to this day is a great injustice that must be acknowledged if we are to find peace.

I ask you to read this account with an open mind and without prejudice or pre-conceived notions. I invite you to put yourself in Saeed's place or my place and think how you would feel if these tragedies befell you and those you love. These pages tell the true story of my family - our suffering and joy, poverty and prosperity, tragedies and triumphs. We stayed together despite enormous hardships. We supported each other no matter what. Each in our own way, we were all loyal to our father's vision of a world where love and respect were more powerful than hatred and violence.

We all bleed the same blood and shed the same tears. I wonder, what would Palestine look like if the political powers at be chose a peaceful and civilized alternative to ethnic segregation? What an incredible nation we could build together, Jews and Muslims and Christians, Palestinians all, if we worked as one in cooperation and peace. I hope in some small way that my family's story will be a step away from an endless, violent struggle that will only produce more suffering and towards a future for the Holy Land based on equality, dignity and the rule of law.

Karim and Sara in Peterborough, Canada

Chapter One

SEPTEMBER 2011

Think of Others

As you fix your breakfast, think of others.
Don't forget to feed the pigeons.
As you fight your wars, think of others.
Don't forget those who desperately demand peace.
As you pay your water bill, think of others
who drink the clouds' rain.
As you return home, to your home, think of others.
Don't forget those who live in tents.
As you sleep and count planets, think of others.
There are people without any shelter to sleep.
As you express yourself using all metaphorical expressions,
think of others who lost their rights to speak.
As you think of others who are distant, think of you and say:
'I wish I was a candle to fade away the darkness'.

Mahmoud Darwish

IN THE MIDST of a crowd of desperate, starving people, the reporter spoke his well-rehearsed lines into the camera. He seemed almost oblivious, detached from the horror that surrounded him. His tone and demeanor expressed that he had done this before, that he knew where he was and it was all too familiar to him.

The walking skeletons all around the reporter were disinterested in what he did or said. They were too emaciated to care about anything other than searching for their next meal. Their wafer-thin, jet-black bodies were covered in rags if they were clothed at all.

"Somalia remains one of the most troubled regions on the planet," the reporter said in the monotone manner of television newsmen everywhere. "Refugees by the thousands are pouring into these camps. The government in Mogadishu has little or no resources available to support the relief efforts here. Time is running out for most of the people living in these camps as—"

Karim clicked off the television and wiped his mouth. Although there was still food on his plate, his appetite was gone. He was both sad and angry. What he watched on TV had triggered memories, some of which he would rather forget but he knew were ingrained in his soul forever. He was conscious of the fact that he had just been blessed with a hearty breakfast—a meal the unfortunate souls in Somalia would look upon as a feast. He was disgusted, not with himself, but with the world around him. There was simply no reason, no valid one anyway, in his mind for such suffering to take place anywhere on the planet. An average North American or large European city threw away enough good food every month to feed all of the needy in Somalia for a year.

But such is not the way of the world. Resources are allocated by economics and the whims of governments, not by genuine need. Most see suffering in faraway lands and ask what is wrong with them. Why can they not take care of themselves?

Granted, Karim argued with himself, as a whole, Western society gives millions every year to charities and tens of millions more in foreign aid, which does help advance progress in the developing world. Perhaps I am too hard on the West, he chided himself. After all he was a Western man now, at least by adoption. Were people from other parts of the world more charitable? Probably less so, he had to admit.

Even though he had never been there, when he closed his eyes and sat back in his chair, he could see the Somali camps in his mind's eye. He stood with the suffering people, heard their cries for relief and felt the hot sun beat down relentlessly on his head. Hope was absent in these places or in short supply. It mattered little if the camp was in Somalia, Sudan or any other place; they shared the same awful common characteristics: tents lined up row after row, parched earth beneath the people's feet and lines of filthy human beings waiting their turn for a quick shower, a bowl of tasteless mush or the slim chance to see a doctor who probably had no medications with which to treat them.

While the world knew all about these horrible places, seeing the suffering on television was like watching a Hollywood film; it just was not real. Someone could not smell the stink of an overflowing outdoor latrine on TV, experience the horror of watching a child die in his arms from malnutrition or dysentery or hear the near constant wailing of those suffering from injury and disease.

As a physician Karim had worked in several refugee camps, doing his best to alleviate whatever suffering he could. By serving the people, he relieved some of the emotional turmoil he experienced. Part of him felt guilty that he was so blessed while others struggled for survival. He was also angry that the privileged people on the planet, those who consumed most of the resources and lived a life of abundance, did so little to help others who wanted for the basic necessities of life.

His wife, Sara, washed dishes and did not pay close attention to what her husband was doing. Her focus was on the day ahead and how she was going to manage her household responsibilities. The sudden silence of the television caught her attention. She looked over and saw Karim first rubbing his forehead and then gazing outside with a blank stare at the fall splendor of their new home's backyard. She knew he was troubled.

"Would you like something else to eat? More tea perhaps?" She put down the dishes and walked slowly towards him, wiping her hands on a towel.

"I'm going to Somalia," Karim said, without offering an explanation. He continued to stare outside at the late fall day. The wind had picked up, and the sky was cloudy; rain was in the forecast.

"What?"

"I'm going to Somalia. I cannot sit here in my comfortable home and do nothing to help them."

From past experience, Sara knew that he was not just talking. He was dead serious.

"Will you consider all the issues involved before you make your decision?"

"Such as?"

"How about our life in Canada? You fought so hard to bring us to this country, Karim. Now that we are here and established and we have a normal, peaceful life, why must you run off and leave us behind?" Sara knew that her tone was not completely fair, but still she thought he should not go.

"No. I would never 'run off.' We have been blessed, no doubt. That makes us all the more responsible to give back, to return a measure of our good fortune to those in such terrific need."

"Somalia is a warzone. It is not just a question of helping refugees; there is real danger there."

"We were both raised in a warzone, Sara. We know how to protect ourselves in such situations."

"Why you?" she continued to protest. "Can't you just raise money, perhaps organize things from here? You could go to the States, maybe—"

"And be like all of the other people I see around me? Turn away from the suffering? Make it someone else's problem?"

"You are making me sound selfish for wanting my husband to be at home. I've sacrificed too, Karim. When is enough finally going to be enough?" Sara was visibly upset now. Behind her somewhat controlled anger was a genuine worry for her husband's welfare. She tossed her dishrag in the sink and walked out through the French doors and onto the patio.

She absolutely loved her backyard. They had two lovely, large oaks in the back, both of which were in their full fall glory; their orange and red leaves were dribbling off in the breeze. The grass was still green. The air was crisp but not cold. Karim followed her out to the backyard a moment later.

"I know you, Karim. Your heart is absolutely in the right place. But so is mine," Sara said, gently removing herself from her husband's embrace. "I am very opposed to you going to Somalia and for many reasons."

"I feel compelled, Sara. Would you have me ignore these people? I cannot turn away from such need when I know that I can help them."

"You are asking me to ignore my good sense, to willingly say, 'Go ahead and go somewhere where human life has little value.' You have a family, Karim. We matter too."

"What if Saeed had said that in 1948? He is my example. We are called to a higher standard."

"Yes, what if Saeed had said, 'I can only give so much'? What if he had retained some wealth for his family? You might not have been raised in such a horrible place, your brothers and sister—"

"You don't mean that, Sara. You're upset and understandably so. My father's generosity saved many lives."

"You start my day off by making such a bold pronouncement? I'll see you later this evening when you return." She respectfully kissed her husband on the cheek, headed for the French doors and then turned. "And you must tell your son. He will not be pleased."

It was nearly 8 a.m. Karim was running late for work. He would have to ask the hospital for an extended leave of absence, but given where he was going and why he was traveling there, he was confident they would grant his request.

Sara's feelings were of great concern to him. He did not want her to think that he was dismissing her out of hand as if she had no say in what he did with his life. He had expected her to have concerns, but she was not just worried; she was adamantly opposed to him going.

Before when he had volunteered to serve as a physician in refugee camps, she had always been supportive. She was worried as a wife was apt to worry, but she was not against his going. Was Somalia so different than the other places he had been to? Desperate poverty breeds violence; Somalia was nothing new.

"So, your studies are going well this term?" Karim asked his son.

"Yes. I am beginning to see the light at the end of the tunnel. Thank God medical school is almost over," Salam said.

"You will probably yearn for the easy days of med school when you experience the long and trying hours of your internship."

"We aren't here to talk about me."

Karim sighed and looked over at his wife. "Yes, that's true I suppose."

"Dad, going to Somalia is a bad idea, period."

"You base this on your vast experience in the world, son?" Karim argued, a bit sarcastically.

Salam knew that he had lost this argument before it began. "I don't have to visit hell to know it exists. I happen to know a few things too, Dad."

"You are anything but stupid, but don't be fooled into thinking that there is any substitute for experience. As you know, I have been to these types of places before. I have no illusions. I know what to expect."

"The camera doesn't lie," Salam said as he opened his laptop. "Let me show you exactly where you're going, father."

He had collected pictures of Somalia from various Internet sites and other sources and also downloaded several articles and government reports on current conditions in the country. The slideshow was indeed gruesome. He showed his father images of shredded Somali fighters tossed in shallow graves by the side of the road, pictures of roaming gangs of thugs who called themselves militia preying on people and beating them senseless and photos of the starving and near dead who were stacked by the thousands, like cordwood into overcrowded tent cities. Then he presented highlights from some reports from credible sources, all of which said that traveling to Somalia was a dangerous proposition.

"That was a very convincing report, son," Karim said. "If I were your instructor, I would give you the highest mark. Salam, I really get it, but you must see my point of view as well."

"Why won't you at least listen to him?" Sara said.

"I have been listening very attentively. I also received permission today to take a six-month leave of absence from the hospital. They will even donate money and supplies to the relief efforts. I leave for Somalia in three weeks."

"I thought we were going to discuss this first, as a family."

"We are discussing it," Karim said.

"This is not a discussion." Tears now welled up in her eyes. "You've made your choice. What we think is unimportant to you."

"Nothing matters more to my heart than what you both think and feel. I love you both very much. This is a question of a higher—"

"You are needed here," Sara said. "You're not young anymore, Karim. Neither am I."

"How can we ask others to do what we are not willing to do?"

"It's pointless, Mom," Salam said, as he closed his computer and returned it to its case. "Dad's going, and that's that. He will not be influenced by us."

"I have been in contact with the umbrella humanitarian organization. They will fly me to Kenya, and from there I can fly to Mogadishu. There is a hotel in town where I can live in relative safety. Rest assured, I will take no unnecessary chances."

Sara rose from her chair, walked over to her husband and kissed him on the top of his head. "Now we shall eat the marvelous meal I've spent all day preparing. No more talk of this. Tonight we enjoy each other in peace."

Mogadishu Beach

Chapter Two

MOGADISHU

I Have the Wisdom

I have the wisdom of one condemned to die,
I possess nothing so nothing can possess me
and have written my will in my own blood:
'O inhabitants of my song: trust in water'
and I sleep pierced and crowned by my tomorrow…
I dreamed the earth's heart is greater
than its map,
more clear than its mirrors
and my gallows.
I was lost in a white cloud that carried me up high
as if I were a hoopoe
and the wind itself my wings.
At dawn, the call of the night guard
woke me from my dream, from my language:
You will live another death,
so revise your last will,
the hour of execution is postponed again.

I asked: Until when?
He said: Wait till you have died some more.
I said: I possess nothing so nothing can possess me
and have written my will in my own blood:
'O inhabitants of my song: trust in water.'

Mahmoud Darwish

AS SARA CAREFULLY packed for her husband, she struggled with competing emotions. Part of her felt ashamed—not ashamed, embarrassed—that she had voiced her views so demonstrably to her husband and son. She was not raised to keep her feelings to herself, but she knew that Karim thought she did not mean everything she said. She was also sure that her husband was confused by her strident objections to his going to Somalia; she believed that he expected more support from her.

Going over her checklist, she made sure that he had all of his prescription medications—for back pain primarily—antimalarial, antacids, instant coffee and tea, mosquito nets, the correct type and amount of clothes, medical texts and ten extra copies of his own authored books on the basics of pediatric medicine to aid the young Somali physicians. Where he was going, supplies would be difficult to come by and tough to ship to him promptly.

Regardless of her fears and desires, Karim was going to Somalia. This was the man she married; he was by no means acting out of character. But it was different this time. This trip needed to be his last one to such a terrible place. Sara felt this with all of her heart. She had never really wanted him to be anywhere but by her side, in their home being her husband, but now she desperately wanted to him to believe as she did—that he needed to settle, that he deserved to settle.

As she finished her work, she said a silent prayer asking that this would be the last time she had to pack for her husband to travel to some distant and dangerous land alone. But that was a hope, not a certainty. Despite how much she respected her husband's motives and actions, she could not shake the feeling that his going to Somalia was the wrong thing to do. This feeling was strong and dominated her thoughts like never before.

On the day of Karim's departure, he and Sara were well dressed. Given their humble past, traveling was still a big deal to them, so a certain amount of respect was due. He had on a suit and tie, and Sara wore a lady's formal pantsuit with a navy blue headscarf that matched the color of her shoes. She never wore makeup—she considered cosmetics to be immodest and for young women only.

As they drove to Pearson International Airport in Toronto, they talked only about pleasant subjects. There was no discussion about the trip itself or what each of them had to do over the coming weeks; those subjects had already been covered in depth. They were not full of joy, but they were not downcast either. They had done this before.

Neither Karim nor Sara was fond of long, elaborate goodbyes. When they reached the airport, he stepped from the car then hugged and kissed his wife respectfully. Like always, he left her on a positive note, telling her to finish her painting and complete her course. If Sara was not painting or writing, she was studying something. Neither of them was fond of sitting and doing nothing; they both preferred to be active all the time. That was part of the reason Karim had to go to Somalia—he was a doer. If they were not people of action, they would never have gotten out of such dark places. Karim turned, gestured to his wife and waved farewell.

As always, she prayed as she watched her husband go. "I bestow on you God's protection, for He is the protector of whose deposits are never lost."

However this goodbye was unlike any other Sara had given her husband before. She was nervous. Smiling at her husband on the outside, inside her thoughts were flooded with unpleasant memories and worries that she might never see him again.

The flight from Canada to Kenya was uneventful except for a stop in London and another in Cairo to transfer planes. All Karim had to do was walk through the customs line and show his passport, and they let him straight through. How different this was from the days when he had Palestinian credentials, which did nothing more than document his status as a refugee. Back then, he had no real citizenship, and everywhere he went outside of the Middle East, the authorities looked on him with suspicion when he showed his inadequate papers. They questioned his every move, despite the fact that he was the same man as today, a physician traveling abroad to help others in need.

His Canadian passport made all the difference. It was such a simple document, something everyone in the Western world took for granted as their birthright. But Karim knew how valuable it was. Now he could not only move, but live, freely. It was a true blessing from God that he could travel to Africa to help his fellow man with the comfort of knowing that his wife and family were safe back in North America.

Once in Nairobi, he had a couple of hours to board a plane for Somalia. Jomo Kenyatta Airport was a relatively modern facility, roughly comparable to a Western airport. He had no trouble retrieving his bags and finding his departure gate. But when he departed from this gate, Karim knew that he was leaving the First World behind. He called and left a message for Sara, telling her that he had arrived safely in Kenya. He also purchased a Kenyan SIM card for his cell phone, a requirement if he was going to be able to use it in Somalia.

Most of the journey was in modern jet, but the final leg would be completed in an old propeller plane. While the aircraft had seen much better days, it appeared sound. The porters loaded the luggage on board. They were anything but delicate in this procedure; they tossed the wide assortment of bags around like they were boxes of rocks. He had expected this, and his bags were packed to withstand rough treatment.

When he walked up the stairs and into the main cabin, he saw that the plane was filled with desperate-looking people. It was brutally hot inside the aircraft, much warmer than it was outside. It was stifling too; there was no air flow and would not be any until the plane started its engines. Within seconds, he began to sweat profusely. People were talking loudly and moving around the cabin with no regard for others. The rancid smell of the unwashed surrounded him. He knew this was but a taste of what was to come.

When the plane took off, it strained to climb into the sky. Karim feared that they may not make it far. Every part of the old crate shook. A frightening rattling competed with the chorus of loud voices from the passengers. He white-knuckled the departure until the plane reached cruising altitude and leveled off, when the clamor abated, at least to some degree. He seemed to be the only one who was concerned for his safety; everyone else was busy shouting and roaming around the cabin like they were in an outdoor marketplace. One patch of rough air, even moderate turbulence, and he would be treating the first patients of his trip on the plane.

For two hours Karim sat in his seat petrified, praying that he would at least get the opportunity to treat a few children before he was killed. Then, thankfully, the plane began its descent. The flight from hell was almost over but not quite yet.

When the plane touched down, he heard violent banging noises. His impression was that the aircraft was crashing. This was not his first time flying in an old prop plane. In the 1990s he had ridden on a few less than sturdy birds operated by the Palestinian Authority, but this experience was far more frightening. Was the landing gear down? Had they hit something on the runway? What could be causing such a terrible, gut-wrenching noise? But again, Karim was the only passenger in panic mode. Everyone else was sitting in their seat, unconcerned. After a moment, he assumed that everything was okay.

He quickly disembarked when the port-side passenger door opened. Karim took a moment to thank God for His mercy, and then he laughed inside knowing that this was only the beginning of his trials. He took a deep breath of Somali air—it was a hot and sticky late afternoon, but it at least it was not the noxious mixture he had been forced to breathe for the last two hours.

Even though he had never been to Somalia before, Karim generally knew what to expect next. Most of the Third World airports he had been to were crowded and chaotic. The main terminal building was a two-story structure with an airport tower on one side. The only paved roads he could see were the runways themselves, and the concrete on the runways was weathered and cracked. He needed to find his contact as quickly as possible to avoid problems and was able to make his way to the foyer near the front entrance of the main terminal, confident that this was where he was supposed to connect with his chaperone.

After a couple of minutes of anxious waiting, Karim saw a man holding up a sign with his name on it.

He was a middle-aged African, and thankfully, he spoke English. "Dr. Karim?"

"Yes, you must be from the aid agency."

"My name is Baako. Welcome to Somalia, Doctor."

They shook hands, and immediately Karim was more at ease. Baako asked Karim to follow him back inside the building. The noise inside the airport was even more deafening than it had been on the plane, an intense mixture of shouting and aircraft revving up their jets and propellers less than a hundred meters away.

They passed rows of people who were lined up for something. A few of them had been on his flight from Kenya. Then airport guards armed with AK-47s were shouting and gesturing for them to move in unison back onto the tarmac. Many resisted being herded and prodded at gunpoint, so they shouted and shoved in protest. Karim thought that a little restraint and even kindness would have gone a long way here. But the guards were simply doing their job, and there seemed to be no malice in their actions.

One of these airport guards stopped Baako and Karim. Baako and the guard exchanged a few words in a language Karim did not understand. Then the guard motioned with his weapon, urging them to move on. Moments later, Karim and Baako walked through a door. They entered what was obviously a baggage claim area.

"What did the guard want?" There was less of a din in the baggage room, although it was by no means quiet.

"They are what pass for police here, Doctor. Once they knew who I was, they let us go. Now, let's check in and then retrieve your bags."

Baako led him to the rear of the baggage area. There was a sign above a door in English that read, "VIP Lounge". They stepped inside. The VIP Lounge was nothing much to speak of—a couple of sofas, a table and a few chairs. Thankfully, it was quiet. They sat down. Baako opened his thermos and offered Karim some tea, which he gratefully accepted.

"How was the flight in?"

"Interesting." Karim tried to be diplomatic. "It has been said that any flight is a safe flight if you're not being shot at."

Baako laughed. "They don't waste their ammunition on passenger planes around here, Dr. Karim. Good thing too; one stray bullet could probably take down most of the relics that fly into Mogadishu. Shortly a customs man will—"

A man in a black uniform with an unreadable name tag walked in the door, greeted Baako and gestured to the doctor. Karim knew what he wanted: his passport. He had handed it to the man, who took it over to the table, quickly examined the document and stamped it. Then he left.

"That's it?" Karim asked.

"Somalia does not have much of a customs service. If you're not carrying weapons and you're from the West, they ask few questions."

"I see. Now we find my bags?"

"They will not be lost for long," Baako said.

"They're lost?"

"In this airport all bags start off being lost. No worries, we will find them."

Karim was worried. The last thing he needed to do was to have to replace his personal items before he even got started at the clinic. They walked back into the baggage claim area. It appeared that there was a minimal organization to the baggage sorting process. People were combing through 15 separate heaps and tossing luggage to and fro.

"Ah," Baako said, after looking around for a few seconds. "Your luggage is over here."

Karim had no idea how Baako knew this because there were no signs indicating which flights were associated with which pile. The mound of plastic bags, boxes and some actual luggage that Baako was headed for was the largest on the floor. A porter of some kind was not so gently tossing luggage onto the unorganized mass. Karim's flight was one of the most recent to arrive, so it might have been logical to assume his bags were in the largest and newest pile.

"I am looking for?" Baako asked.

"A black, hard-shell suitcase and a red fabric bag. Both pieces are locked and tagged."

Baako dove into the pile along with the ten or so other people who were also searching for their luggage. It was not long before he spotted Karim's bags and pulled them out for inspection.

"Is everything in order?"

"Yes, thankfully," Karim said. The luggage was intact, the locks still firmly in place.

"Then we should go. Remaining here too long is not a good idea."

"Problems?"

"Not yet, but people with real luggage attract attention. We do not want to become a target for thieves. Let's go," Baako said.

They walked from the baggage area for a short distance to the curb. The chaos in front of the airport was equal to that inside.

"We're over here." Baako gestured towards an older Toyota Land-cruiser that was parked on the outer rim, away from the crush of vehicles that were trying to get close to the curb.

Inside the car were two armed men, who smiled at them when they approached. Baako and Karim stowed the bags and then climbed into the back seat.

"Where to?" Karim asked.

"The hotel. Let's get you settled in. We will take you to the camp tomorrow."

Camp Amal, Somalia

Chapter Three

HELL ON EARTH

Brand of Slaves

Rome is skin to us as if imposed fate
Its name is branded on our backs yet
As prisoners' numbers and scourges that's Rome
Rome dismantles our brands under her want
Unarmed slaves smashed the royal court
Babylon is around our neck,
As branded returning captive prisoners
Attires of tyrant were changed entirely
That he was survived after death.
If they still believe on him, he won't die
We died and lived but the way is the same
Africa at our dancing party is as drum and naked fire
It is as songstress desire nearby the smock of her fire
One day I played pipe fluently of fallen trunks.
I let the snake dancing until sleep
And I threw its canine away
Africa and Asia then shall meet at a new dance.

Mahmoud Darwish

MOGADISHU'S ADEN ABBE Airport borders on the Indian Ocean. The city is a mile or so to the north and east. As the Toyota pulled out of the terminal and headed towards the main road into town, Karim noticed wrecked homes and buildings, many with no roofs and interiors. They looked as if a bomb had exploded inside. Everywhere he saw worried, black faces on slim, tired bodies—it seemed as if the entire country was in desperate need of food, clothing, shelter and, inevitably, medical care.

He had looked at these images recently—on his son's laptop. Seeing the wasteland that was once a very different Mogadishu up close and personal reminded him of places he had been before. The scene around him was appalling but not unfamiliar. Whether it was Palestine, Kenya, Sierra Leone or Iraq, in many ways it was all the same. If people were hell-bent on destruction, they often got what they were after.

There were exceptions to the ruins—enclaves of intact buildings, most surrounded by high walls and armed soldiers. Security was the top priority here. The only way to protect property was by constant vigilance and force. Again, this was what Karim expected to see. In every Third World society there were a few elites who managed to thrive amidst chaos.

Inside the city proper the scene was the same—most of the buildings were completely gutted, except for those guarded by militants. In the center of town was their destination, a hotel called Shamo. It was a modest place by Western standards, but it was the best hotel in Mogadishu. Karim's first impression was that it was better than he had hoped for, at least from the outside.

The Landcruiser pulled over quickly to the curb across from the main door. The hotel was relatively well finished, but the street was only sand. A man opened the door, and they got out. Both Baako and the driver were carrying AK-47s as they escorted Karim inside. Once he was safely delivered, the driver ran back to the Toyota and sped off as if he was fleeing gunfire, creating a sand cloud in his wake.

It was early evening, but Karim was tired. He had been traveling for almost 30 hours. In the lobby of the hotel, as Baako was checking him in, Karim was greeted by some young Somalis who worked in the relief organization. They were healthy, or relatively so, by Somali standards, and they were overjoyed that he had agreed to work at the camp. They briefly talked about what they would do tomorrow and how best to get him set up in the clinic.

There were also a few Western businessmen off in a corner by themselves in the lobby. Armed escorts kept an eye out for anyone who might disturb their evening conversation. They were in a bubble, sequestered in a little world all of their own amidst the chaos. Without question Karim knew what they were doing—where there was scarcity, there was potential for great profit. No doubt these men and others like them were stepping in to fill a void in commerce, to supply anything and everything wanted and needed by the few Somalis who still had the money to pay.

Baako came back with the room key, and they went upstairs to the hotel room. It was small but tolerably clean. The linen looked like it was regularly washed. When Karim turned on the water in the bathroom sink, it flowed and was not too brown.

"Are you hungry?"

"No. I have some food in my bag if I need to eat." Karim pointed at his duffel. "I would like to take a shower and get some sleep."

"Yes, that's a good plan. Doctor, I—"

"Karim, please. Call me Karim."

"Karim, please do not venture out of the hotel unescorted. Not in the daytime and certainly never at night. In here you're safe, as safe as you can be, but the streets are very dangerous."

"I'll stay put, I promise."

"Also, gunfire is not uncommon in the city—again, more so at night. If you hear AK-47s going off, do not panic. They are likely not directing their attention to the Shamo."

"I have heard gunfire many times. This is not my first trip to a war zone."

"Until tomorrow." Baako extended his hand.

Karim shook his hand. "Be safe. See you in the morning."

All he wanted to do was unpack, take a shower and pass out. But he knew that he must do something else first. He opened his backpack and removed the small package he had purchased in the Nairobi airport. He took out his ancient Qteck and inserted the new SIM card. The only reliable cell service was from Nairobi; there were no Somali cell networks.

The phone sprang to life. He had service. This was another relief. At least now he knew that he could keep in touch with his wife and family on a regular basis. He dialed his home in Canada.

Sara answered after one ring. Before Karim could say a word, she said, "Thank God you are safe. Are you all right?"

"Yes, I am fine. What matters is you. How are you doing?"

"There is no problem here. Salam asked me to tell you to be very careful. He is watching the events in Somalia on the Internet. He is very concerned."

"I am being protected. Tell Salam he need not worry."

"May we speak daily?" she asked.

"If we keep it short, we can do so. Sara, you take care. I will do the same."

"Call me tomorrow evening then?"

"Yes, God willing. I'm off to the shower now and then to bed."

"Sleep well. Good night."

"All my love, Sara. Always."

He hung up the phone. He had to keep the conversations short, but for his wife to rest peacefully, he needed to reassure her that he was alive and well on a daily basis.

The shower was lukewarm, and the water did not have the freshest aroma. But he loved it nonetheless. He dried off, put on his nightclothes and passed out as soon as his head hit the pillow.

A little after 7 a.m. Karim was up, ready and waiting in the lobby. There were a few volunteers from the relief organization in the foyer with him, a couple of whom he recognized from the night before. But the room was filled mostly with heavily armed men. They were not in uniform—they were militia, not part of the regular Somali army. Karim was not sure if Somalia had an organized national armed force. Certainly groups, factions, did. Clearly they were in charge here, not the central government.

Around 7:30 a pleasant looking young man, perhaps 30 or so, came through the door. He introduced himself to Karim.

"I'm Doctor Mensah," the light-skinned African said. "You must be Dr. Karim."

"Pleasure to meet you."

Dr. Mensah led Karim into a back room of the Shamo on the main floor where breakfast was being prepared and served. A nurse, a social worker, an administrator and a driver joined them, and they talked as they ate.

"We are so pleased that you are here, Dr. Karim," the nurse said. "You are a true blessing."

"Where are we headed today?" Karim asked.

"To Camp Amal," Dr. Mensah replied. "That is where your skills are most urgently needed."

"How far is the camp from here?"

"Forty-five minutes, depending on the conditions. The amount of checkpoints and interference varies from day to day," the administrator answered.

"We have a security team in place to escort us to and from the camp. The factions generally leave medical teams alone. There have been exceptions," the social worker added.

"Exceptions?" Karim asked as he sipped his tea.

"Six months ago a medical convoy was attacked by an unorganized group of thugs. Five of our people were killed. When the organized factions found out about the attack the retributions against those responsible were severe. We have not had a repeat of this ugliness though, thanks to Allah," the administrator explained.

After breakfast, the group assembled in the lobby and then climbed into the waiting vehicles. Idling in front of the Shamo was a medium, cube-style truck, carrying supplies Karim assumed, an old SUV and two small pickup trucks filled with armed men.

As the convoy made its way through the streets of Mogadishu going south towards the camp, the pleasant aroma of saltwater coming through the open window lifted Karim's spirits a bit. But he knew where he was.

He had no illusions about the desperate conditions in Somalia. Drought, famine and war had ravaged this country for years. That was why he was here.

When people saw the trucks and the insignia identifying them as medical relief vehicles, they chased them. They were running through the streets and shouting at the convoy, begging for help. Karim's heart went out to them, but prudence was a virtue for a reason. The trucks could not stop to assist them. If they did they would quickly be overrun by a hoard of black skeletons with sunken eyes. Even here, perhaps especially here, there had to be some order to the madness, or no good could be done.

As he watched the surreal world of Somalia pass by him from the relative safety of the truck, his heart was filled with empathy. The concept of injustice weighed heavily on his mind, as it always did when he arrived in forlorn places. Given the abundance of the earth, no one on the planet needed ever go hungry. People created this horror, not God or nature; greed, international indifference and the scourge of war were responsible for this pocket of abject misery.

How long will we allow this to continue? Karim silently asked himself. The answer to Somalia's problems was not simply more aid. At best his efforts were like putting a gauze bandage on cancer, but that was all he could do. Until people made the decision to quit being cruel and violent towards each other, there would always be places like this: open sores infecting an otherwise beautiful planet, shameful reminders that human beings are often selfish and shortsighted creatures. He was not interested in assigning blame; he wanted solutions. All the blame game did was infect an already serious wound.

The eyes of the people staring at him as they passed were passive and dark, seemingly resigned to the fact that their lives would be short and painful. When they opened their mouths to yell, Karim saw their missing and yellow teeth. These mouths may never have been blessed by a toothbrush, he said to himself silently. Certainly none of these poor souls had ever visited a dentist.

Kilometer after kilometer, the view was the same until finally the crush of people shuffling through the rubble was interrupted by a stretch of open countryside. The effect of the drought was most noticeable here. It looked as if the rains had never fallen in Somalia. The ground was yellowish brown, cracked and obviously parched. Food could not be grown under such conditions.

They reached a checkpoint and stopped. The soldiers wore different identifying clothing here, clearly not part of the faction that was escorting the convoy. For a few minutes, Karim watched nervously as the soldiers—all of them had to be less than 25 years old, and most were teenagers—inspected the vehicles and spoke with Dr. Mensah. Shortly after that, the convoy continued on its way.

A short time later a throng of people appeared again. This time the crowd was headed in a definite direction, and they did not chase after the convoy. That meant that they were getting closer to the camp.

Karim and the children of Camp Amal

Chapter Four

INNOCENT CHILDREN

Hope

Still there is on thy saucers remains of honey
Kick out the flies so that you can protect the honey
Still there is on their vines clusters of grapes
O, guarders of vines, drive foxes out,
Therefore, grapes will be ripe healthy.
Still there is at thy houses mat and door
Close up the way of wind away out of thy children
Perhaps they can sleep
Wind is very cold and you should close doors.
Still there is effluent blood in their hearts,
You may keep it and don't throw away
A new fetus is still unborn waiting the dawn
Still there is at thy hearth remains of firewood
Still there is coffee and a bundle of blaze

Mahmoud Darwish

WHEN THEY PULLED up to the rusty metal fence of Camp Amal, the soldiers jumped out of the trucks and opened the gates. It was a huge open-air prison, one where the inmates begged to get inside. The barbed wire fence was there to keep people out, not to keep people in. Amal was a crude form of temporary salvation. Inside the dirty brown gates, which had been battered and repaired several times, was rudimentary food and shelter. After they had driven inside, the militia soldiers closed the gates behind them.

Karim tried to get a sense of where he was. He was surrounded on all sides by rows of white tents. They were separated by a distance of only half a meter. Small bushes, some with a hint of green on them but most only dead sticks, dotted the landscape. There was nothing like pavement for the refugees to walk on other than the stony ground. Most were barefoot.

As soon as they arrived, the refugees began to assemble. They knew that every truck entering the camp had something they desperately needed: food, water, medical supplies or other basic provisions. From experience, they also knew that if they waited too long to gather at the appropriate place they would likely miss out on whatever was being distributed.

One of the militia soldiers then shouted something in a language Karim did not understand, but the meaning was clear: we have nothing to dispense; go back to your tents. Most of the crowd complied, but more than a few stragglers stood by, intent on judging for themselves if the new convoy was carrying anything they valued.

Dr. Mensah then gave Karim a brief tour of the camp. It was not a tour really but rather a sampling of the living conditions; the camp was huge and far too big to be walked in a short period of time. They moved to where the rows of tents ended and a cooking area began. Above fires, men stirred large pots of what he assumed was food. The smell was anything but appetizing. Away from the cooking area, mothers and children were lining up to receive their food ration. In their hands they held dirty plates and bowls that were beyond unsanitary.

A signal from one of the cooks started the women and children moving towards a cooking pot. He walked over to investigate what was being served. This cooking pot, and the others as well he soon discovered, was filled with a thick, gray colored substance.

"What is this?"

"Beans cooked for hours in boiling water. It's the best meal we can serve here right now. They eat it two or three times a day, if it's available," Dr. Mensah answered.

Although Karim found the beans repulsive, one by one the refugees lined up for the gruel and received their share. No one complained about the mush or even made a negative expression. Children were dressed, half-dressed or mostly undressed. Women wore traditional Somali clothes with bright colors, including drapes and scarves. Some wore blankets around their heads and shoulders. Karim wondered how many had lived decent lives until recently. How many had lost loved ones and homes? Were they suffering more from the memories of things lost or from their current circumstances?

"Can we move on?" he asked.

"Yes, let's keep going. Over there are the water towers." Dr. Mensah pointed to two metal towers with tanks on the top. "They help themselves to the water. We try to replenish the supply daily."

As they walked away from the cooking area Karim asked, "What about garbage?"

"We collect it and dump in a central collection area. That is a major challenge, though. I take it you do not wish to see the dump right now."

"I'll pass. Thanks. Human waste?"

"We have portable facilities, separate tents for men and women. Over there." Dr. Mensah gestured towards two small, conical tarp structures. "There is always a line of people waiting to use the facilities."

"How often are the bathrooms cleaned?" Each question had an intention behind it; the more information he gathered, the better able he might be to combat infectious diseases.

Unable to help himself, Dr. Mensah laughed. "Sorry, I… We do not have the luxury of cleaning things much around here, Dr. Karim. You must not think of the camp as a modern living space. Conditions here are primitive. We do what we can."

"The clinic?" He had seen enough. While the conditions were not unfamiliar or unexpected, he did not wish to dwell too long in the camp proper. Not only was it depressing, he felt valueless just being an observer of suffering.

"Yes, of course. You are anxious to get to work. There is plenty to do," Dr. Mensah said. "Follow me please."

They walked back through the camp to an area near where they first arrived. There were a few buildings, or what passed for buildings in Amal. They were little more than tilt-up, plywood structures with tin roofs. On the door was a sign in English and other languages that read, "Clinic."

Inside the small entry room were 50 people crammed into a space that could uncomfortably accommodate 20. The doctors somehow made their way through the front room and into the back. An armed guard manned the door between the front room and the treatment areas.

"I can see patients in here?" Around Karim were a few plastic chairs and a crude examining table that had been pieced together from scraps of waste lumber. On top of the table was a stethoscope.

"Yes, I will be in the other room. Remember, medications are extremely limited. Here is our supply for the day." Mensah handed him a list.

Karim spent a minute reviewing his pharmaceutical stock. It was a truly pathetic cache, little more than a few antibiotics and a small amount of nonprescription meds used to treat the most basic of ailments.

"We must improve our medical supplies. I can help in this area."

"Wonderful. Ready to begin?"

"Yes. Who sends in the patients?"

"Just tap on the door twice, and the guard will send them in," Mensah explained. He left through a side door to begin seeing patients in an adjacent room.

After Karim tapped twice on the door, it opened, and a mother brought her child into the treatment room. The boy was 2 or 3, but he looked like he was 1. He was suffering from exposure, malnutrition and severe dehydration. His eyes were sunken, and he was generally unresponsive. Karim briefly examined him and found what he knew he would find—rapid heartbeat, fast, shallow breathing, low blood pressure and skin that looked like a dried prune. The boy's dehydration had caused an electrolyte imbalance. Signs of hypovolemic shock were evident.

The boy was dying. There was nothing Karim could do to stop that now, even if he had access to modern intensive care medical facilities. Still he said aloud, "Your child needs to be in a hospital."

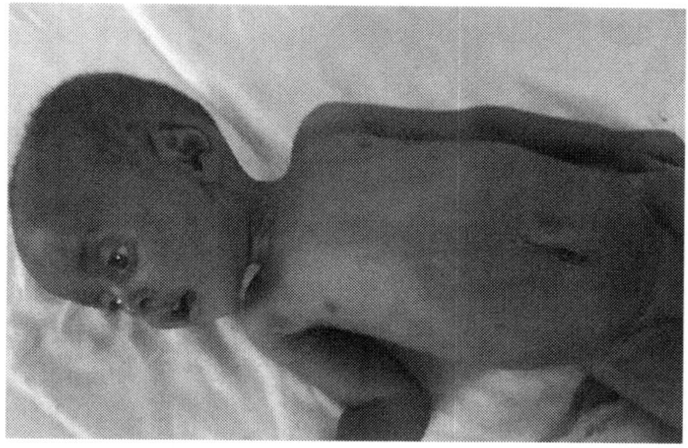

The mother looked at Karim. She had no idea what he was saying because she did not speak a word of the languages Karim spoke fluently:

English, Arabic and French. But she did see the care, concern and empathy in his eyes. She sensed in him a burning desire to give comfort, a willingness to try to do something to relieve her suffering.

She held her son and started to cry. Karim touched her gently on the forehead and gave her a candy bar from his backpack. A chocolate bar to comfort a mother whose child was dying of exposure and hunger—it was overwhelmingly sad.

All he could do was give the mother a couple of bottles of water and some dried food rations. He sent them on their way, hoping that perhaps some of the patients he would see today could be saved from an immediate trip to the grave.

After he closed the door, Karim did not immediately tap for another patient. He was here to be strong, to show mercy, to be a physician. But for a brief moment he was not able to be a doctor. He had seen this kind of suffering before. Karim was once on the other side of the door, a desperate child lost in a nightmare of war, hunger and poverty. At certain times, like now, he was taken back to those days in his mind.

He was seven years old again, back in Al Shati, called the Beach Camp in English, in Gaza. He and his family were Palestinian refugees who were forced to flee when the new state of Israel took their home and lands. Although he was a small boy, he had duties to perform for his family. Today he was tasked with watching his baby sister while his mother took her turn fetching water from the public well.

The AlShaikh family lived in a small, two-room shack. Their only roof was a rusty piece of metal that covered the bedroom, but it offered no real protection from the cold, wind and rain. There was no electricity, no running water and no floor other than sand.

Karim's baby sister was a year and a half old. She was able to walk and could speak a large number of words in short sentences. He loved to watch her play with their mother's comb, her only toy. She always had the comb in her hand; her favorite game was to comb her soft, thin hair constantly and to comb the hair of anyone else who came within her reach.

"I'll be back in a few minutes with some water," their mother said. "Keep an eye on your sister and don't let the flies come on her face."

Before she left, she had changed his sister's diapers three times in a matter of minutes. Clearly the baby was not well.

Karim performed his task perfectly; not one fly was allowed near his sister's face. She lay there peacefully, not making a sound. He thought this was unusual because she was normally far more vibrant and vocal. When their mother returned after a few minutes, she took one look at her daughter and became upset. She picked up the baby and ran outside shouting for her husband to help her. Saeed was quick to respond. Together they took the baby away. Karim waited patiently at home.

Hours later his parents returned, but his sister did not. The neighbors all came over, and everyone cried. His sister had died from dehydration and diarrhea, a direct result of the miserable conditions their family was forced to live in.

Young Karim thought he must have done something wrong. His parents assured him that he had not, but the truth was that his sister had gotten really sick when he was watching her. Maybe he should have done something differently, he thought. Maybe he should have taken her in his arms and run for help. Maybe if he had done that she would still be alive.

Sitting in a plastic chair trying to compose himself, Karim had to disengage from his troubling memories to help the patients waiting to see him. He could hear them arguing in the other room. They were trying to get the guard to open the door.

Palestine was his homeland, a place he loved, but it was also his perpetual nightmare. His past both inspired and haunted him—it urged him to be the best, but at times it tried to pull him back into a pit of despair.

At a young age, he had learned that the best way to get over your own troubles was to help someone else. Dr. Karim AlShaikh was a fighter for love, a warrior in the never-ending battle to heal and comfort those in the world who had nothing.

On the other side of the thin plywood door were hundreds of children who desperately needed his assistance. So he wiped the tears from his eyes, took a couple of deep breaths and tapped on the door two times.

https:www.facebook.com/palestine.our.homeland

Jaffa, Palestine circa 1930

Chapter Five

BEIT DARAS, PALESTINE 1923-1947

Earth Presses Against Us

Earth is pressing against us, trapping us in the final passage.
To pass through, we pull off our limbs.
Earth is squeezing us. If only we were its wheat, we might die and yet live.
If only it were our mother so that she might temper us with mercy.
If only we were pictures of rocks held in our dreams like mirrors.
We glimpse faces in their final battle for the soul, of those who will be killed by the last living among us. We mourn their children's feast.
We saw the faces of those who would throw our children out of the windows of this last space. A star to burnish our mirrors.

Where should we go after the last border? Where should birds fly after the last sky?
Where should plants sleep after the last breath of air?
We write our names with crimson mist!
We end the hymn with our flesh.
Here we will die. Here, in the final passage.
Here or there, our blood will plant olive trees.

Mahmoud Darwish

A CHILD WAS ABOUT to be born. As was the tradition in Palestine, the house was full of family, friends and neighbors to celebrate the birth. While Abdullah AlShaikh, the nervous father, paced in the reception hall, maids carried buckets of water and linen to an older woman standing on the balcony at the top of the wooden stairwell. In the field across from the front yard, young servants ran back and forth preparing things for the party. More servants brought supplies in through the back doors. Carriages delivered guests to the east entrance.

Beit Daras was a small village located a hundred kilometers west and a little south of Jerusalem. For centuries, people had lived there in relative safety and peace. Since the 13th century when the last of the European Christian Crusaders left or were vanquished, Palestine had been part of a larger Islamic state. From 1517 to 1917 Palestine was a province of the Ottoman Empire. The Ottoman Empire had sided with Germany in the First World War. After the Allies had won the war, Palestine had become a British protectorate. While life in Beit Daras had so far changed little under British rule, the Palestinians were still adjusting to living under English control.

The AlShaikh family farmed—they grew crops and tended olive trees. They employed a large number of people from the village. Their house was bright yellow and gray, constructed with Jerusalem Mountain stone. As was obvious from the architecture of the home, the family was prosperous.

Houses in Beit Daras were constructed of either stone or clay or made of some combination of the two. It was common for the larger houses to have an open air hall in the middle where the family gathered to eat and sit. There was not a separate yard for each home; rather there was an open area, either grass or sand, that was shared by all the neighbors. The children from the neighborhood ran and played in these open areas. Behind a group of homes there was always a common stable. In front of the big houses, like AlShaikh's residence, there was a large reception room where guests gathered. These adjunct rooms also served as places for men in the village to meet and discuss issues vital to the community.

Saeed AlShaikh was born on August 6, 1923. Abdullah AlShaikh had definite plans for his son's life; Saeed would become a leader in the community, take over the family business and pass on his rich cultural and spiritual heritage to his children. There was no separation between the family, the land and their community; they were one in the same, all part of a greater whole. He would be taught the laws of God by his father and be raised to live in peace with his neighbors and to be kind, generous and merciful. Abdullah was overwhelmed with joy at the thought of his son growing up by his side.

There was a definite rhythm to life in Beit Daras that was centered on prayer, family and community. Palestinian villages were comprised of mostly extended relatives. A person's cousins, in-laws and grandparents were his neighbors, coworkers and friends. Young people were taught the old ways and brought up in a culture that required them to work hard. Children learned their trades by serving others in the community and working with their elders. To earn respect, a young man had to prove himself by completing the tasks given him.

As Saeed grew older, Palestine was changing. Decades earlier, in the 1880s, large numbers of Jews had begun to immigrate to Palestine. They were part of the Zionist movement, a political philosophy centered on the idea that Jewish people should return to their ancestral homeland and establish the State of Israel with Jerusalem as its capital. As World War I ended, events in Britain and America had facilitated the Zionist cause.

The British issued the Balfour Declaration in November 1917, which both allowed and encouraged Jews to immigrate to Palestine in large numbers. For centuries Muslims, Jews and Christians had lived in the Holy Land together in relative peace. Now both the population and the politics were changing. The increasing Jewish presence in Palestine created conflicts. Both the Jews and the Palestinians chafed under British rule, but when Saeed was young, Palestine was still relatively at peace.

His parents had a definite daily routine. Abdullah AlShaikh woke before dawn and prepared for the Morning Prayer. Amna, his wife, also got up at that time and stood with her husband as he performed his ritual cleansing for prayer. Then she walked him to the bedroom door, said goodbye and began her day.

He enjoyed the fresh morning air as he walked across the balcony on the second floor and moved down the stairs to the open hall in the middle of the house. From there he headed to the sitting room and from behind the door picked up his Abaya, a long outer garment with wide half-sleeves trimmed with a golden strip. He put on and adjusted his Kufiya, making sure that his headwear was perfect, and then headed toward the mosque.

As Abdullah walked toward the mosque, the sky was still dark, the sun not yet up. He was not alone at this time because all of his neighbors were also headed to morning prayers. He greeted each of them in turn with a wave or quick handshake. As soon as the prayers were over, work began for most of the village.

Most days he went straight to his farm. When he arrived there, the workers immediately rose from amongst the bushes and trees and greeted him. The most striking feature of his farm was the olive trees, which were not organized in rows but rather scattered throughout the property. These trees were not deliberately planted, at least as far as anyone knew; they were as much a part of the native Palestinian landscape as were the families that had also lived there for centuries. According to family lore, one of the olive trees mid-property was over 400 years old.

The olive trees did not need much tending. They required water and some pruning, but for the most part, unless the olives were ripe the farmworkers could concentrate on other crops. Some plowed the ground, and others mixed seeds with sand. Other workers tended to water canals that fed each field. An old water pump made an annoying pounding sound every few seconds as it moved water from a dark brown stone well to the canals.

Amna brought her husband breakfast around 8 a.m. at the farm. Breakfast usually consisted of butter and honey, a small plate of zatar, a bowl of olive oil, green olives, cucumbers, sliced tomatoes and boiled eggs. The bread was baked in a stone oven. Tea was also served with fresh milk. The food was shared with the other farmworkers as a daily morning ritual. She never stayed long because work was done on a tight schedule.

Abdullah always had his morning meal under the biggest olive tree, with its meter-wide trunk and low-hanging branches. It was large enough to provide shade for 20 or more farmers. Around them, small fig trees were scattered in between the olive trees. Figs were sometimes picked and eaten with the butter and honey.

Most men were finished with their work by noon or in the early afternoon. The rest of the day was spent having lunch with extended families and socializing. This was an important part of village life. News of the day, including national and international politics, was discussed, along with matters directly related to the community such as who was getting married to whom and when, which young person was headed to high school and villagewide financial concerns.

The older men socialized in the form of a village council. Beit Daras, like all Palestinian villages, did not have a structured municipal government. The British knew about this centuries-old practice and did not interfere in local affairs. The village council was an effective form of governance because the community respected the elders' decisions and their judgments of disputes.

Drinking tea in the late afternoon in the village café was a longstanding tradition in Palestine and other Arab countries. Abdullah could not participate in this daily, as most of his farmworkers could, because he had many other responsibilities. After spending time with his family until sunset, he would go to evening prayers and then retire about 9:00 or 10:00 p.m.

Abdullah AlShaikh distributed salaries to his workers on the last Friday of every month. When he did so, he usually had a feast for the workers. He would put the salary money in a sack and tuck it in a pocket of his vest. He was known to give out a little extra each month to each of his workers when times were good. If there was a feast at his home, his employees were always invited to attend.

The relationship between him and his workers was not simply boss and employees; it was far more complex. Most of his workers were younger and distant relatives. He considered it his duty to look out for their wellbeing in every sense—financial, spiritual and physical.

As the Imam of the village, Abdullah led the mosque in daily prayers. He was an educated man, a graduate of Arabia's most prestigious university, Al-Azhar University in Egypt. After morning prayers, he usually gave a short motivational speech to the men who had gathered to pray. He often reminded the prayers who gathered during his evening class, reciting the Prophet, to "Fear God wherever you are. Follow an evil deed with a good one to erase it. Treat people with good conduct always." He loved to discuss the connection between man and his Creator and the duty we all have to understand the weight of our actions, both good and bad. He both taught and believed that the village was the home of one, big family. Despite differences and troubles, everyone was knitted together by common bonds.

Saeed worked on the farm from an early age. He preserved the traditions and was prepared to one day take his father's place as the head of the household and as a village leader. Abdullah AlShaikh passed away when Saeed was 8 years old. By the time he was 18, Saeed was basically running the family business. He regularly traveled north to Syria and Lebanon and west and south to Jerusalem and Gaza. He was often seen in Jaffa, Haifa and Akko. He formed a network of friends in these places and became well known for his business acumen and integrity.

The only real regret he had by the time he reached age 25 was that, due to his father's early death, he was obliged to look after the family business and was unable to attend university. To compensate, he did his best to read and study on his own. He became knowledgeable in many subjects.

For over two decades, Saeed grew and prospered in Beit Daras, surviving through both the rough years of World War II and the immediate postwar disturbances when the British relinquished control of Palestine.

One day in 1948 everything changed. With one knock on the door, the world as Saeed AlShaikh knew it came to an end.

Palestine on the move in 1948

Chapter Six

THE EXILE (NAKBA) MARCH 1948

Victim Number 18

Once the olive grove was green.
It was.
And the sky a grove of blue.
It was.
My love, what changed it that evening?
At the bend in the track they stopped the lorry of workers.
So calm they were.
They turned us round towards the east.
So calm they were.
Once my heart was a blue bird, a nest of my beloved.
The handkerchiefs I had of yours were all white.
They were, my love.
What stained them that evening?
I do not understand at all, my love.
At the bend in the track they stopped the lorry of workers.

So calm they were.
They turned us round towards the east.
So calm they were.
From me and you'll have everything,
Yours the shade and yours the light,
A wedding-ring and all you want,
And an orchard of trees, of olive and fig.
And as on every night I'll come to you.
In the dream I'll enter by the window and throw you jasmine.
Blame me not if I'm in a little late;
they stopped me.

Mahmoud Darwish

SAEED ROSE TO answer a loud knock on the door. These were perilous times. Who was on the other side? A British soldier? A Zionist terrorist? A number of possibilities ran through his mind as he opened the large, wooden door on the main floor of his home.

He was greeted by three of his neighbors. They told Saeed that they had important news.

"More terrorist attacks in Palestine?" Saeed asked.

"I'm afraid it's even worse than that," one of the neighbors said. "May we come inside so that we can listen to the radio while we talk?"

"Of course." Saeed's family had the only radio in the village. Although he was just 25 years old, he was often asked to participate in meetings with the village elders.

The news was grim. Palestine was in turmoil. Recently there had been attacks on nearby villages, skirmishes between Palestinians and Jewish groups who were trying to assert control.

"There were gunshots heard in Beit Daras last night," one of the council members reported. "The violence is coming here."

The village elders discussed the situation and made plans. The radio and newspapers reported that groups of Zionist militia roamed the countryside looking for trouble. Until now it had been relatively peaceful around the village.

A political power vacuum existed in Palestine. The British were leaving, and they had no interest in getting militarily entangled in the conflicts of the region on their way out. After World War II ended the new United Nations decided to partition Palestine into two states—one Palestinian, one Jewish. This international decree was met with resistance from the native population in Palestine. What right did some international body that met in America have to create a separate Jewish state in Palestine? Did these world leaders not know or care that Palestinian people lived in the areas they were ceding to the Jews?

Saeed knew many Palestinian Jews. For the most part they were kind, God-fearing families who wanted only to live in peace with their neighbors, but there were other Jews in Palestine with far more evil intent. Those were Zionists, and they had no problem burning homes and murdering innocent Palestinians to take what they perceived to be something they had a God-given right to expropriate: Palestinian land.

Less than a month later, on April 10, 1948, there was another ominous knock on his door. This time Arab soldiers were on the other side. "We need you to evacuate and seek refuge. There will be serious fighting here, and civilians will become targets if they remain in their homes."

The elders gathered again. Options were discussed. The one thing everyone initially agreed on was that no one was leaving. The men expressed the desire to die fighting rather than to evacuate.

"If the damned Jews attack, we will fight back against them to the last person standing," Judah, one of the elders, said. The other village leaders echoed his sentiments, except for Saeed.

"It's not the Jews, my uncle." Although Saeed was the youngest in the leadership group, he was educated in the ways of the world and well-traveled. He regularly went to neighboring cities and countries both north and south to buy goods and sell his farm's products. Saeed was the only person in the village who owned trucks; everyone else used horse drawn carriages.

"There are terrorists among the Jews," he explained. "My father told me this, and he warned me that while the Holy Land should always remain under Muslim guard, no one should be prohibited from entering it."

The elders of Beit Daras decided to assist the Arab soldiers who were fighting against the Israelis. In theory, the armies of Jordan and Egypt were in Palestine to defend the Arab population from attacks and exploitation by Jewish extremists. Saeed agreed that giving these Arab armies food and shelter was the right thing to do and would help protect their homes and land.

There was no way for him to know that the Arab soldiers would be gone within days. Protecting small Palestinian villages was simply not a priority for the Arab armies. Saeed could not possibly have anticipated that the new Jewish state was going to ban Muslims from Palestine for years. How could he even imagine that he would never see Beit Daras again if he chose to take the soldier's advice and evacuate?

But what he did know was that yesterday, April 9, the Irgun Zwei Leumi, a Jewish militia group, attacked the village of Deir Yassin near Jerusalem. Jacques de Reynier, at the time the Chief Delegate of the International Red Cross in Palestine, reached the village shortly after the slaughter. He reported to the international media that "300 persons were massacred without any military reason or provocation of any kind; old men, women, children and the newly-born were savagely murdered with grenades and knives by Jewish troops of the Irgun, entirely under the control of their chiefs."

Four days earlier Saeed had visited Deir Yassin. Whenever he went on a business trip to the eastern parts of Palestine, he stopped by this village. The woman he intended to marry lived there. The village he left only days before was now gone, razed without mercy. His fiancé was murdered in the senseless slaughter.

The objective of the Deir Yassin attack was to terrify the Arab population of Palestine and force them to flee. The plan succeeded. Under British rule, Palestinians had no national army to defend them; they were forced to rely on the armies of neighboring countries. Despite their opposition to British rule, the Jewish forces fighting now as the new nation of Israel were backed by de facto, pro-Zionist British policies and American arms, especially heavy artillery. On the other hand, the armies of the Arab countries, who had only recently freed themselves from British rule, were poorly armed and not well trained. They had the advantage of numbers against the Israelis, but a significant numerical advantage was not sufficient to win battles against the well-equipped Jewish force.

The Arab soldiers were positive and reassuring; they were absolutely sure that the Jewish terrorists would be vanquished in short order. They made a compelling case for a quick victory—Egypt, Jordan and the other Arab states would simply not allow the Jews to form a nation from Arab lands. How could the Jews possibly defeat the combined multi-national Arab forces?

The people of Beit Daras defended their village and fended off several assaults from Zionist invaders. But when the Zionists, with logistical support from the British, brought heavy weapons to bear upon Beit Daras, Saeed and the other village elders had no choice. It was time to go. They could not risk a catastrophe, such as the one that just occurred in Deir Yassin. There were women and children to consider; it was obvious from the recent carnage that innocent lives were at risk. The Israelis had a clear objective and simple tactics—they wanted all of the Palestinians to flee so they burned everything to the ground and shot anyone who remained.

Saeed ordered his extended family to pack up everything they could and load it onto trucks and horsedrawn carriages. Their destination was Gaza, the only place he thought was relatively safe and close to Beit Daras. He knew the area well—he had been to Gaza many times on business trips—so he locked the doors and took his house keys with him, expecting to return in short order.

He and his family were a part of a mass exodus. Since they were wealthier than most, they arrived in Gaza in a big truck. Most of the refugees either walked in or rode on mules or donkeys. Those who were able brought small pieces of furniture with them, but they were limited to what they could carry.

Despite his best efforts, Saeed was unable to rent or buy a home for his family in Gaza City. He was turned down not because he did not have the money, but rather because the building owners said, housing was "too expensive" for him. They feared that because his farm and livelihood had been taken from him, they would have to evict him from whatever home he rented after his money ran out.

There was more to consider. His extended family—aunts, uncles, nieces and cousins—were all in desperate need. So, despite his gut telling him that it was a mistake, Saeed chose to enter Al Shati, or Beach Camp. The camp was situated about one kilometer from the Mediterranean Sea just north of Gaza City. Their house only a short time earlier had been a magnificent stone structure and was now a camp slot with simple brick walls and no roof to protect them from the elements. The entire area of the camp was less than one square kilometer. Soon over 20,000 refugees would cram themselves into this small space.

The Zionist strategy, called Plan Dalet, to first depopulate and then slowly settle on seized Palestinian lands was succeeding. In 1947 and earlier, the pre-state Zionist leadership outlined an explicit strategy for taking over Palestinian communities and displacing the Palestinian population. Plan Dalet called for "...destruction of villages (setting fire to, blowing up and planting mines and debris) especially those population centers which are difficult to control continuously" with the goal of "wiping out" any armed Palestinian resistance because the "population must be expelled outside the borders of the state."

The Palestinians were now political orphans without rights or property, with no means to defend themselves and no nation to secure their legitimate claims to land that had been lovingly passed down to them through the generations by their ancestors. The harsh reality was this—Western Palestine had been ethnically cleansed of its Arab population, at least to the extent that the Zionist armies had been able to do so.

Days and then weeks went by. As more refugees poured into the camp, Saeed became all too aware of the magnitude of the crisis. All of the bold talk about quickly vanquishing the Israeli army proved to be nothing but empty blustering. The Israelis were a formidable enemy. The Arab forces were unable to retake the lands absorbed by the new Jewish state. As the Nakba year, the year of great tribulation 1948, drew to a close, it was apparent to Saeed that he and his family were stuck in Gaza for the foreseeable future.

Everyone in the camp had in common that their property, their livelihood and their communities were gone. From the beginning the residents of Al Shati had no means to support themselves other than what they brought with them; they were completely dependent on aid from the United Nations and other charitable benefactors to survive.

On December 11, 1948 the General Assembly of the United Nations resolved that "[Palestinian] refugees wishing to return to their homes and live in peace with their neighbors should be permitted to do so at the earliest practicable date." The new Israeli state had different ideas. Through a series of measures passed by the newly formed Knesset such as The Land Acquisition Law and The Abandoned Areas Ordinance, 1949 the lands and property left behind by the fleeing Palestinians became by fiat the property of others.

Saeed had keys to a house that no longer existed. For him, and for hundreds of thousands of his Palestinian countrymen, his nation had been usurped, conquered by an invader from within who was actively supported and armed by the most powerful nation on the planet. Once rich, Saeed was now stateless, desperately poor and surviving on a day to day basis.

Palestinian Refugee Camp—Early 1950s

Chapter Seven

LOVE IN THE MIDST OF MISERY

On the day when my words
were earth
I was a friend to stalks of wheat.
On the day when my words
were wrath
I was a friend to chains.
On the day when my words
were stones
I was a friend to streams.
On the day when my words
were a rebellion
I was a friend to earthquakes.
On the day when my words
were bitter apples
I was a friend to the optimist.
But when my words became honey
flies covered my lips!

Mahmoud Darwish

THE WORLD DID not seem to care. For whatever reason or combination of reasons—the slaughter of Jews in German World War II death camps, the noble ideal of creating a home for a long-suffering people or the powerful political influence of Zionists in the United States and Great Britain—the international community largely ignored the plight of hundreds of thousands of displaced Palestinians. There were outcries, empty statements made by posturing politicians and diplomats that the Palestinians had the right to return to their homes, but no action was taken other than by the Israelis.

For Saeed, it was as if the world had lost its collective mind. Did one million people living in Palestine before 1948 not count for anything? Who has the right to displace an entire people who had lived in a land for centuries? Did Zionist might make Zionist right? It was as if the Palestinians simply did not matter, that somehow they were less than human.

During the previous decade, the world had united to crush oppression and labeled those who systematically tortured and killed a particular race of people as the vilest of criminals, as enemies of all humanity. Yet as German Nazi leaders were being tried and convicted at Nuremberg for attempting to exterminate the European Jews, the new State of Israel was forcibly exiling hundreds of thousands of Palestinians from their ancestral homeland. Saeed wondered, how could the world not see this irony, this gross hypocrisy? Where was the indignation, the outrage?

Life for Saeed was a continuous struggle for survival. The conditions at the Beach Camp were miserable in every respect. He had an extended family to look after and providing for their basic needs consumed every minute of his day. While his village was barely more than 30 kilometers away, it might as well have been on another planet. He could not go home and even if he could, there was no home to return to; the Israelis had leveled every building and wiped Beit Daras from the face of the earth.

Nonetheless, Beit Daras and hundreds of other Palestinian villages and towns still existed in the hearts and minds of the people in the refugee camps scattered across the Arab countries that bordered Israel. They were still alive, so Palestine also lived on. Many of the refugees vowed to take back their homes by force, to repel what they considered to be a foreign occupying power. Others, like Saeed, had no choice but to focus on the immediate needs of their families rather than on the armed struggle against Israeli oppression.

Saeed set up a small business in Al Shati selling sweets and a few other food products needed by his fellow refugees. He and a couple of other young men traveled biweekly to the nearest town and bought what merchandise they could and brought it back to the camp.

After four years of exile he had nearly given up on the dreams of his former life—to expand the family farm, improve the house and make Beit Daras a better community. He was almost 30 years old. Since the forced emigration, he did not aspire to anything other than to make life easier and more comfortable for his family and friends. He did not plan for the future or think of himself. His horizon was limited to what was immediately around him.

Every day Saeed went to the Beach Camp's Community Square, which was half a kilometer from his home. The main attraction in this area was a water pump, which every woman in the camp visited at least twice a week. He and his business partners knew that when families got their water, they might also be interested in purchasing sweets and food.

One morning, after he finished his dawn prayer called Fajr, he lay on his thin mattress with his eyes wide open. His mind was active. The day before had been exhausting, and he had not been able to sell many of his sweets.

Perhaps in a time when so many tears are shed, people do not crave happy foods, Saeed told himself. A cloud of negative thoughts crowded his mind, contrary to his general personality of being a positive man intent on pursuing happiness.

Today, like many other days, he could not stop thinking about all the difficulties facing his family. When he closed his eyes, he saw the troubled look on his mother's face and the effect of her recent illness. All around him was poverty and suffering, and there seemed no way out of his miserable conditions. Where could the family go? They had no money. Saeed and others still held out some hope that if they waited long enough and prayed hard enough, God would restore their homes to them. They were

Palestinians. Why should they leave? It was the Israelis who should leave, not them.

He thought about poor Salma, the young woman he was close to marrying only a few years earlier. She was dead now, killed in the Deir Yassin massacre. As his memory produced clear images of the terrible incident, a wound in his heart reopened, and an ache spread all over his body. It was Allah's will, he reminded himself after a few torturous minutes of sorrow.

"May she be embraced in Allah's love and mercy, dwelling in His paradise," Saeed prayed.

When he rose to the rooster's call, the glint of determination normally found in his dark brown eyes was missing. He felt heaviness all over his body and was filled only with misery. A cover of darkness had grasped him, and not even the chirping of the morning birds could bring back his sweet temper and easygoing smile.

He greeted his mother as was his habit. She sensed his distress and expressed her concerns, but she did not discuss his dark mood with him. As he left for work, his mother called out to him, "May Allah open doors for you, my son!"

When he met his friends and fellow merchants, Saeed wearily shook their hands and had less to say than usual.

"How is my aunt, your mother, doing?" Saeed inquired halfheartedly of one of his friends, whose mother was sick. It was common for young people to use the words aunt and uncle when they referred to their neighbors.

"I'm glad to say she is getting better," his friend replied. A faint smile appeared on Saeed's face, but the heavy weight on his heart was not lifted.

The men walked to the Community Square in silence. They reached their destination, set up their goods for sale and waited for customers. Saeed sat on the side selling the sweets while his two friends took charge of the other products. Today his friends were busier than he was. As he sat waiting for business to pick up, he wished to God that something would make his people happier and that it would be the norm again to enjoy some sweets. A few minutes later, a conversation at the water pump caught his attention.

"Miriam, I can't take this anymore. Our life is miserable. I wish I could see my little brother laughing and playing as a little boy ought to. He cries all the time. My dad hasn't laughed in years, and my mom sheds countless tears." Saeed had not seen either of these women before.

"Have patience my friend, hold peace," Miriam said, with a distinct tone of hope in her words. "Your father will laugh, and you will notice. With hardship comes ease; we've been promised good times amidst difficulty."

"Glory to God! Miriam, how patient you are. I don't know how you can smile when your own mother is sick and you have to come down to the water pump in addition to managing all the day's work by yourself. I hope my aunt is getting better?"

"Thankfully she is. My father is doing a wonderful job of looking after her." Miriam's turn came to fill her water jug.

Saeed was a naturally positive person. All he needed to hear was someone expressing sincere hope in a better future, and a measure of his innate courage and determination came back to him. He instantly felt better as he watched the two young women fill their containers with water. When they were done, the one named Miriam said to her friend, "How about some sweets for your little brother?"

Saeed snapped out of his trance and silently thanked God for his remarkably quick change of mood. He set the products in line and prepared for the approaching customers. The women bought their sweets and went home. He could not help but notice Miriam's soft hazel eyes. He thought that the young woman was the most beautiful girl that he had seen around the camp. For hours after he first gazed at her across his merchant's table, he could still hear her speaking in his mind. When it was time to go home, he left the Community Square determined to smile and be hopeful.

The next few days brought more encounters with the young woman. Her repeated buying of sweets was a sign to Saeed of her determination to be happy. Her words whenever she spoke to any of her friends had deep meaning and brought joy to his heart. He slowly felt his interest in the young woman increasing. After a few more days, Saeed was sure that he was in love with her.

For the first time since being forced to leave Beit Daras, he could see a future for himself other than constant misery. Now he had a goal beyond the limits of today and even tomorrow. His love reenergized his soul. He thought it was possible to taste pure happiness once again.

As he packed up the merchandise, Saeed brought up the subject of marriage with one of his two friends, who was about his same age.

"Are you in love?" The friend was a keen observer with a quick wit. He knew that Saeed was not one to discuss serious subjects in a frivolous manner.

"You have always been like a brother to me." Saeed let out a deep sigh. "I am interested in the new lady, Miriam. Do you know anything about her?"

He had already found out that she came from a wealthy background. Back in Isdood, her home village in Palestine, her father was a community leader. Nothing but praise was said concerning the family's manners and reputation as a whole; hearing this made Saeed admire the young woman even more.

"She is not engaged, and according to my aunt, she is very mature for her age. Her father is well respected."

Amna laughed that evening when her son told her all about Miriam. She was delighted that he had found someone so special and that it had renewed his hope in life. After Salma's brutal death, she was worried that her son might choose not to love again.

"Have you inquired about her?" his brother asked.

Saeed relayed all he had heard about Miriam and her family. His brother urged him to ask her parents for permission to get to know her better and promised to go with him to visit her father tomorrow. That night, after Saeed finished his evening prayer, called Isha', he had nothing on his mind but the sweetest of thoughts.

The next day they went to visit Miriam's father. When they announced themselves, her little brother opened the door. Her father greeted them and welcomed them inside. When he heard Saeed propose for permission to get to know his daughter, he laughed and called Miriam into the room. Saeed was well-known around camp and had a commendable reputation, so her father approved of the proposal without hesitation and invited his daughter in to meet him.

When Miriam came into the living room and saw Saeed, she gave a brief look of recognition. Upon hearing his proposal, her face lit up with happiness, and she smiled, blushed and gave him her consent. From that moment on they were engaged and brought nothing but happiness into their families' and neighbors' hearts.

Every minute Saeed and Miriam spent together strengthened their belief that they were soulmates. Two months into their engagement, they announced their intention to be married, and the entire camp prepared to celebrate the event.

As the time for the wedding drew near, thoughts of the day Saeed met Miriam crossed his mind. He remembered how he had sat hopeless, pondering at the slow selling of his sweets and wishing that people had more reason to enjoy them.

How ignorant man can be as to the affairs of tomorrow. Praise to Allah the All-Knowing, for today brings reason for everyone to rejoice, he said silently to himself. He considered the many happy prospects for his future as he showered, got his hair cut and then donned the traditional Palestinian attire worn by grooms on their wedding days. The outfit was comprised of baggy-fitting pants and a loose white shirt that was tucked in. A colorful belt was wrapped around his waist and the Palestinian black-and-white Hatta was secured neatly on his head.

When Saeed was done getting ready, the wedding celebration was only a couple of hours away. He had tea with friends and neighbors who had come to celebrate. While he tried to calm his anxiousness, his friends made his task harder by their jokes and remarks.

The day before the wedding, the Ma'thoon left Miriam's home after writing the marriage contract between her and Saeed in the presence of the two families. In the evening, several women from the neighborhood came over to help her prepare for the wedding. They had their own small celebration with the bride, and they each got a share of Miriam's henna.

The flowering henna plant was grown in one of the neighbor's gardens, and she had the pleasure of bringing it to the party. The leaves were ground, mixed with water and lemon and left to ferment while the party went on. Hours later the henna dye preparation was ready, and the most experienced of the elder women embellished Miriam's hands and arms with the most beautiful of designs. The women sat around, watched with admiration, sang songs and laughed. Hopes and well-wishes of finding their own soulmates were passed on to the bachelorettes.

Miriam was full of joy as she awoke on her wedding day. Her hair was beautifully styled and her eyes decorated with Kohl eyeliner. She was helped into her Palestinian Thoab—a traditionally black, long dress that is covered with colorful, embroidered designs—and her head garment was applied. Just as she finished getting ready, it was time for the event to begin.

The people of Al Shati camp gathered in the community square. Young men occupied one corner with their musical instruments. Neatly dressed children ran around freely. The older men sat comfortably on chairs on one side of the square while the younger men sat on the ground. The women sat on the opposite side of the square from the men. Chatter and laughter were plentiful, and there were plenty of lemonade drinks and sweets to go around.

The talking ceased when Saeed and Miriam came in hand-in-hand and sat on decorated plastic chairs in the middle of the square. Then the music played, and the young men got up to do the Palestinian Dabka, a traditional Arab and Palestinian dance, while the rest of the crowd watched. After that, the women sang their best of wishes for the couple and gave their blessings.

The public square at the camp may have been small, but to Saeed it felt huge. He could not have hoped for a better wedding.

No one was focused on their misery on this day. Not when Saeed and Miriam, two lanterns of hope joined together forever to augment one another's light, filled their hearts with great joy.

Karim and his brother on the beach in Gaza

Chapter 8

1965
BEACH BOY

Those who pass between fleeting words

O those who pass between fleeting words
carry your names, and be gone
Rid our time of your hours, and be gone
Steal what you will from the blueness of the sea
And the sand of memory
Take what pictures you will, so that you understand
That which you never will:
How a stone from our land builds the ceiling of our sky.
From you steel and fire, from us our flesh
From you yet another tank, from us stones
From you teargas, from us rain…
It is time for you to be gone
Live wherever you like, but do not live among us
It is time for you to be gone
Die wherever you like, but do not die among us

For we have work to do in our land.
O those who pass between fleeting words
It is time for you to be gone
Live wherever you like, but do not live among us
It is time for you to be gone
Die wherever you like, but do not die among us
For we have work to do in our land
So leave our country
Our land, our sea
Our wheat, our salt, our wounds
Everything, and leave
The memories of memory
those who pass between fleeting words!

Mahmoud Darwish

ON A FRIDAY afternoon in the spring of 1965, eight-year-old Karim was walking with his father on a beautiful white sand beach in Gaza. The tide was low.

"There are higher tides in other places," Saeed told his son, "making them especially fun. When we were children, we used to go to the beach just north of here. I jumped into the tides just as those kids are doing over there."

Several children walked to the top of the surf line and then waited for the tidal surge. When the surging wave arrived, they jumped into the water. The small waves carried the kids for a few meters and then deposited them further up the beach. They rode the tide waves over and over again, laughing, carrying on and having a great time.

"You know what else I liked to do?" Saeed asked, clearly trying to provoke his son's curiosity. Everything Saeed said to his son had a deeper meaning. Saeed enjoyed spending time with Karim because he loved him dearly and enjoyed his company, but he also used their time together to instill values in his son.

"What?"

"My sister and I, when we were your age, used to go out in the rain and jump in my father's fields on the farm. We called it the flood season, not because it really flooded, but because in the fall when the farmers anticipated the rain, they plowed the land in deep furrows. Only after the rain fell and flooded this plowed sand and the ground absorbed the moisture could they plow again and plant.

"We made a mess out of ourselves every time," Saeed went on. "Your grandmother was not pleased when we came home covered in wet sand. The funny thing was that when we jumped in the soil during the rain, we prevented the soil from absorbing enough water. When the crops grew, we knew the area we messed up because the crops growing there were shorter than the rest. They also died earlier."

They sat on the beach. Then Saeed asked his son, "Where do you think the sea ends?"

"Beyond the horizon," Karim said, pointing to the west.

"Who lives there?"

"People?" Karim replied hesitantly.

"Other nations, yes, like us."

"What type of nations?"

"They are different, yet they are the same. They live similar to us; they have families and friends, and they work. Their skin may be a different color than ours, and they speak other languages," Saeed explained.

"Are they good people? Do they pray?" It was only natural for Karim to ask about whether or not they prayed because his father had carefully instructed him about the importance of prayer—how it teaches you to organize your time around five prayers a day, how to wake up and go to sleep early and to fear God in everything you do.

"There are good and there are bad people in every nation, son. And there are those who pray and those who don't, even though other nations may pray differently than we do. Religions differ, but I don't mind people of other faiths as long as they believe and practice good values."

Saeed looked into Karim's eyes and said in a serious tone, "Son, never do injustice in the name of religion. Justice is the language spoken by all religions when they are correctly understood. Variety adds richness to the world. One nation has the solution for some of another nation's problems and vice versa. Our differences make us complete and allow us to learn from one another.

"That's why God created us," Saeed said, quoting the Quran, "'and we have made you into nations and tribes, that you may know one another.'" Saeed made him repeat the verse after him. From that moment on Karim dreamed of traveling the world and learning about other people.

Karim dug his fingers into the sand and cupped his hands. Then he lifted them up and dumped the sand back onto the beach. He came here often, both with and without his father. Saeed gently placed his hand on his son's head and ran his fingers through his hair. They smiled together as they gazed in silence as the sun began to slowly sink into the sea.

Bathed in the orange light of sunset, Karim returned to his sand scooping but became purposeful and began to build something.

"What are you building?" Saeed asked.

"A sand house," he replied "a big one!" He could see the house taking shape in his head. He had imagined it and built it before, a comforting ritual that took him away from the curfews, the everpresent soldiers and the poverty and into a brighter, freer future where he would have a real home.

Karim loved the beach. The clean water and the fresh, salty air helped him think. He brought his math problems from school here and etched them in the sand with a stick to solve them. He liked math because if he thought long and hard, he could always solve the problems. There was always an answer, and that was comforting to him.

"Is your sand house like our home in Beit Daras?" Saeed asked.

Karim was confused. "We have a big house? Is it far away from here? Can I see it?"

Saeed smiled awkwardly and looked sad. But Karim also glimpsed something else in his father's eyes, something warm and bright, like love or longing.

"Unfortunately, son, we cannot visit it, but I can explain something to you while we are walking back home but by a different route this time."

Karim nodded, thinking about how his father's words were always carefully chosen. When his father spoke with other adults, Karim thought that he sounded formal. He often used big words Karim did not understand.

Many of their wealthier neighbors and friends were nervous when they talked with Saeed. Karim used to wonder why this was, but now he knew—his father was held in high esteem. Saeed was respected, and although Karim did not know the whole story behind why this was, he was sure that his father's extraordinarily good character and keen sense of justice were the main reasons. Saeed often told Karim, "Respect yourself and respect everyone else. Never look down at anyone, and never let anyone look down upon you. That way you earn others' respect."

They walked northeast. The sunset transformed the sand into a rich golden color. As they moved away from the sea, the small hills gradually got bigger. The larger hills were dotted with green plants. The greenery was vividly contrasted by the setting sun's rays coming from the west, which laid down long shadows from the trees. Birds sang melodies from their branches.

They approached a rise in the land extending a kilometer or two in front of them. A few ancient homes were built there. They were constructed of fist-sized irregular stones, each bearing a different shade of gray or brown, asymmetrically arranged on their fence walls and stuck together with a brown cement-like material called sand clay—mud mixed with naturally occurring chemicals. This was a traditional Arab way of building houses in Palestine and elsewhere.

From the top of the rise, the view was spectacular. The sun to the west was united with the horizon, and only half of its orange disk showed. To the east, the city houses were neatly stacked, and behind them was the Beach Camp.

"Beit Daras," Saeed said as he pointed to the north and a bit to the east, "is right there."

"Where?" Karim was not sure what he was looking for. All he saw were trees when he looked north.

"Can you see those high buildings there near the horizon?"

"Yes, I see them," Karim answered, now looking in the correct direction.

"That is Ashqelon. Beit Daras is just northeast of it, only 32 kilometers northeast of where we are standing right now. Beit Daras is connected with a network of old trade roads to the villages surrounding it like Isdood and Hamama. The Crusaders built a fortress on the hill that looks down on the village and towards the coast. The Mamluks, who ruled Palestine from 1205 to 1517, made it a mail station between Damascus and Gaza.

"Your grandfather was a farmer in a community of farmers who grew grains and citrus fruits, like lemons and oranges. He had olive trees too. He also raised livestock, mainly poultry. Most of the village citizens were farmers or understood how to farm when they needed to help their families. The crops and fruits they grew were exported; that's what your grandfather did for a living, Karim. That is your heritage."

"Father," he said. "I don't understand. How did we lose our home? How could the Israelis just take it from us? Don't they know right from wrong?"

"I feel that I have not done my job in properly educating you."

"Father, no… what do you mean?"

"You have been told about our history, but it is not yet ingrained in you. You are a Palestinian with a very long, proud and rich heritage."

"I know about the Ottoman Empire and how we were a part of that for centuries. I know that Palestine has been a nation for a long time."

"Yes, but you need to know more about our recent history. Let's sit over here for a minute." Saeed pointed to a nearby pile of large building stones. Father and son sat in the now rapidly fading light.

"You know about the two world wars, don't you, Karim?"

"Yes," he said proudly. "The First World War ended in 1919 and the Second World War ended in 1945."

"After the First World War ended, Great Britain took over many nations that were once part of the Ottoman Empire—Palestine, Egypt, Jordan, Iraq and others. The British allowed the Jews to come and live in Palestine in ever increasing numbers. They also allowed them to form militias, armed groups. The British even trained the Jews on how to become good soldiers.

"Some of these Jewish groups, like the Haganah and the Ergon, attacked and terrified Palestinians. The British kept the Palestinians under close control; they would not allow us to own guns, and they taxed us heavily. So the Jews gained in military and political power in Palestine after World War I, and the Palestinians diminished in power."

"Why did the British do that, Father?"

"The British were misguided more than they were evil. The Zionists were pressuring them to allow them to form a nation in Palestine. For many centuries, the Jewish people have been displaced, forced to move from one country to another."

"Why?" Karim asked.

"There are many reasons, but almost 2000 years ago the Palestinian Jewish nation was destroyed by the Roman Empire. Since then the Jews are people who come from many different countries."

"But that was a long time ago, Father."

"Yes it was, and it was before the coming of the Prophet. For the past 19 centuries, Palestine has been a nation. Jews, Muslims and Christians lived here in relative peace since the beginning of the 13th century. Until the last 50 years or so, that is."

"So, why did they take our land?"

"They want to claim the land of their ancestors, the Palestinian Jews," Saeed explained. "We are the decedents of Palestinians who were followers of different religions for the past 6000 years. There were Palestinians living here before the time of Moses. When Aaron came to Palestine, many Palestinians became followers of Judaism. Centuries later Jesus came, and some of the Jews became his followers, the Christians. Then the Prophet Mohammad came and prayed in the holy mosque in Jerusalem. By the time of Omar bin Al Khattab many of the Christians became Muslims. Other Palestinians, who had remained Jewish after the time of Jesus, also then became Muslims."

"So, this whole thing is nonsense?"

"Somewhat," Saeed hesitated. "It's about ideologies."

"What are those?"

"The way people choose to think and feel about the world. Each ideology has its own version of the truth."

"So, who is right?"

Saeed smiled and looked into his son's eyes. "The one that is just and better still, the one that is just and kind."

They went back to talking about Beit Daras. Karim was too young to fully comprehend the lesson that his father had taught him, but with time Saeed had confidence that his son would understand.

"But our family has owned land in Beit Daras forever. How can the Jews just take it?" Karim asked.

"The Zionists believe that they had a right to take it. The British left in 1948, and when they did the United Nations in New York said that the Jews had the right to form the nation of Israel on Palestinian land."

"That's just wrong. The Jews could live with us in peace, but they had no right to take our land."

"No, they did not, but they have done so," Saeed said. "Son, make sure you understand the difference between Palestinian Jews who are on our side and Zionist Jews. It is the Zionists who did you an injustice. Jews are believers in Allah, just like us. Our problem is not with Judaism, it is with injustice."

"I want to see the house in Beit Daras!" Karim exclaimed.

"I hope and pray every day to see my house again. I want to return home and start over, but I fear that only more bloodshed is coming, perhaps with no good purpose." Saeed paused and looked at the sky. "It is getting late. We must walk home now, or we will miss evening prayers."

"Yes, Father."

He took one last look in the direction of Beit Daras and reminded himself that he had no idea who was living there now, if anyone. He had been in exile for 17 years. The Israelis had not allowed him to return to his village even once. Would this incredibly unjust and sad set of circumstances ever change?

When Saeed looked at his son, he hoped that things would change, that his land would be restored to him, but his greatest fear was that the cost of seeing justice done might be more than he could bear.

Moshe Dayan and Ariel Sharon

Chapter 9

SIX-DAY WAR (NAKSAT HUZEIRAN) JUNE 5TH, 1967

Earth

A dull evening in a rundown village
Eyes half asleep
I recall thirty years
And five wars
I swear the future keeps
My ear of corn
And the singer croons
About a fire and some strangers
And the evening is just another evening
And the singer croons
And they asked him:
Why do you sing?
And he answered:
I sing because I sing…
And they searched his chest
But could only find his heart

And they searched his heart
But could only find his people
And they searched his voice
But could only find his grief
And they searched his grief
But could only find his prison
And they searched his prison
But could only see themselves in chains

Mahmoud Darwish

KARIM WAS TEN years old and had just finished fourth grade at the local primary school when the Six-Day War started. He was home when the news broke, so he watched as relatives and neighbors gathered to discuss the situation. The radio was the moderator of their conversation.

Half a dozen men sat on the sandy ground inside Saeed's "house," the slot in the refugee camp that had a couple stones added to it over the years. They debated about the information they heard over the airwaves and the possible implications of the war on the Gaza Strip. Each man projected his own fantasies over the "facts" as stated in the broadcasts.

Karim felt danger like never before. The men were usually strong through the occasional skirmish, but now they were frightened. Their fear was mixed with a certain level of excitement.

From 1948 to 1967, the West Bank, including East Jerusalem, was ruled by Jordan. During this same time period, the Gaza strip was mostly under Egyptian military and United Nations administration. In 1967, Egypt ordered the United Nations troops out of its lands and blocked shipping routes in an act of political protest. The leader of Egypt ordered a concentration of Egyptian military forces in the sensitive Suez zone—adding to the already high levels of tension between Israel and its neighbors.

The Israelis viewed these moves in only one way—Egypt was preparing for war. When Egypt declared that United Nations troops were to leave Gaza, most of the people in Al Shati believed that conflict with

Israel was likely, but few expected it to start so soon. In fact, the war started before anyone could make sense of what was going on.

As the adults talked inside, Karim went outside the front door to the unpaved streets of the Beach Camp. His best friend Zohair, his next door neighbor and classmate, was waiting for him along with some other boys and girls. In Karim's hands was a hand drawn map of Palestine. He did his best to explain the situation of the allied Arab forces to Zohair and the other youngsters.

"Here is Jordan to our east. Egypt is in the south, and Lebanon and Syria are in the north. They will attack from all sides. We will win! Very soon we will go back to our house!" Although he had never been there, he considered his true house to be the family home in Beit Daras.

Karim was echoing the hopeful fantasies he heard from some of the adults, but everyone was not so blindly optimistic. After the children had gone their separate ways, he overheard his mother talking to Zohair's mom from behind the thin, poorly built brick wall that separated their two homes.

Miriam said, "You know, if we survive this, we might have to start all over again."

"Yes, that's possible," Zohair's mother agreed. "God knows what horrible camp we would have to flee to next should we be evicted."

"Here I am feeling sorry for maybe losing this miserable camp, but it is all the home we have now." Miriam giggled.

"God help us! How can you giggle? Where do you get that strength from?"

"The worst of tribulation is the one that makes you laugh!"

The vast majority of the refugees in Al Shati camp were certain that their day of liberation was finally at hand. The camp had existed for almost 20 years—two decades of exile, misery and loss.

Spirits rose in the Beach Camp as they listened to the "news." The only source of information for the people of Al Shati was Egyptian radio. On the radio was a well-known broadcaster who never reported anything but good news. He broadcast story after story of Arab victories over Israel. Most of what this broadcaster reported was untrue, but there was no other source of information available to the residents of Al Shati.

There was a gleam in the eyes of the children. Karim and his friends were sailing on the frothy waves of hope and dreams. Victory appeared to be certain. The Arab armies were on the march, they were winning the war and soldiers were coming to rescue them. Now the evil people who took their homes would be vanquished, and they could return to their cities and villages.

Saeed remembered the last time the Arab world and Israel went to war. He was assured then that an Arab victory was a certainty, but that turned out to be untrue, so he was understandably skeptical about all the premature claims of triumph. Mostly he was worried about how to protect his family, so he and the men who lived close to him in the camp decided to dig a trench in the ground in front of their homes for use as cover during possible attacks. They also planned escape routes. Each child had the emergency plans simplified and explained to them by their parents.

"The trench is just a preventative measure. When the Egyptian soldiers arrive they will protect us." Saeed did not necessarily believe his own words. He chose to be optimistic, despite the fact that the Egyptians had treated them horribly under their military rules, preventing them from adding even a stone to their miserable slots or even building private restrooms that were not preallocated by the camp in the early 1950s.

Saeed did not wish to unduly frighten his family, but Karim saw something in his father's eyes and heard something in the tone of his voice other than complete confidence in victory. Did he think the Arabs were not going to win? How could they possibly lose this war?

He helped his father and his older brothers Ali and Omar dig the trench in front of his house. It was not very impressive, only about 1 meter by 10 meters and 70 centimeters in depth. There were 12 people including children who would have to make use of this trench during an emergency. Whenever they heard the noise of the fighter jets, missiles or explosions, they were to lie in the trench and wait for things to clear.

For the first three days of the war, unbridled optimism pervaded the camp. Beginning on the fourth day of the war, people started to realize that what Mr. Egyptian Broadcaster had tried to make them believe was a lie. Palestinian-Israeli skirmishes were taking place near the camp. Every few hours or so soldiers ran up and down the streets. Fighter jets tore through the skies back and forth continuously, dropping their bombs on nearby targets. Karim and the other children were scared, but Saeed and Miriam kept them as calm as possible as the family huddled together in the trench that in reality offered little or no real protection.

As the battle intensified, Saeed decided to temporarily move his family to his nearby brother-in-law's bigger house, which was about 400 meters away. He divided his family into three groups of two; one group was to leave home every ten minutes and run to their cousins' house. Karim and his five-year-old sister Leen were the first to go, to be followed by the rest of the family. Karim knew the way well; he assumed that his father had him run with his sister because she was very attached to him.

As Miriam stood by the door watching, Karim and Leen took off running for their cousins' house. As they ran, they heard explosions and the sounds of incoming missiles. People ran past them in terror with eyes wide open, like zombies. Soldiers were taking off their uniforms and putting on whatever civilian-looking clothing they could find. Other soldiers were burying their weapons in the sand, sometimes alongside dead bodies. Al Shati was now a battleground.

For Karim and his sister, those 400 meters seemed more like 10 kilometers. With his sister screaming in fright, he ran towards his uncle's door and pounded on it, praying to God someone was on the other side.

"Who is it?" said an anxious voice. Karim yelled out his name. The moment the door opened, he started to cry out of both fear and relief. It took a while before they were calm and quiet. They did not completely stop weeping until the rest of the family arrived in about 20 minutes. Saeed's family spent the remainder of the day with their relatives in their trench, which was similar to the one they had left behind.

The Six-Day War started on June 5, 1967 and was fought until June 10. The result of the war was that the Israeli army now occupied the remaining parts of Palestine—the West Bank including East Jerusalem and the Gaza Strip and its refugee camps.

The war was a military disaster for the Palestinians and a massive blow to Arab public morale. Three of the strongest Arab nations were defeated by Israel in less than six days. Faith in government as well as the media was severely weakened.

A few days after the war ended, Israeli troops appeared in Al Shati. Military cars raced through the streets leaving large dust clouds in the air. It was the first time Karim had seen Israeli military vehicles with heavy machine guns on top and troops marching around in their organized, fast motions. There were tanks too: Centurions, Pattons and AMX-13s. They were large and intimidating. Karim was astonished by the size of the guns on the tanks and their tall lung pipes.

Troops, cars and tanks crisscrossed the Beach Camp from east to west. Then the first curfew was announced. On their vehicles the Israelis had mounted loudspeakers from which they made the announcement—people were to stay in their homes; there was not to be any unauthorized movement on the streets. If anyone violated curfew, the consequences would be dire. The decrees were made in well-spoken Arabic.

As the afternoon of the first day of Israeli control came to a close, more cars driving through the streets made a second announcement, "All males between 16 and 60 should report to the west side of the camp."

There was a vacant area there that the residents knew well. The men were expected to report immediately.

When they arrived at the vacant lot, hundreds of men were told to sit in rows close to each other. They were not allowed to speak or stand. The men were sorted out—those immediately deemed to be an "enemy of Israel" and the remainder of the soldiers in Gaza, most of whom announced themselves, became detainees. The rest of the men were interrogated individually in turn, to either be released or added to the detainee list.

Saeed returned home an hour or so after sunset. He smelled of sweat and was exhausted. He was thirsty but thanked God he was unharmed.

The residents of Al Shati were now forced to endure constant curfews, which restricted them to their home for weeks on end. During these strict curfews there was only an hour of release time per day for the refugees to fill water at the community square; an Israeli soldier's M16 was pointed at their heads as they did so.

Resources, which were already scarce, became harder to obtain. Men were not able to work. After the first couple of curfews people learned to buy nonperishable food whenever possible—dried fish, herbs that could be stored, rice, flour and items of that nature. Almost no families had the luxury of canned food or refrigerators. People devised coping strategies. Supplies like salt, bread and olive oil were passed from one neighbor to another over the walls of the refugee camps. Neighbors made sure to sustain each other so that no one went without the basics. Meals were getting smaller and food simpler. During the summer of 1967 sometimes the only food the family had to share was a bowl of lentil soup for the day.

When September 1967 rolled around, security restrictions had eased somewhat at the camp, and Karim and his brothers were able to go back to school. Saeed instilled in them the idea that "if you want to make a change in this world for the better, you have to be highly educated. Real progress is made by brains and hearts and not by muscles and guns."

After the Six-Day War, in many ways life became harder that it had ever been before. Rather than living under United Nations or Egyptian military rule, the Israelis were now their overseers.

Saeed vowed to God that Karim and his brothers and sister would not live their entire lives and die in Al Shati. Regardless of whether or not he ever saw Beit Daras again and no matter what he had to do, how hard he had to work, how much he had to sacrifice, his children would not remain stateless refugees.

Al Shati Camp

Chapter 10

DAILY LIFE IN AL SHATI 1968-1971

I have a name without a title

I have a name without a title
Patient in a country
where people are enraged.
My roots were entrenched before the birth of time
and before the opening of the eras
before the pines, and the olive trees
and before the grass grew.
My father descends from the family of the plow
not from a privileged class.
My grandfather was a farmer
neither well-bred, nor well-born!
Teaches me the pride of the sun
before teaching me how to read
and my house is like a watchman's hut
made of branches and cane.

Are you satisfied with my status?
I have a name without a title!
Therefore!
Record on the top of the first page:
I do not hate people
Nor do I encroach
But if I become hungry
The usurper's flesh will be my food
Beware… Beware…
Of my hunger and my anger!

Mahmoud Darwish

AL SHATI SHOULD have never existed because there never should have been Palestinian refugees to fill it. Now the second generation of these refugees was coming of age—the sons and daughters of those who were directly displaced. Saeed often wondered how long it would be before the refugees found permanent homes, either in Gaza or elsewhere. Would the Beach Camp always exist? That was the horrible possibility: that the tragedy of the Palestinian people was an unending saga never to be resolved.

Gaza City was well populated before the refugees arrived. The people already living there were Arab Palestinians too. In a sense, the refugees were unwillingly invading their home. Some of these native Gazans considered the refugees to be a lower class. This within-Arab discrimination was obvious to the adults and to the children as well. It made a bad situation even worse for the refugee families.

After the Six-Day War, there was a period of a few years when life in Al Shati settled into a somewhat predictable pattern. The constant threats of a new Arab-Israeli conflict breaking out or violent oppression from the occupying Zionist soldiers remained, but nevertheless what passed for a normal life went on. Saeed's family adapted to their circumstances as best they could; there was a rhythm to these times, and not every day was bleak or even unpleasant.

For Saeed and his family, victory was now redefined. He no longer held out any realistic hope of ever returning to Beit Daras or having his property restored to him, but he had high expectations for a brighter future—if not for himself then certainly for his children.

The only way out of Gaza for Saeed's kids was through education and achievement. Ali, Omar, Karim and Leen were taught history—they needed to know exactly what happened to them and why—but their eyes were always kept focused on the future. The future was not a sandy-floored refugee hovel; it was somewhere else living in a proper home with a family of their own.

Young Karim's daily life was centered on his family and his schoolwork. Unlike his father, Al Shati was the only home he had ever known. Although he intellectually understood that most families elsewhere in the world were not forced to live in a small, roofless, makeshift house and that most nations were not saddled under the heavy yoke of military occupation, Gaza was the only reality Karim had ever directly experienced.

Zohair was born in a different refugee camp but later came to Al Shati. Karim could not recall exactly how they met, but it was probably when the kids were playing together in a large group when they were six or seven years old. Zohair's father was a school teacher in Gaza City. The boys did many things together. Over time, they became inseparable.

Karim loved to watch the sun set into the sea. From his house in the camp it was only a short walk to the beach. He tried to be in the same place every day when the sun went down—standing on his street looking west.

Although he saw it happen every 24 hours, each sunset was a new event for him. The colors were slightly different, the reflection on the water a little brighter or duller than the previous day and the clouds in the sky formed ever changing backdrops. He felt at peace as he watched the reddish orange ball disappear into the blue water. There was also surety in each sunset; no matter what else happened, Karim would always be able to enjoy this beauty. No one could take this simple pleasure away from him.

After the last rays of sunlight faded away, if there was no moon it was very dark. There were no streetlights to illuminate Al Shati, but if there was sufficient moonlight Miriam often went outside and sat with other women from the neighborhood. If his mother was outside after dark, Karim ventured out too. On those moonlit nights, he would run around with the neighborhood kids or sit by his mother's side and listen to her discuss the events of the day with her friends.

When it was time for bed he and his older brothers would lie down on thin sheets and piles of old clothing across the room from his father, mother and sister. When the kerosene lamp was extinguished, it was time to go to sleep. Ali and Omar were in high school so, like Karim, they had to rise early to make it to school on time.

Most nights after the lamp was put out, Karim waited a few minutes and then moved across the room to be next to his father. When he did this, Saeed would often whisper a bedtime story to him. Mostly, these stories were about Palestine and what life was like in Beit Daras before the Israelis stole their land. He never tired of hearing his father talk about Palestine, but many nights Karim fell asleep before the story ended.

But he would not always stay asleep. Often his slumber was interrupted by nightmares of soldiers attacking him and taking him away. When he had these bad dreams, he moved closer to his father, who would comfort him and assure him that, at least for the moment, all was well. But when someone is 12 or 13 years old and his world is ruled by people in green uniforms with guns, many of whom despise him simply because he is a Palestinian, fear is his constant companion.

Karim was repeatedly insulted and humiliated by Israeli soldiers on the street. Some of them were cruel and capricious. Some days the soldiers would make jokes about him as he walked back from school with his friends; on other days he would be thoroughly searched and sometimes beaten for no reason.

Out of desperation, the Palestinian children demonstrated against the Israelis. After these demonstrations had begun in earnest, soldiers stormed into the school, charging forward with their heavy batons and M16 assault weapons. All of the children screamed and ran ahead of the shouting soldiers, who eventually caught up with them. The children who were caught and deemed instigators of the demonstrations were severely beaten and, in many instances, taken to jail at the tender age of 12 or 13. Surprisingly, jail did not upset these children much because the Israelis only kept them there for a few hours or a couple of days. Many of them went back to jail several times.

Living under such oppression, Karim became a shy, withdrawn child except around his parents and close friends. He was confused by the divisions and injustice he saw between people and conflicted because of the disharmony between what religion taught and the inequality that existed all around him. His mind refused to accept and come to terms with what he saw. His personal crisis was highlighted by the fact that while he was the top student in his class, nothing in his overall status changed for the better because he was still a refugee.

His parents knew how tragic it was to have to raise their children in a small house in a miserable refugee camp. They taught their children that the present circumstances of their life were the result of a monumental injustice, but they also made sure that they did not become consumed by that injustice. Their family was in need of almost everything—food, clothing, shelter, security—but they always had an abundance of love.

Saeed got up every morning before dawn to participate in the community Fajr prayer. His routine did not vary—he lit the fire so the house would be warm before his wife and children arose. Then he would make some toast over the fire and eat it, after dipping it in olive oil, of course. Sometimes Miriam would wake up and make his toast for him.

It was difficult for Saeed to find steady, long-term employment. The economy in Gaza was at best uncertain, and it was difficult for any of the refugees to prosper given that they had nothing to work with—no money, no land and no status. This proud man who once owned large tracts of land and a beautiful family home was now reduced to finding any type of manual work to support his family. Every day was a sad reminder that his birthright had been stolen from him.

But he never gave into the temptation of despair. His faith in God was his bedrock. He got out of bed, ate his simple breakfast and went to work or to look for work. His life would now be lived through his children, and that was enough for him.

In 1970, Saeed's family enjoyed the "luxury" of tap water in their small home for the first time. There was no such thing as hot water, though, unless it was heated on the stove. In the morning, the children had to wash in cold water. This was a hated thing to do, especially in the winter. But Miriam insisted that they went to school with clean faces and hands.

Breakfast was usually toast and tea. There was no money for anything other than the bare essentials. The family ate one large meal together in the late afternoon, but between meals there simply was not a lot of extra food to go around. As the sun was rising in the sky, Karim and his two brothers ate their bread, drank their tea and headed out. Sometimes they took a little bread with them for a midday snack, but that was not always available.

The boys wore modest clothing. Miriam did her best, but her boys wore hand-me-downs that were often pieced together from multiple sources. Their clothes were always clean, but they were basic. Since all the other children at the school were dressed the same way, they did not feel out of place. Their shoes were shibshib, an Arabic slang word that describes an open-toed and open-heeled sandal.

When it rained, which was not uncommon in the winter in Gaza, Karim would have to seek shelter on his way to school. He knew right where to stop on his route, a high wall with a partial roof that he could duck under to avoid getting drenched. If he stayed exposed for any length of time, all of the books and papers that he carried in his cloth book satchel would get soaked and ruined.

Karim was ahead of everybody else in his class at school. Soon his academic achievements gave him status; then his success became an ingrained habit. The school in Gaza City was a 30-minute walk from home. Karim was lucky; many students had to walk two hours to get to school. Feet were the only means of transportation for everyone in the camp.

The school was set up in a U-shape, with a sandy courtyard in the middle. Each classroom held 40 to 50 students. The building itself was hastily built, and the roof and walls leaked. When it rained, the students often had to shift positions to dodge raindrops.

Before school began, the children lined up in the courtyard for a brief period of morning exercises. If there was any news to share, such as security issues that needed to be discussed or other matters vital to the student community, the principal or a teacher would address the kids at this time.

There were six periods of the school day. After the third period, the children were let out for recreation time. If he had some, this was when Karim would eat his midday snack of bread. More often than not he had nothing to eat so he would spend this time talking with friends or playing.

Getting home from school was usually not a problem, but there were times when Karim and his friends were stopped and harassed by Israeli soldiers. Usually this was a brief encounter where Karim was berated and perhaps roughed up a bit, but for the most part he was left alone. Still, every journey home was an uncertainty. When tensions were high, the Israeli soldiers often arrested primary school children for supposed acts of defiance, such as protesting or throwing stones at the soldiers. If a small child was taken into custody, usually he was returned to his family in a few days—but not always.

Given this constant threat of detainment and violence, if Karim was even a few minutes late getting home from school, he had to answer to his mother. Saeed and Miriam's greatest fear was that one or more of their sons would be in the wrong place at the wrong time and end up in an Israeli jail—or worse. So on those days when Karim was delayed for a while—a meeting with a teacher after school, a run in with a soldier or even just spending a few minutes with a friend—he would come home to see his mother waiting at the door for him with a worried look on her face.

As soon as Karim got home, the first thing on his mind was food. Actually, food had been on his mind all day—bread and tea are not enough to satisfy a young man's hunger until late afternoon. Miriam had started the evening meal by then so the house was filled with a delicious aroma when he walked inside. He was supposed to wait until his brothers got home to eat. They usually arrived an hour or more after he did. Although he was told not to, he often stuck a spoon into the pot when his mother was not looking to steal a snack.

In Saeed's house the rule was homework first, play time second. The same small portable table, called a Tableya, that the family used to eat their meals on was Karim's workstation. After dinner, his mother would wipe off the table and set it back up under the olive tree in the middle yard of their simple house. Karim and his brothers would finish their assignments and then be released to play until darkness fell.

Miriam was illiterate. Despite this handicap, she took a great interest in all of her sons' homework, especially Karim's. She would sit across from him and watch him complete his studies. When he did, a broad smile would emerge on her face. It was this smile that told Karim it was okay to go outside and play.

Miriam—the best teacher ever

Karim and Zohair organized the neighborhood boys into two competing football teams. Their soccer field was a sandy expanse in front of their house, and their ball was a bunch of rags shoved into a cloth bag that was tightly wound with rope. The two teams would battle it out for hours. While Karim loved playing, he was not skilled at soccer, and his team usually lost.

Such was not the case with racquetball. Karim excelled at this makeshift combination of tennis and squash played against a wall. He made himself a couple of racquets out of discarded wood. These racquets were Karim's prized possessions and they served him well. Karim's friends and brothers would bring older boys or even grown men to play, but only rarely could they defeat him.

The day ended as the previous one had started, at sunset. Racquet or soccer ball in hand, young Karim stood on his street and watched the sun slide into the sea.

Life in Al Shati was all Karim knew, but whether it was from his father, a neighbor or a relative, he had been told many stories about Beit Daras. Because he had heard so much about it, he could close his eyes and see his father's home, the olive trees and the farm. In his dreams, he walked by his father's side as Saeed paid his workers or took a load of citrus or olives to market in a nearby town. He vividly imagined himself living in the big house made of Jerusalem stone and playing in the open spaces with the other children from the village.

Karim lived in two worlds, each of them in their own way very real. As a refugee, he knew want, struggle, violence and oppression. As a citizen of Palestine and a resident of Beit Daras, he had a beautiful home, a prosperous life and a proud and noble heritage.

Once or twice a month the United Nations Relief and Works Agency (UNRWA) Store House that had been set up in Al Shati issued rations to the refugees. These rations consisted mostly of food, but on occasion donated clothes were also given out. The refugees received their monthly allotment of flour, rice, sugar, cooking oil and sometimes lentils, peas and powdered milk based on their home village. While not everyone from

Beit Daras ended up at Al Shati, on a certain day each month, the former residents of Beit Daras who lived at the Beach Camp all congregated to receive their sustenance.

The Store House was on the southwesternmost edge of the camp, near the Mediterranean Sea. Saeed's home was in the northeast section of the camp, on the opposite side from the storehouse. Whether he went with his father or mother, Karim loved to go to the storehouse when the people from the old village gathered there.

Each family was given a ration card by the UNRWA. The blue card was issued in the name of the head of the household and the name of the refugee's city of origin. It entitled the bearer to their allotment of supplies from the United Nations. A lost or stolen card was difficult to replace, so the blue UNRWA laminated card was the family's most important asset, equal in standing to the house keys Saeed kept on him to the family home in Beit Daras.

On their appointed day, Saeed, Karim and perhaps one of his older brothers would get up early in the morning and make their way to the storehouse. By the time they arrived it was already a noisy and chaotic scene. People tried to get as close as possible to the point of distribution. While there were usually enough supplies for everyone, one could never be sure when the doors might close and someone would yell out, "Everything is gone!" Also, because they were picking up 50-kilogram sacks of flour and other commodities, the refugees often needed to arrange for transportation of their goods back to their homes.

Although he was young, when he went with his father to get their supplies Karim always asked him the same adult-like, intelligent question, "Why doesn't the United Nations use their money to give us the means to help us feed ourselves rather than just hand out food?"

Saeed's response was always the same. "Yes son, that makes sense, but that is not the way the world works." Jobs in Gaza were scarce, and there was little being done by the United Nations and nothing being done by Israel to help improve the infrastructure of the Gaza economy.

Since many of the families had no outside source of income, unscrupulous traders set up a makeshift marketplace adjacent to the storehouse where the refugees could exchange some of their food rations for much-needed cash. The prices these buzzards gave the refugees for their commodities were far below market prices. They took full advantage of the situation without pity or remorse.

Saeed did not engage in the practice of selling his food allotment, but many of his friends and neighbors were forced to do so. At times, getting cheated was the only option available to those desperate for cash to buy medicine or clothes or to help a sick relative. Seeing people who had nothing get swindled out of the true value of their meager amounts of flour or sugar made Karim both angry and sad. These were his villagers, the same people who would have likely worked for his father and been paid a just wage by him for a day's work on the farm. That they were reduced to begging and scrounging made him not only angry but also ashamed.

The only source of transportation from the storehouse to the refugee's homes was donkeys and mules. Some of the animals were loaded down with sacks and satchels, others pulled makeshift carts. These poor animals were often mistreated. It broke Karim's heart to see people whipping the beasts when they could barely stand, much less walk, because of the excessive burdens they were forced to pull or carry. Of course he was too young and his father would not allow it, but he wanted to run up to the poor animals and pull the heavy sacks off of their backs.

Usually Saeed and Karim would have to wait a couple of hours for a donkey or a mule to become available for transportation. When it was their turn to go home, Karim loved to sit on the back of the donkey and pet its neck. Sometimes he would be allowed to ride one for a short while. As Karim guided the animal with the reins, he imagined what it would be like to fly an airplane or drive a car. He always made sure that their donkey never carried too much and no one ever hit the animal while it was in their care.

Nothing about Al Shati was sustainable, yet somehow it endured. It was like living in a life raft with no chance of ever reaching the shore. Worse, the people who came to their rescue brought them food and water, but they refused to tow them into port.

Karim knew that his life raft was being kept afloat but just barely. Yes, it was a long way to land, but he had to try to swim to shore. He knew that most likely he would drown before he reached safety. The waters were filled with hungry sharks looking for a quick and easy meal. But staying in the life raft, staying in Gaza, meant remaining a refugee forever.

That was a fate he was simply unwilling to accept. He wanted to leave and then return with the means to help his people, with a big motor boat to take at least some of them to shore.

Unidentified Palestinian boy being arrested by Israeli soldiers for demonstrating against oppression

Chapter 11

NIGHT TERROR

Defiance

Tighten my fetters.
Confiscate my papers
and cigarettes.
Fill my mouth with dust.
Poetry is blood in the heart,
salt in bread,
moisture in eyes.
It is written with fingernails,
with eyes,
with daggers.
I shall proclaim in my detention cell,
in the bathroom,
in the stable,
under the lash,
manacled,
in the violence of chains,
that a million birds

on the branches of my heart,
are singing fighting songs.

Mahmoud Darwish

EVERY MORNING AFTER breakfast Karim was off to school but not before receiving the same admonition from his mother: stay out of trouble. The trouble she was referring to was run-ins with the Israeli security forces. He gave his mother a hug goodbye and promised to do his best, but it was becoming increasingly difficult for Palestinian youngsters to avoid problems with the Israelis.

Palestinian children were tired of the abuse, the constant harassment and the occupation of their homeland by what they considered to be a foreign power. The conditions under which they were forced to live—crude shelters for homes, little or no economic opportunities, being directed to do this and that at gunpoint by the Israeli military—were a breeding ground for discontent and radical and sometimes violent retaliation against oppression.

Despite difficult conditions, the Palestinian teachers at Karim's United Nations sponsored school were incredibly dedicated. Rain or shine, heat or cold, they taught the children without interruption. There was a consensus in the Palestinian community that regardless of their exile and domination by the Israelis, their children would be well educated. If Palestine was to have any future, it was the children who would have to create it.

During breaks in between classes, the children would gather in the school's courtyard and chant slogans like, "Freedom, justice and equality." If a larger group of protesters were doing the same just outside the school walls, which was often the case, the kids would climb over the short walls and join the larger group in the streets. From late 1969 onward, protests in one form or another in Gaza were basically ongoing. Periodically, the Israelis would react against these protests.

One day Karim was standing in the courtyard with his fellow students chanting in protest when big, dark green vehicles pulled up in front of the school. Other vehicles deposited Israeli soldiers around the perimeter. Soldiers then stormed onto the school grounds and arrested the students who were protesting. If a child resisted, he was beaten and then tossed into a waiting vehicle to be transported to a detention facility.

As the soldiers manhandled their way through the school, grabbing students and carrying them off, Karim and a group of his classmates moved towards the principal's office. Normally the principal's office was a place to be avoided, but now it seemed the only potentially safe place on the compound.

When he arrived at the office he found that the principal and the teachers were already engaged with the soldiers, arguing with them in loud voices that they should not be so violent with the children and that what they were doing was not justified. The soldiers were not interested in listening to the complaints. Rather, they shouted orders to them that needed to be followed immediately or threatened to arrest them as well.

Karim was 12 years old and scared to death. All around him was noisy chaos and men with guns and batons looking for more victims. So he decided to climb out of the back window of the principal's office. Behind the school was a one-meter high wall with barbed wire strung on top of it. In theory, the wall was designed to prevent anyone from leaving or entering school property without permission. However, the wall was low, and the wire was not too carefully positioned. Karim was able to crawl over the wall and through the wire without getting cut too badly. Some other students followed his lead and similarly escaped.

But they had not reached safety yet. Waiting for them on the other side of the wall was an armed soldier. When Karim saw the soldier, he turned and ran as fast as he could in the opposite direction. It was a rainy day, so there were puddles on the street, and the sand was thick and sticky. He took off his sandals so he could move faster. He felt that he was literally running for his life. There was no doubt in his mind that, if he had stayed on the school grounds, at a minimum he would have been arrested and carted off with the other kids. Now he was afraid that he might get shot in the back or be bludgeoned to death by an angry Israeli infantryman.

After running for a couple of blocks, Karim looked behind him and saw that the soldier was not following. Either he had eluded capture or the soldier had lost interest in him. Momentarily relieved, he took a deep breath and was about to put his sandals back on when a military vehicle came around the corner and started moving in his direction. So he started running again, faster this time as the vehicle pursued him.

He ran towards a small grocery store and dashed inside. The middle-aged man who owned the shop stood up quickly, and his chair fell back, knocking some food items off of the shelf. Then the man said, "There is a door in the back behind a box of lemons. You can get out from there, and you will be on the other side of the neighborhood."

Karim was frightened beyond words, so he stood there frozen for a moment.

Then the man shouted, "Quickly!"

The shop owner was only doing what every other Palestinian in Gaza would have done; he offered refuge to someone fleeing the Israelis. There was solidarity among the people. No one gave anybody up, ever. The man knew that within a few seconds armed and angry Israeli soldiers would burst through his door demanding to know where the "rebel" was hiding.

But before Karim could make his escape, he was caught as two soldiers rushed in and saw him standing there preparing to flee. Part of him was glad that they caught him because he did not want the shop owner to be assaulted or arrested on his behalf.

The Israeli soldiers beat Karim with thick batons. They cursed him and detained him for hours. He was a sixth-grade boy who was simply frightened to death, yet they treated him as if he was an armed militant. The only crime he was guilty of was peacefully protesting against the Israeli occupation of Gaza.

They released him later that night. He arrived home feeble and weak with bumps, bruises and scrapes all over his body. He had lost his sandals too, which was a major problem since the family did not have extra money for new shoes.

Miriam wrapped him in blankets, fed him lentil soup and tended to his wounds. He cried and cried until he could cry no more and then went to bed. However, soon after he fell asleep Karim woke up with a start. The

Zionists were invading his slumber with nightmares, horrible visions of being chased, grabbed and beaten for the crime of being a young boy who dared to speak out against his oppressors.

The Israeli military ran Al Shati with an iron fist. They considered every refugee to be a potential enemy. Strict nighttime curfews remained in force. All of Gaza, not just Al Shati, was heavily patrolled by Zionist soldiers. What the soldiers called terrorist activity— and the Palestinians considered fighting for their freedom—was steadily intensifying.

In 1970, over 200 soldiers and Palestinians were killed when multiple bombs exploded in Gaza in public places—attacks carried out both to intimidate Palestinians cooperating with the Israeli authorities and to send a message to the Zionist military commanders that the Palestinians in Gaza would not stand idly by in response to oppression.

At the end of a beautiful summer day in 1970, Karim relaxed at home. The sun had dipped below the horizon, leaving behind a spectrum of colors ranging from red to dark blue. Stars rose in the night sky, decorating it with their mysterious twinkles.

He lay on his back, his eyes fixed on those distant, magical stars and wondered whether there was another planet out there that supported life. He also wondered if he would ever be loose from the vise grip of the refugee camp and its poverty, strife and the continuous protests.

The family had a Sony radio, which was their main source of entertainment. In the evenings, they would sit around the radio and listen to various news and entertainment programs. Around 9 p.m. every night, after the radio programs were over, the family went to bed.

Karim fell asleep for a few hours until he was startled by strange sounds, flashes of light and loud knocks on the door—not on the door outside the home but the doors within. He opened his eyes and saw his family's humble ceiling-less foyer powerfully lit up by bright electric flashlights. A large number of armed Israeli soldiers had jumped over the short wall that surrounded their two-bedroom home and forced themselves inside.

Now fully awake and terrified, he heard his father protesting against this unwarranted invasion of his family's privacy. Saeed's exclamations were responded to by a rough push from one soldier, followed by two other soldiers holding him to face their captain. The captain told Saeed that if he did not calm down, they would arrest him.

While all this was going on, Miriam was in a bedroom trying to calm her baby, who was crying in protest. Karim's ten-year-old sister Leen was tightly glued to her mother with a look of terror on her beautiful little face. She cried and shivered in fear as she listened to the soldiers shouting in the main room.

Karim remained where he was and attempted to appear asleep, to somehow escape reality by taking cover underneath his blankets. He was denied this false sense of security when a soldier pulled the covers away from him and yelled in a strange, incorrect Arabic accent. "Get up! Get on your feet!"

He stood there motionless, incapable of uttering a word.

"Where is Omar?" the captain yelled, inquiring about Karim's 16-year-old brother.

"Why do you ask?" replied Saeed.

"Don't ask. Just answer!"

"He's in the room next to you."

The captain gave instructions to his soldiers in Hebrew. The soldiers went into the other bedroom. Karim could hear them ask, "Are you Omar?"

Seconds later, his brother was brought out to the foyer where a couple of soldiers handcuffed and blindfolded him. They started to drag him out of the house against Miriam's loud protests. She cried out that he was just a young boy and a student and that he did not have any record of causing trouble. Her pleas were met with heartless commands to remain silent and an occasional shove out of the way. Nothing she said affected the soldiers, so she put her crying baby on the ground and ran after her son who was being abducted before her eyes.

"Have some mercy! Have you no mother?" Miriam cried, pleading to the captain. "Would you care for your mother if she were in my position?" She repeated this statement several times.

The captain answered her with an Arabic proverb which he pronounced in his own strange accent. "A hundred eyes cry, but not my mother's," meaning that he cared for his mother's tears but for no one else's. Then he added, "This son of yours is a terrorist."

Omar was escorted outside and locked up in a military truck. But that did not conclude the soldiers' mission; they had not done enough. They tossed Saeed's small house and turned it head over heels, searching every corner and drawer, scattering their clothes and other belongings. They ransacked the kitchen, throwing the family's meager food supplies of flour, tea and sugar on the ground. In response to Miriam's pleas for mercy, the soldiers only offered a terse command of "Silence!"

These events took place between 2 and 4 a.m. Zohair's father knocked on the Saeed's door immediately after the soldiers left. His son was by his side.

"They took him?" Zohair asked Karim, already knowing the answer.

"Yes, they forced their way in here. They have no respect for anything."

"I know. I saw most of what happened looking over the fence."

The conversation between the two friends continued as the house filled with inquisitive neighbors, all seeking answers to the same questions: What happened? Why Omar? "Your son is well mannered; he doesn't deserve this," along with expressions of sympathy and condolences were mostly directed towards Miriam, whose tears had not stopped flowing.

Over the past couple of years, such midnight raids had become more common. Several of the neighbors recalled how a son or a husband was taken and did not return for months. Friends could offer condolences but no real comfort. Everyone in Al Shati knew that the Israelis did what they wanted with no real accountability. The refugees had no meaningful civil rights.

Midmorning Saeed decided to go to the Red Cross Center. His neighbors told him that he might be able to locate his son through the Red Cross but they had no information to give him, although they assured him that they would try to find Omar. Going through the Red Cross was the only way of finding out anything about those taken away by the Israeli military.

Three months passed. Saeed's family was in a constant state of anxiety and sorrow because they knew nothing of Omar's fate. Finally, they received a short letter from the Red Cross informing them that Omar was being held in Almajdal prison in Ashkelon, which was about 25 kilometers north of Al Shati. They knew nothing more.

Days after the letter arrived, Saeed went to the Red Cross Center in Gaza to see if they had any updates on Omar's status. As soon as he returned home, Miriam asked, "What did you learn?"

"Omar will be put on trial in two months."

"Why? What is he charged with?"

Saeed offered no response. He was upset and having great difficulty expressing his thoughts as words. He did not really need to say more. Everyone in Al Shati knew that Israeli trials of Palestinian suspects were almost always followed by convictions and long prison terms. The specific charges were irrelevant.

"What are we going to do?"

"I don't know," Saeed said, his eyes focused on the floor.

"We have to find Omar an attorney." Saeed said nothing. Miriam repeated her statement, and he nodded.

"And where do we find the money to pay this attorney?" he finally said.

"Allah will provide," she answered with total confidence.

A friend told Saeed that an Israeli lawyer might be willing to defend Omar. Her name was Felicia Langer, a German-Israeli human rights advocate who was defending several Palestinians accused of political crimes, such as protesting against the occupation.

A lawyer took Omar's case and argued that he had done nothing wrong other than to speak out against injustice. Omar AlShaikh was convicted of the crime of belonging to a resistance group. He was sentenced to two years in an Israeli prison. When he was arrested, he was only 16, just a boy.

The Al Shati community was increasingly enraged. But what could they do? How could they defend themselves? Their options were limited.

Karim and Zohair discussed these matters when they were walking down the sandy streets of the camp or playing soccer or when they were at school. Although they were still young boys, the circumstances of their lives had forced them to grow up way too quickly.

"I think there will be another war soon," Karim said.

"The radio says that the Arabs are traitors," Zohair responded. "They did not protect us in '67. They only looked out for themselves."

"That's why the next war will be between us and the Israeli military."

"There will be so much blood."

Unlike a few years earlier, no one in the camp was hopeful. The future for the refugees looked bleak. While another war did not start as quickly as some anticipated, conflicts and riots became a normal part of daily life in Gaza.

The Palestinian families who called Gaza home before 1948 were increasingly worried and resentful concerning the refugees. A large rift was growing between rich and poor because the refugees were not being assimilated into the larger community.

Over dinner one evening Saeed told his family, "Palestine is nothing like it used to be. All the rules have changed, and they continue to be rewritten."

Part of Karim believed that it must be possible to break free of his situation, but another part of him worried that his fate was sealed, that he was somehow destined to live a life of desperation and want. Like his father, the better part of him was naturally optimistic. While the suffering all around him weighed heavily on his soul, he did not allow this burden to defeat him or cast him into deep despair.

After Omar's arrest, Karim began to see everything in his life as a challenge. He vowed that he would somehow rise above the injustice, strife and constant conflict. The only other option was to quit and give into the fear, to accept the false and evil premise that because he was born a Palestinian, his life was worth less than another's life.

Although he was only a boy of 13, from this point forward Karim was a young man with a singular purpose—to rise above the pain, fear, violence and hate to become the person Allah intended him to be.

Tel Aviv beach near the soap factory

Chapter 12

THE SOAP FACTORY 1975

Palestine

This land gives us
all that makes life worth living:
April's blushing advances,
the aroma of bread at dawn,
a woman's haranguing of men,
the poetry of Aeschylus,
love's trembling beginning,
moss on a stone
mothers dancing on a flute's thread
and the invaders' fear of memories.

This land give us
all that makes life worth living:
September's rustling end,
a woman leaving forty behind with her apricots,

an hour of sunlight in prison,
clouds reflecting swarms of insects,
a people's applause for those who laugh at their erasure,
and the tyrant's fear of songs.

This land give us
all that makes life worth living:
Lady Earth, mother of all beginnings and endings,
She was called Palestine
and she is still called Palestine.
My Lady, because you are my Lady, I deserve life.

Mahmoud Darwish

OUT OF NECESSITY, Karim entered the job market at the tender age of 13, even though up to that point he had not been away from his parents for more than a couple of hours other than to go to school. The best manual labor jobs were found in Israel, not Gaza. Because he spoke Hebrew, Karim had an advantage when looking for work in the occupied territories.

His first summer job was working on a farm inside Israel picking apricots from 6 a.m. to 6 p.m. Karim was the youngest laborer in the group—some of his coworkers were over 60 years old. The dried apricots were packed in boxes and both consumed locally and exported to Europe.

When Saeed heard of this job, he initially did not allow Karim to return to the orchards. It hurt him to see his son working so hard for so little, but he was also afraid that a manual labor job might be a distraction from Karim's education. However, he relented when he could see how determined Karim was to earn money for the family.

Karim's next job was at another farm some two hours' drive inside Israel. It was similar to the first one in terms of picking fruit. The biggest difference was that he had to stay on the farm for 17 straight days. He worked 12-hour shifts and then slept under the sky at night. At dawn he would wake up and start working again.

After the first 17-day cycle, Karim could not take it anymore and asked to go home. The problem was how to send him home because the farm was far from the main highway. The Israeli orchard owner, who was an emigrant from the Soviet Union, was kind enough to arrange for someone to take Karim to a main road that connected to other cities. There he caught a bus and returned to Gaza. When he returned, he was welcomed as if he had come back from the dead.

For a while, he worked as a manual laborer in the construction business just outside of Tel Aviv. His job was to mix the cement and carry it on his shoulders to the construction worker who would then apply it on a wall. He also carried tiles on his head. Sadly, after he had worked on this job for a couple of weeks, the subcontractor disappeared without paying him or the other workers anything. Karim was not in a position to complain to the police because he was supposed to go through Israeli labor offices to get employment, something he did not do. Official work permits were avoided at all costs by the Palestinians because it meant that more than 50 percent of their pay would be taken from them. So Karim was part of a large, unofficial and illegal Palestinian workforce.

Shortly after this fiasco, he landed another job working on the construction of prefabricated houses. He started as a manual laborer and closely observed how the people handling the materials guided the men working on the cranes and directed them to precisely position the suspended walls of a house. This process was interesting to him, and he quickly moved up the ranks. But when the construction was complete, the work was over.

Until he graduated from high school, Karim never kept a dime of his wages—every penny he made went to his father to help support the family.

Palestinian high school students completed their final exams at the end of June. In July 1975, the final marks and ranking of students were released. The announcement of where the students ranked in terms of their class and their cumulative GPA was big news in Gaza—the results were broadcast over the radio as soon as they were available. Karim was ranked among the top students in all of the Gaza Strip. It was a high honor for both him and his family.

There were no universities in Gaza. Higher education had to be pursued in other countries. Due to the political situation, there was no direct way for prospective Palestinian students to apply to Egyptian universities, so they sent their applications through the Red Cross. Generally, Egyptian universities did not accept new Palestinian students until a year after they completed their high school education.

There was never any question that Karim would go to college; it was a matter of when he would do so. It was his desire to keep working to help support the family until his siblings had completed their higher education, but Saeed vetoed that plan. Karim applied to study medicine and was accepted. He was set to begin studying at Tanta University in Egypt in November 1976.

So in July 1975, Karim was once again looking for employment. It was just past 7 in the evening, right after sunset. There was a knock at the door. Miriam gestured to him with her eyes to see who it was. He opened the door.

"Hello, Zohair, come right in." Karim was always pleased to see his best friend. It was obvious from Zohair's face that he had news to share. Karim hoped it was not of another crackdown by the Israeli military.

"There is a factory, a soap factory, in Israel. They need more workers, and they pay well."

"How do you know?"

"I have been working there for a week. I want you to come and work there too." Zohair's pleading eyes suggested that he would not take no for an answer.

Karim looked at his mother, and she tilted her head as if to say, "It's up to you; you know best."

This was welcome news. His face lit up with joy. Good paying jobs were difficult to find. To make it even more attractive, he was going to be working with his best friend. Life had certainly taken a turn for the better.

He wanted to get his father's approval for his new plan, so later that evening after Saeed came home from work, they had a discussion.

"It's a great opportunity. I need to save some money for school; we both know that."

"Karim, I understand what you are saying. I'm not trying to argue with you. I suppose I am frightened more than anything else."

"Father, I can handle myself in Israel. I will not get into trouble," Karim promised.

"I'm not overly concerned about you getting into trouble, although that is always a possibility," Saeed explained. "I am worried that you will start making money and for whatever reason choose to keep making money rather than pursue your dreams."

Karim looked his father squarely in the eyes. "I'm going to Egypt next year. I will become a physician. Of this, you should have no doubt."

"Life is uncertain, Karim. Only God knows what will happen tomorrow."

"You have my solemn vow, Father. I will go to university next year. I promise you."

With that, Saeed let out a big sigh and gave his son a hug. While he was not completely happy about what Karim was doing, he knew that it was being done with the best of intentions. Karim had to save money for school expenses. There was simply no other option.

Zohair told Karim that they had to leave early in the morning, around 4 a.m., to get to work. The factory was two hours inside Israel. That meant getting out of bed at 3 a.m., so Zohair left and Karim did his best to retire early. But the excitement of his future prospects kept him awake until late into the evening.

The next morning Karim met his friend at the appointed place at precisely 4 a.m. They were not the only people there. More than a hundred workers were also trying to get on the bus at the same time. Zohair had some experience at finding a seat on the bus through the crowd, so Karim followed him. The two skinny 18-year-olds nearly had to crawl under people's legs before they finally made it to the bus floor. Karim wondered if he would be required to go through this contest every day before work.

Zohair and Karim spent most of their two-hour journey to an industrial area outside of Tel Aviv taking short naps. They crossed the Israeli border check post around 6 a.m. and arrived at the factory an hour later.

After they had climbed out of the bus, they surveyed their new place of employment.

The factory was about two-thirds the size of a football ground. Inside, the facility was divided into three parts. The front section was dedicated to offices and chemical storage. The largest area of the factory was in the middle, which housed six large mixing units. The production floor was splattered with chemicals and was slippery. The back of the factory was separated by a plywood partition from the production area. Here they stored the finished product in various sized containers.

Karim stood on the production floor waiting to be called upon by the manager. He looked around at the dirty, chemical-stained floor and noticed the excessive clutter. The high roof of the plant was held up by tall pillars and a crisscrossing mesh of steel girders going all the way down to the far end of the factory. The overwhelming smell of the chemicals was nearly too much to stand.

The superintendent walked over to greet Karim. After brief introductions, Karim asked, "Where are the factory workers?"

Jacob, the superintendent, was a Yemeni Jew. It was clear from the start that Jacob did not like to answer questions and that he did not like Karim.

"They are all here," Jacob replied tersely. Karim looked at his friend, question on his face. Zohair nodded in response, confirming that Jacob was telling the truth.

After a brief further exchange of information, they walked over to the plant manager's office. Jacob pounded on the door, and someone inside with a deep voice yelled, in Hebrew, "Tekanais!" which means, "Enter!"

Inside seated behind a desk was a tall Polish man with a long face named Abraham. He had wide eyes and white skin, a peaked nose, receding hairline and dark, hornrimmed glasses. His eyes were glued to a big ledger. Without looking up from his book he asked, "Your name?"

"Abdul Karim." Karim said with a tone of confidence in his voice.

Abraham looked up to see who in the hell this refugee boy was who spoke like he was someone. His look was piercing, but he was more curious than angry.

"Abdul will do just fine. Abdul, this is a business. I pay for work, not for idling. I don't simply let the idle people go; I deal with them my way, and they don't like my discipline. See that you do your job properly and quickly at all times." The threat in Abraham's voice was crystal clear. "Jacob, show them what to do."

Karim and Zohair then became Jacob's new recruits. The superintendent was having a field day with the boys; they were his favorite toys. Karim soon realized that there was nothing much to making soap. Both he and his friend had studied chemistry in high school and were familiar with how to make the three types of liquid soap produced by the factory.

One type of soap was for cleaning window glass, another was for cleaning dishes and the third was for washing floors. All of them were almost exactly the same product except for the concentrations of chemicals and differences in perfume. Jacob made it seem like making soap was rocket science. He was a bit disappointed to see that Karim and Zohair grasped the simple concept and process in a couple of hours.

The job was not difficult. Once the quantity of soap to be produced was given, the proper amount of ingredients was loaded into the six mixers. All Karim and Zohair had to do was fill the mixers with the correct amount of water so the concentration of water to chemical matched the category of the liquid soap being produced. Perfume was added during the mixing process.

What came as a rude shock to Karim was when he discovered that each of the huge 500-liter capacity mixers had to be mixed manually. He and Zohair had to stand on a platform holding long instruments like oars and mix the soap with their arms in a circular motion. While they were mixing, they could hear Jacob and Abraham shouting at them to ensure that they did not miss a beat.

If any one of the factory workers made a mistake, the response from Jacob and Abraham was more than just shouting. Karim and Zohair refused to be humiliated. However, since they had no authority, all they could do was work hard and not give the superintendent or manager a chance to say anything. Jacob was an idiot, but Abraham was another story. He was a shrewd, authoritative and intelligent man. He soon saw that Karim and Zohair did not want to be told what to do.

When he shouted at them, they slowed down a bit. When he left them alone, the boys worked harder. Abraham proved his intelligence by understanding the personalities of his workers. He backed off. He did not say anything if nothing needed to be said. He walked quietly past behind them most of the time.

The friends kept doing their best. The days were long and arduous. By the time they got back to Al Shati, it would be past 9 p.m. A few hours later, the whole cycle would be repeated.

Karim started questioning the wisdom of being home for a few hours only to sleep. Their schedule needed to change, so he came up with an idea. Perhaps they could sleep at the factory during the week and avoid the bus trip home. At least that way they would be less exhausted and be able to spend quality time with their families on their days off. Zohair agreed that it was a good plan, but there were risks.

The day they tried out their new plan they were making detergent for washing floors. This was the simplest product to make in terms of mixing chemicals, but it was the one they dreaded the most because chemical acid was added to the mixture. The noxious fumes that emanated from this combination were a severe irritant to the eyes and lungs. They covered their faces with a cloth, but this was not enough protection.

The end of the shift came. Karim and Zohair stayed behind. They found Abraham just as he was ready to leave for the day. After a brief discussion, he agreed to let them spend the night in the factory, provided that they stayed out of sight and kept quiet. Things had to be organized before it was completely dark. They could not turn on the lights at night for the risk of being spotted by the police. The Israeli authorities were always on the lookout for illegal workers.

They separated off one corner towards the far end of the factory, close to the storage area. To avoid being spotted in case someone entered the premises, Karim and Zohair made a wall of plastic sacks containing jerry cans. Then they found wooden planks and stacked them one on top of another creating a crude elevated bed. They had a couple of blankets hidden away to use as covers. This hideaway was just big enough for the two of them. They were exhausted and quickly fell asleep.

As time went on, Karim developed a good relationship with Abraham. Both boys proved that they were reliable workers and extremely bright and capable. They designed an automatic mixer for the plant, and Karim helped Abraham devise a new product distribution plan.

One day while Karim was working on top of a mixer, an electric wire broke free and created a hazardous situation on the plant floor. He was in serious danger of being electrocuted unless someone immediately came to his aid. Seeing the situation, Abraham instantly bolted out his office, jumped over a wall to avoid getting electrocuted himself and rescued Karim using a large wooden stick.

Weeks and then months passed. Abraham began to trust the boys, and it was obvious that he liked them too. He started to leave almost everything up to them—the plant production schedule, for example, and he also entrusted Karim and Zohair to sell his goods and receive cash and checks from his vendors. Abraham's customers came from all over the region—some were Sephardic Jews, others were Ashkenazic and so on. Karim got on well with all of them because he spoke both Hebrew and Arabic fluently.

To his surprise, Karim made friends with these customers. Once they got to know him and could see what an upstanding young man he was, the customers were nice. This made him wonder, were these the same people who stole his father's land? They did not seem to be evil people at all—just the opposite.

Karim's new friends told him about their immigration to Israel from the United States, Europe and other Arab countries. The European Jews told stories about the Holocaust and something called "pogroms." These affable and open people came to Israel seeking a place of refuge. He wondered if they knew their country was built on land stolen from Palestinians.

For obvious reasons, Karim did not discuss politics with his new friends. Almost all of them were considerably older than he was, and almost all of them were Jewish. For the first time in his life, he felt comfortable around adults other than his parents and close relatives. He learned how to handle himself in social situations, what to say and what not to say, how not to offend and how to communicate effectively in a business context.

Karim and Zohair also got the chance to see a great deal of Palestine. Abraham often took the boys with him when he went to places like Haifa, Jaffa, Netanya, Herzliya and Tel Aviv to deliver product. It was awkward for them to see Palestine from a seat in a Polish Israeli immigrant's work truck. At times they wanted to shout at Abraham, "Do you know this land is not yours?" But they liked and respected Abraham, so they kept their opinions to themselves.

On one of these trips, Karim delivered boxes to a building where a Jewish lady operated a small trading company. He carried two boxes on his shoulder, each one containing 24, 1-liter bottles. He was required to carry these boxes up six flights of stairs. Because it was Ramadan, a fasting month, and a hot summer afternoon, when he arrived at the sixth floor with the boxes, he was exhausted, short of breath and sweating profusely.

When the lady opened the door, the first thing she said was, "Abraham, this chap is exhausted, and he looks dehydrated! Why did you ask him to carry these boxes by himself?"

Abraham smiled but did not comment. The lady ran towards the kitchen and brought a glass of juice for Karim. "Sit down and drink this, son." She extended her hand towards him.

"Thank you," Karim said, "but I am fasting."

"You should not work on such a day."

"I have to work, but do not worry ma'am. I will be ok. Thank you for your kindness." As he turned to walk away, Karim noticed a few teardrops coming out of the nice lady's eyes.

One day Abraham walked out on the factory floor at midday and said, "Karim and Zohair, be prepared this evening. You are invited to attend a party."

"Are you planning to marry again, Abraham?" Karim joked while stirring the soap solution.

"I am not kidding. Finish what you are doing and come to my office with Zohair. I will explain."

Ten minutes later during their lunch break both boys went to see Abraham.

"What is the matter?" Zohair asked.

"Tell us what you have to say quickly because we want to get our meal from the cafeteria next door. We have no time," Karim added.

Abraham smiled. "My newest son is eight days old. We will be performing a bris ceremony this evening."

Karim knew a lot of Hebrew words, but not this one. "What is that? What do you mean?"

"Like you Muslims, we Jews also have to circumcise our newborn sons."

"At least we have that much in common," Karim commented in a lighthearted, teasing manner. "What will we be doing there?"

"Sharing the occasion and celebration with us."

"Come on, Abraham. You know us, but your guests do not," Karim said, unconvinced that an important Israeli businessman would invite two Palestinian refugees to an intimate family celebration.

"Most of my guests are good people, and they accept others without prejudice. Besides, most of them already know about both of you," Abraham explained.

"Wow, so you told them that you have two 'terrorists' working for you," Karim replied, referring to how many Israelis stereotyped all Palestinians. He looked at Zohair, and he could tell they were both thinking the same thing. "Abraham, we appreciate your kind invitation, but I think we shouldn't go. We would not want to embarrass you on such an important occasion."

"You have to come. If you appreciate me, you must attend my son's bris," Abraham asked kindly.

Zohair and Karim looked at each other and nodded in agreement.

"Be ready at 5 p.m. I will come and pick you up. Now go get some lunch."

So Zohair and Karim, two young Palestinian refugees, attended the bris of Abraham's son. They had a wonderful time and were treated with kindness by everyone at the event. Again Karim wondered to himself, what did these people know about the Palestinians? Were they aware of their suffering? Were they simply "out of sight and out of mind"?

By September 1976 Karim and Abraham had developed a genuine friendship, so it was with more than a bit of sadness when Karim came to tell his manager that he was quitting. Abraham was in his modest office with his friends, Heyeem and Rahamaim, the two owners of an adjacent window factory where both Karim and Zohair worked at times until midnight to earn extra money.

"I must give you my termination notice," Karim said. "I will be starting university soon. I'm going to become a doctor!"

"Could Karim become a doctor?" Heyeem asked.

"Why not?" Abraham said as he smiled.

At the end of the month, Abraham paid Karim's salary in full. Abraham, Heyeem and Rahamaim met him on his way out of the plant to bid him goodbye. They wished him all the success in the world.

Then Rahamaim said, "I will not go to any other doctor! I will wait for your return and come to you only!"

Karim joked back, "Then make sure you remain alive until then!"

During his time working at the soap factory, Karim had learned some valuable life lessons. He had earned the respect of and befriended Abraham who, as it turned out, was not only a factory owner but also a general in the Israeli army. Karim worked hard for him, and Abraham in return treated him with kindness and with dignity.

Abraham reinforced the lesson Saeed taught Karim as a young boy—those who treat others kindness and justice are deserving of our goodwill and friendship, whether they are Muslim, Jew or Christian.

Karim with his brother at Gaza beach

Chapter 13

LEAVING GAZA 1976

Psalm 31

Have mercy on me, O Lord, for I am in trouble;
My eye wastes away with grief,
Yes, my soul and my body!
For my life is spent with grief,
And my years with sighing;
My strength fails because of my iniquity,
And my bones waste away.
I am a reproach among all my enemies,
But especially among my neighbors,
And am repulsive to my acquaintances;
Those who see me outside flee from me.
I am forgotten like a dead man, out of mind;
I am like a broken vessel.
For I hear the slander of many;
Fear is on every side.

IT IS ONLY natural to flee from suffering. No one in their right mind embraces oppression or is pleased to be an unwilling servant to an unwanted master. So on November 2, 1976, Karim was thrilled when he received his final acceptance letter and permission to cross national borders to attend university. His thoughts went immediately to what life might be like for him in Egypt.

Getting accepted to medical school was beyond a dream come true; it was liberation in every sense of that word. Despite this great news, it was a day of mixed emotions. November 2 is a black day in Palestinian history because it was on this day in 1917 that the British Foreign Minister Balfour issued his infamous declaration allowing Jewish people to immigrate to Palestine in large numbers. For Palestinians, November 2 is a day of mourning because it marks the beginning of their suffering.

Since 1948, the Palestinian people had no government body to issue them passports and visas. Depending upon who was in charge of Gaza at the time—the Israelis, the Egyptians or the United Nations—getting permission to study abroad or to immigrate was either extremely difficult or impossible. Other nations feared that if Palestinians were allowed to travel for any purpose, they would simply choose not to return to whatever refugee camp they came from. In effect, this made the vast majority of Palestinians prisoners in small geographic areas.

Karim was released, but when would his people be set free? His heart would forever remain with Palestine. He knew that he was leaving a tragedy behind, but there was no other choice. His parents did not want him to stay, but they were hopeful that when he had completed his education it might be possible for him to return.

Al Shati was the only home Karim had ever known. Ideas like freedom of movement and freedom from oppression were things he intellectually understood but had never experienced. While Egypt was not a democratic society like Western Europe or America, it was dramatically more prosperous and open than Gaza.

As he finished packing his belongings, he wondered if he would miss Al Shati. Would he be able to return home? Yes, in theory, but the political situation in Palestine and Gaza was always uncertain. Would the Middle East explode in conflict yet again? Would his family become casualties in the next war? If the past was any guide, he had to prepare himself to deal with some unpleasant possibilities.

On those few nights when Karim was able to be in front of a TV at a neighbor's home, he watched Egyptian TV. The films and shows from Egypt depicted a country where people lived in relative peace, free from the iron grip of military rule. Like many other young Palestinians, he idolized former Egyptian President Nasser. Karim grew up listening to Nasser's inspirational speeches on the radio. Now he was heading to Nasser's homeland, to a better place where the possibility existed that he could become all he was capable of becoming.

But what was Egypt really like? He had no way of knowing, no frame of reference and no experience to draw upon. While he read voraciously and tried his best to learn all he could from talking with others, he still had serious doubts that Egypt was all he hoped it would be. He trusted that God was not leading him astray and that He was mercifully sending him to a place of deliverance, not to a place of even greater suffering.

Karim was headed to Tanta, Egypt, located north of Cairo and south of Alexandria. It was well known for its sweets and textile industries, but its primary fame was as a university town. Tanta University's medical school was highly regarded. Top students from many Arab countries came there to complete their medical degrees. He felt best about the medical school aspect of his new life. He had little doubt that the university itself was everything it was represented to be.

There were a few Palestinians in Gaza who had been to Tanta. Karim had found some distant relatives who were able to tell him what life was like in the city, but no one could tell him what it would be like to go from being a factory worker and a refugee who was accustomed to taking orders and being on the bottom of the social tier to a medical student at a prestigious Arab university. He would have to discover what that was like all on his own.

Although he had saved almost all of the money he had earned working at the soap factory, his supply of funds was meager. His existing financial resources would have to see him through the next year, so he carefully budgeted only for essentials like food and clothing. He would not be well dressed by the standards of his peers, but he was not concerned by this. Karim was accustomed to doing more with less, so making do was second nature to him.

The day before he left, the entire neighborhood came by to see him off. Everyone shared in his and his family's joy. Any young person who had worked hard enough to earn the right to study abroad had triumphed not just for himself but also for the entire community.

This final sendoff was bittersweet. Karim wondered about his peers, those young men and women about his age. What would become of them? Many of them had chosen a far different path than the one he was on; they were determined to fight for the liberation of their homeland. There was no doubt that violence would come again and again to Gaza and all of Palestine. Until there was justice, there could be no peace.

Thirty years earlier the equation was simple—Karim's people lived in Palestine as they had done for centuries. To uproot them, to take their homes and force them to flee was evil. Now, however, an entirely new generation of people existed—refugees like him who had never lived in Western Palestine and Israelis who had known nothing but the State of Israel as their country. What did justice look like now? More violence and death? A never ending cycle of repression and resistance, of attack and counterattack?

Karim thought that perhaps Gandhi was right when he said, "An eye for an eye only makes the whole world blind." Yet there was no escaping the fact that his people had been wronged and viscously persecuted. What was the answer to such a seemingly insoluble problem? The answer for him seemed to involve healing, not inflicting pain, in the acceptance of differences, not judgmental prejudice. These are the lessons Saeed had taught his son.

Around 100 kilometers south of the Al Shati camp was the border crossing at Al Areesh. This was a chaotic place and heavily militarized. Since there was no functioning airport in Gaza, the only way out other than through Israel proper was through this border crossing. Although the

Israeli military controlled all of the Sinai from Gaza to the Suez Canal, Al Areesh was still considered a border to be crossed.

Saeed and Miriam took their son to the Al Areesh bus station. Once there, Karim's papers were checked and rechecked to be sure that everything was in order. Waiting in line to board the bus were 200 or so other students and young people also headed to Egypt.

The bus looked like a rolling cage, not a transport vehicle. All of the windows were shaded black. Karim wondered what exactly the Israelis were afraid of. Surely none of the students boarding the bus had any violent intentions. Who would wish to harm them? Were there Zionist terrorists along their route who intended to do them harm? Looking at the bus through the lens of Gaza, it made sense at least in one respect—in Gaza, everything and everyone were suspect. Violence could erupt at any moment; there did not need to be any specific reason because tensions were always high.

No matter how foreboding it was, the bus was Karim's only ticket out. With his suitcase in hand, he looked at his father. They embraced, but they both withheld the tears that were welling up in their eyes. This was a proud day for Saeed. All of his sons were becoming professional men—doctors and engineers. He had hoped for so long that by some miracle his sons would raise their families by his side in Beit Daras, but now he knew that would never come to pass. But Allah was merciful. Now his beloved Karim was going to Egypt to become a physician.

Miriam could not hold back her tears. They were tears of joy but also of sadness. She would miss Karim. No longer would she be able to just have a long talk with him, look at him across the dinner table or gaze at him as he studied. He was leaving home, which was natural and proper, but it was still difficult.

Karim finished saying his goodbyes and got on board. Through the dark tinted window, he saw his parents standing where he had left them moments ago. His mother was still crying, and his father looked sad. He kept looking at them until the bus pulled away from the station.

From the moment the bus began moving, he could tell that this was not going to be an ordinary ride. Once in the Sinai, the bus moved at even slower speeds, stopping at every one of a seemingly endless number of military checkpoints.

The black windows could not be opened more than a sliver. There was no air conditioning, and the small fans were inadequate. At every checkpoint the passengers begged the driver for permission to use the restroom because there were no restrooms on the bus. In between checkpoints, the driver asked a Red Cross worker who was also on the bus to speak with the soldiers about the passengers' need to use a toilet. A couple of times the soldiers gave in to these repeated requests and told the driver to stop the bus. When the doors opened, the soldiers allowed a few of the passengers to walk out into the desert and relieve themselves as long as they hurried and did not utter a sound.

Along the way, Karim noticed the debris from the last Arab-Israeli war in 1973. Destroyed and abandoned military equipment—burned out tanks, shattered transport vehicles, mangled artillery pieces—lined the road. In some respects, he now understood why his bus was a rolling, black cage. A war had been fought here and not so many years ago.

The remnants of war made Karim recall sitting by the radio in his home in Gaza in October of '73, listening to accounts of battles in the Sinai. It made him sad to think that, despite the fact that the Egyptians regained the Suez Canal and the Sinai, Arab armies were again unsuccessful in liberating Palestine. He believed that Palestine would never be liberated by an invading army. If three efforts to defeat Israel had failed, how could any reasonable person believe a fourth war would produce a different result?

The bus pulled onto a ferry that then pulled out into the Suez Canal. What a magnificent experience this was. While it was not an impressive body of water, the Suez Canal was only 200 meters wide and 20 meters deep, the massive ships that moved up and down the canal were a sight to see. Karim watched in fascination as a large freighter made its way south to the terminus of the canal at Port Tewfik.

Crossing the Suez Canal was a milestone in many ways. For the first time in his life, he was not under the direct control of any military force. While still a Palestinian refugee, he would now call an Arab country home, one that was not occupied by a foreign power. Through a slight opening in one of the black-painted windows of his soon-to-be-forgotten bus cage, Karim took a deep breath of the salty air. It reminded him of being home on the beach at Gaza with his father.

When the ferry reached the Egyptian side of the canal, the bus drove off the boat and into a secured parking area. Karim and his fellow travelers got off the bus, grabbed their luggage and started to walk the 500 meters to the official border. In the distance, they saw a new set of buses that they would board to continue their trip to Cairo.

Karim had arrived. He was thrilled to hear the Egyptian accent being spoken. All of his life he had heard this accent on the radio, on television and in movies. Now he was here among these people.

Thankfully, he was carrying only a medium-sized bag. Most of the other students had to pull, or in some cases drag, heavy cases towards the new buses. When Karim got close to the waiting buses, a young Egyptian about his age came rushing towards him and said, "Let me carry your bag, sir."

Karim was taken aback. Why did this man want to carry his bag? Why was he calling him sir? He was used to being the one who carried others bags, who bore burdens for other people.

"No, thanks," he replied, trying his best to be polite. "You're kind, but I will carry my own bag."

Despite Karim's response, the young Egyptian put his hands on the bag and removed it from his grip. He carried it to the bus and stored it in the bottom luggage compartment.

The young man returned. "I didn't want you to exhaust yourself." The man extended his hand.

Karim stopped and shook the young man's hand vigorously. "Thank you very much."

His smile faded. "Anything kind would be accepted from you."

Only then did Karim realize that the man wanted a tip for his services. Miriam had given him some Egyptian pounds before he left. She had instructed him to keep loose change in his pocket and told him that he might need it along the way.

Karim pulled some coins from his pocket and gave them to the young man. His smile returned, and he thanked Karim and was on his way. Karim smiled back, but he was not thinking about the young man; he was thinking about his mother. Even though she had never been to Egypt, she had prepared him to do so. He said a short prayer for her and realized how much he already missed her.

Karim by the Nile River

Chapter 14
TANTA

In Egypt, One Hour Isn't Like Any Other

In Egypt, one hour isn't like any other…
each moment is a memory renewed by a bird
of the Nile. I was there. The human creature
there invented the Sun-God. No one calls himself
by name: 'I'm a son of the Nile, that's name enough
for me.' From your first moment, you call yourself
'son of the Nile' to avoid the heaviness of the abyss.
There, the living and the dead pick clouds of cotton
from the land of Upper Egypt and plant wheat
in the Delta. Standing between the living
and the dead, two guards take turns watching over
the palms. Everything romantic is within you,
you walk on the edge of your soul in time's labyrinth,
as if before you were born Mother Egypt
had given birth to you first, as a lotus flower.
Do you know yourself now? Egypt sits with itself
in stealth: 'Nothing is like me.' And mends

the battered coat of eternity with a wind blowing
from any direction. I was there. The human creature
was writing the wisdom of Death-Life. Everything is
romantic, moonlit… except for the poem
as it turns around to look for tomorrow, thinking
of immortality but speaking only of its frailty
before of the Nile…

Mahmoud Darwish

THE EGYPTIAN BUS was much older than the Israeli one Karim rode from Gaza to the Suez Canal, but from the second he boarded it, he loved the crowded old ride. He was excited to be where he was, on the way to his future. The noisy rattle of the engine and the grinding of the gears as the driver navigated through traffic were sweet music to his ears, a symphony of liberation. The windows were clear and wide open. A cool breeze refreshed tired bodies weary from having spent hours locked up in a jail on wheels.

Now free from their former oppressors, the Palestinian students erupted in songs and shouts of joy. Nobody told Karim and his new friends to sit down or be quiet. The few Egyptians on the bus were peppered with questions by the Palestinians and were treated like ambassadors of goodwill. The Egyptians talked and joked with their new friends, and everyone was in high spirits.

The bus traveled through the city of Suez and then on towards Cairo. Karim watched in fascination as Northern Egypt passed before his eyes. He saw cinemas, grocery stores, people driving their own cars, couples walking—normal, everyday life. This was fascinating to him because he had not seen this before; he had only glimpsed it in on occasion in Gaza City through the tarnished lens of his former life as a refugee. Egypt was indeed what he hoped it would be. People here were living in peace. He saw no heavy military presence of any kind, which both relieved and encouraged him.

However, once the bus arrived in Cairo, his situation took a turn for the worse. The students were taken off of the buses and put through a series of medical tests and screenings. This was done in an old warehouse-type building that had no amenities. There was no place for anyone to comfortably rest and no indication from those in authority how long this screening process would take to complete. The joyous bus ride had ended. Now the students were stuck in a type of purgatory, waiting for those in charge to release them and send them on their way.

Fortunately for Karim, his older brothers were already attending university in Cairo. To his great joy and surprise, Ali and Omar showed up at this medical screening facility and rescued him. Several other people also arrived and took charge of their friends and family members. Evidently this medical screening point was well known by the Palestinian ex-pat community in Egypt as a place to be avoided.

After they signed him out of the screening area, his brothers and their friends showed him the Nile River. As a child, Karim had read about this magnificent river, and he had watched countless shows about it on TV. He was not disappointed; the Nile was everything he imagined it to be and much more.

Then they showed him the five-star hotels in downtown Cairo and exposed him to the richness of the city. He was overwhelmed. Only a day and a half earlier he was living in a squalid refugee camp. Now he was driving around Cairo with his brothers and their friends looking at the bright lights and staring in wonder at the finely dressed people as they made their way through the downtown area.

After driving around the streets of Cairo for a couple of hours, his brothers took him to Omar's apartment. It was a small place, and he had to sleep on the couch, but he was grateful to his brothers for looking out for him.

The next morning Karim had only one thing on his mind. He wanted to get to Tanta as quickly as possible. Omar asked him why he was in such a hurry, and Karim answered that the current school term had already been in session for over a month and he needed to catch up with his classmates. Omar told him not to worry, that he would take him to Tanta the next day.

Their first stop in Tanta was at a university gathering center where Karim met several other students from Gaza. He knew a few of them at least enough to call them by name, but most of the faces were brand new. This was his new circle of support. The Palestinian students looked out for one another and formed a tightly knit community within the broader university student body.

Everything seemed to be falling into place. Months ago back in Al Shati, when they learned that they were both admitted to study medicine at Tanta, Zohair and Karim had agreed to live together. Zohair had arrived in Tanta a few weeks earlier and had already found a place to live. Omar drove Karim to where Zohair was staying. They got out of the car and walked into the apartment.

The outside of the building looked dilapidated. The interior was in worse shape. The furniture was old and broken, the walls had holes in them and the apartment was infested with cockroaches and other insects.

"How do you live here?" Karim asked his friend.

"It is difficult, but it was the best I could find on my own. Without a roommate, I could not afford a better apartment."

Karim took another look around. "I'm very sorry, but I cannot live here. I know that I just came from a refugee camp, but this place will not work for me. Would you consider moving if we could find a better apartment?"

"I'd love to move!" Zohair said. "If we can find another place we can both afford, I'll move out today."

So Omar took them around Tanta to look for a suitable place to live. They saw many nice flats, but most were too expensive. Towards the end of the day, they came to an apartment that was both clean and affordable. While it was not new, it was acceptable. They rented it immediately.

Omar had to get back to Cairo, so he did not stay the night. Karim thanked his brother and also thanked God that even in his new home in a new country, his family was still caring for him and making sure that he had everything he needed.

As soon as Omar left and Karim put away his belongings, he began to worry. For the first time in his life, he was on his own. If things went wrong at the university, he could not easily return home. Who would cook for him? How would he manage his own affairs? While he had become remarkably self-sufficient at an early age, now he was completely on his own.

Sitting on the edge of his new bed, he was grateful that he was in Tanta and settled with his best friend, but he was also afraid—afraid for himself and for the family he left behind. One by one his siblings were leaving Gaza and venturing out into the world. He knew that he could not afford to go back to Gaza once or twice a year for a visit. It might be several years before he saw his parents again.

As he sat there in a state of unease, wondering about all these issues at the same time, Zohair came in. "Karim, let's go for a walk and check out the neighborhood."

His old apartment was several miles away, so he was also unfamiliar with the area.

"Sure. That would be good."

They set out as the sun was setting. They visited an ironing shop and several other local businesses. At first people looked at them a bit warily, but as soon as people found out they were students from Gaza, they were friendly to them. As it turns out, the university was only a 20-minute walk from their apartment. Everything they needed was nearby. While Karim was still suffering from a serious case of homesickness, he felt a little better knowing that while Tanta was not Gaza, there were people of goodwill here that he could go to for help.

Karim and Zohair bought a simple meal at the grocery store and took it home to eat it. After their meal, they went straight to bed because the next day both of them had to be at the university early. Karim's pillow was wet with tears that night. He missed his family and was worried about them. He wondered if he would ever see his mother and father again. He slept fitfully, unsure what tomorrow would bring.

The next morning, they got up and dressed in their best clothes. Just as they had been told, it took them 20 minutes to reach the university on foot.

Walking through the grounds and the buildings, Karim noticed how casual and comfortable the students were. He felt uncomfortable because he had never been to a university before, even for a visit, because there were no universities in Gaza. After asking some questions, he was directed to the Office of Student Affairs. They gave him the basic information he needed, including his class schedule. Within a short time, he was ready to attend his first class, botany.

He walked in a bit late because of his delay at the Student Affairs Office. The tutor chastised him for being tardy, but once he told her that he was a new student from Gaza, she smiled and nodded.

That day the botany class was taking tomato slices and looking at the plant's cells under the microscope. The tutor gave Karim a piece of tomato and asked him to look at it through the microscope.

There were no microscopes in Gaza classrooms. He certainly knew what a microscope was from pictures he had seen but had no idea how to use one. The tutor prompted Karim to look at the tomato, so Karim put the entire piece of fruit on the viewer and then tried to examine it. Of course, this was the wrong method—a small slice of the tomato needed to be placed on the slide and then it could be examined.

Karim tried his best to look at the tomato under the microscope, but all he saw was darkness. With his eye still in the lens of the microscope, he heard the tutor's voice.

"Are you making a salad?" She stood right next to his desk. The tutor was an attractive young lady, perhaps 25 years old or so.

"No, I… I do not know how to do this properly."

"We went over this several weeks ago."

"Unfortunately I was delayed in getting to Egypt. It is difficult to travel here from Gaza." Karim believed that he would soon die from embarrassment.

The young tutor smiled and sat next to him. "Here is how you prepare a sample to be viewed under the microscope." With a blade, she carefully sliced off a paper thin amount of the tomato and mounted it on a slide. Then she put the slide on the viewer and asked him to look at it now.

When Karim looked through the microscope this time, he clearly saw the plant cells and could identify the parts that were required for today's lesson.

"Thank you," he said meekly.

The tutor smiled at him. "Do you know where to go to buy the textbook required for this class?"

"No."

She then took the next few minutes and told him the things he needed to know about buying textbooks and how to get around the university. Grateful, he returned the tutor's smile and promised that he would quickly get up to speed with the rest of the class.

The next class was English. There he found that despite missing a few weeks of school, he was actually ahead of the other students in most respects. The older male instructor took an instant liking to him and called on him several times that first day. Karim's Palestinian-accented English seemed to please the teacher. He left that classroom smiling.

In fact, when he was done for the day and walking home, he still had a smile on his face. He had met some new people and discovered that the University was a nice place, not somewhere to be feared. He had some catching up to do in some of his classes, but he was confident in his abilities to do the work required.

The only thing missing was Karim being able to tell his parents all about his first day at the university. His lifelong habit had been to tell his parents everything that went on during the day. Phone calls to Gaza from Egypt were expensive and had to be arranged through a third country through a three-way call well in advance, so as much as he wanted to, he could not simply find a phone and call home.

When he went to bed that night, his pillow was not full of tears. He drifted off to sleep with the happy image in his mind of telling his mother all about his first day as a medical student and of her saying to him how proud she was of her son and how much she loved him.

Karim with his friends by the pyramids

Chapter 15

STUDENT LIFE AND SARA
1979

From me and you'll have everything,
Yours the shade and yours the light,
A wedding-ring and all you want,
And an orchard of trees, of olive and fig.
And as on every night I'll come to you.
In the dream I'll enter by the window and throw you jasmine.
Blame me not if I'm in a little late;
they stopped me.

Mahmoud Darwish

KARIM SPENT HIS first year at Tanta studying general education subjects like botany, biology and chemistry. Once he successfully completed his first year, then he could move on to pursue a purely medical curriculum.

Daily life was an adventure. Most of the ways of the world beyond Gaza were brand new to him. For any young university student, adjusting to living away from home is a serious transition, but in his case these challenges were magnified by his previous life as a refugee. Common, everyday things that most of the students at Tanta took for granted, like putting money in a bank for safekeeping, Karim had to learn about through experience.

From an academic perspective, his greatest challenge was language. All of his textbooks were written in English. While he was fairly proficient in English, he soon realized that he needed to go from fairly proficient to an expert in a short period of time, so he purchased a large English dictionary. This book quickly became his closest companion. During his first year as a university student, he painstakingly added to his English vocabulary word by word. Reading the texts for his various classes, Karim came across as many as a 50 words a night that he needed to look up and memorize.

In some ways, this burden was also a blessing. He did not have the time to pursue any sort of social life beyond getting to know a few people and occasionally interacting with them outside of the university. Any awkwardness he felt was not as relevant as it might have been if he had more time on his hands. He did not have the luxury of being frustrated, angry or lonely—there was simply too much to do.

There was no option for him other than success. He had no comfortable existence to return to if he did not make it at Tanta. Gaza was not a hundred kilometers down the highway. Not only was it far away geographically, it was an alien world compared to Egypt—one Karim could simply not return to before achieving his goals.

Day by day, class by class, marathon study session by study session, he began to adapt to his new life. University was a refuge. His mind, body and soul were free and being fed by the nectar of science and discovery. He excelled in school despite the handicaps he had to overcome. He completed his first year of general studies with an A average in all of his subjects. Many of his fellow students received far lower marks or failed university altogether. This encouraged him and gave him confidence as he entered his first year of formal medical school.

The first year of medical school was far more challenging academically than were his general studies, but Karim again got high marks. He was now convinced that he had the general attitude and temperament required to be an outstanding medical student and a good physician.

For his entire life, he had thought of himself as a healer. While he was by no means a pacifist, he was interested in healing wounds, not inflicting them. Now he was in a place where he could express himself without fear and become all that he was capable of becoming. He soaked in knowledge like a dry sponge placed in water. His natural curiosity took him where he needed to go.

Saeed had instilled in his son respect for all life and the Creator. Through medicine and science, Karim now had the opportunity to look at the handiwork of God in great detail. Embryology was particularly fascinating to him. He marveled at the stages of fetal development and the miracle that occurred when a woman became pregnant. It both humbled him and filled him with a sense of awe.

The first year of medical school was 12 months straight, September through September. The second year was September through June. At the end of the second year medical students were given a series of difficult examinations. It was common knowledge that many of the students would not pass these exams and would be forced to either take courses over and then retake the test or simply quit school.

Karim received an A on all of his exams. Some of his classmates were envious of his success. They made fun of him and tried to make him feel bad because he did not have a girlfriend or a large number of casual acquaintances at school. None of this teasing bothered him in the least. By now, after three years at Tanta, he felt comfortable in Egypt and in his own skin. What others said about him was of little importance.

What was of importance in 1978 and 1979 was the historic effort by Anwar Sadat, the President of Egypt; Jimmy Carter, President of the United States; and Menachem Begin, the Prime Minister of Israel, to forge a permanent peace in the region. The results of their efforts were the Camp David Peace Accords and the subsequent Egyptian-Israeli peace treaty.

The peace process had an unintended consequence for the Palestinian students studying in Egypt. The Red Cross was removed from the travel equation when the Israelis withdrew from the Sinai Peninsula. Without the involvement of the Red Cross, it became impossible to return to Gaza and incredibly difficult to communicate with people living there. While this situation would work itself out over time, for a while Karim and his fellow Palestinian students were cut off from home.

Karim's funds were running low. His "treasure," as he called his meager savings, was nearly depleted. He could not communicate with his father to arrange for further support from him. To finish university, he would have to make other arrangements.

Omar still lived in Cairo. He was in the same apartment Karim had visited three years earlier when he first arrived in Egypt on the bus. They decided that the best thing to do was pool their resources and live together. That meant that Karim would have to leave Tanta and finish his medical degree in Cairo.

With Omar's assistance, Karim moved and enrolled at The University of Cairo. It was a major center of learning and a step above Tanta in terms of facilities and academic stature. The students were generally from more upscale families than the students at Tanta. They wore fancier clothes and drove more expensive cars. Once more Karim found himself on the bottom rung of the social ladder, but again this was not important to him.

Perhaps the biggest benefit of the move from Karim's perspective was living in Cairo. He loved the city and what it had to offer; the activity and beauty inspired him and made him dream of big things and better days. The Nile River flows through the heart of the city and the upper part of the Nile River delta begins just north of Cairo. He loved the river and never tired of spending time just looking at it or walking on its banks. The hot summers and the mild winters appealed to him too.

Not long after beginning his studies at The University of Cairo, Karim fell in with a small group of Palestinian medical students who were one year behind him in school. They looked up to him because of his achievements, and in turn he enjoyed mentoring them and their friendship. For the first time since he arrived in Egypt, he had a social life, albeit a limited one, given the demanding nature of his academic program.

One of these students was a lovely young lady named Sara. She was beautiful with long, dark hair, fair skin and green eyes. Sara was a serious and outstanding medical student, just like Karim. While her beauty brought joy to his eyes and his heart, it was her dedication and intelligence that attracted his attention.

Sara was from a Palestinian family who lived in Jordan. She and Karim shared a common cultural history, but she was not raised in a refugee camp. Her parents were employed and had settled in Jordan.

It was not long before the couple took long walks along the Nile River and spent hours discussing a future together. As these romantic feelings were building, Karim's financial resources were dwindling. By late 1979, he was borrowing books from other students and eating sandwiches to survive. Hot meals were a luxury he could not afford. He had not purchased any new clothes in over a year.

It was still impossible in the fall of 1979 to either travel from Egypt to Gaza or to communicate with Palestine. While there was a peace treaty in place between Egypt and Israel, the previous infrastructure that allowed for phone, mail and travel between Gaza and Egypt had been dismantled before another system could be put in its place.

Sara noticed that he was not eating properly and that his clothes, while clean, looked increasingly worn. She offered to help him, but he politely refused. He was too proud to accept help from someone other than family, and while feelings of love were growing between them, she was not yet family.

It was acceptable to borrow money from male friends. Karim was forced to do this to survive. He only borrowed the absolute minimum required. This left little money to spend on entertaining Sara or doing anything other than studying, sleeping and eating.

This was a trying period for him in a new way—for the first time he felt inadequate socially. He had nothing but the most sincere and deepest feelings for Sara, but he did not have the means to support her. Not yet. She was patient because she had these same, deep feelings for him. They would have to struggle for a period of time, but in a few years they would both be physicians, and then financial resources would likely no longer be a problem.

As the fourth year of medical school came to a close, Karim once again passed his exams with high marks. He was nearly broke, but his goal of becoming a physician was firmly in sight.

In early 1980, Egypt and Israel finally established a system to regulate travel between Egypt and Gaza. Karim was allowed to return home. With his father's assistance, he was able to replenish his money supply, at least to some degree. Shortly after this blessed event came more good news. Omar had finished his business degree and had gotten a job in the United Arab Emirates. At least financially, the burden for his family was easing somewhat.

Karim returned to Cairo University to finish medical school. He would have to study medicine for three more years and then complete a fourth year of medical internship before he officially became a doctor.

He and Sara continued to see each other, and their relationship developed to the point where they were ready to announce to their families their intention to marry. Karim's parents were thrilled at the prospect and approved wholeheartedly. In 1983, Sara went to Jordan to discuss her marriage plans with her parents.

When Sara returned, Karim met her at the airport, and they took a ride to one of their favorite spots on the Nile River, a place where they had spent many happy hours discussing everything from science to the names of their yet to be born children.

"Karim, I do not know how to say this other than to tell you. My parents will not permit me to marry you," Sara said as she held his hand.

In an instant, the joy he felt from seeing Sara again was replaced by sadness and anger. "Why not? Do they think I'm unworthy?"

"No, not exactly. They are afraid that you will take me back to Gaza once we earn our medical degrees. They do not want me to live in Gaza."

"But Gaza is my home."

"My parents are afraid of what might happen to me there. You've told me yourself, many times, how dangerous Gaza can be. War, violence and death are very much a part of Gaza and it seems to them like it will always be that way."

"Did you tell them that we were in love? That we both share the same values and love of family?"

"They know that I would never have asked them for permission to marry you if you were not a good man. I pleaded with them, Karim, but they said no. They will not change their minds." Sara started to cry.

"What will we do?" Karim said as he stood and looked at a boat passing by on the river.

"What can we do?"

"We can get married anyway and hope that they change their minds."

"I cannot do that… You would not want that either… I… take me home please." Sara asked.

"Yes, of course."

Karim escorted Sara back to her apartment, and they said goodbye. They were still medical students and would have to spend time together for the next year and a half, but they were no longer together as a couple.

Ignoring the wishes of the bride's family and getting married despite their objections was not something he was prepared to do. For a Palestinian, marriage is a union of two families and not a completely personal decision for the couple alone.

Karim was devastated. He continued his education and completed his degree, but the last year of medical school was tortuous. He was depressed most of the time. Whenever he ran into Sara at the school, which frequently happened, his heart would sink like a rock in a pond. Looking at her, he knew that she felt the same.

On the day of his graduation from Cairo University, Karim accepted his medical diploma from the Egyptian Minister of Health and the Provost of the University. It was a proud moment for him. Less than a decade earlier he was a refugee with nothing to his name other than a suitcase full of old clothes and some cash stuffed in his shoe. Now he was a physician, but he had a broken heart. He hoped that someday, sooner rather than later, he would meet someone else who would make him feel like Sara did.

There was no doubt where he was going now—back to Gaza. Whatever future lay in store for him, it would be realized through his family. Thankfully, his parents were alive and well. His brothers were professionals now, and the family was no longer suffering as much financially.

The Gaza Karim was returning to was in many ways exactly the same one that he left. The Israelis were still in charge, seemingly now completely entrenched. Tensions were rising. While some people, the select few like Karim and his brothers, left Gaza and were educated abroad, the vast majority of the Palestinian population remained in a state of poverty and disenfranchisement.

As it turned out, Sara's family was right in at least one respect—Gaza was a tinder box just waiting to explode. The world had not yet addressed the root cause of the problem: injustice to the Palestinian people. Israel was determined to rule Gaza with an iron fist and increase the pressure on the refugees to accept the status quo as the way things had to be. While some in the West were becoming more sympathetic to the plight of the Palestinian people, no one cared enough to rein in the Israeli military and political machine that was crushing the people of Gaza without mercy.

The Proud Father
Saeed AlShaikh holding Karim's medical diploma

Chapter 16

DR. KARIM RETURNS TO GAZA 1984

In Jerusalem, and I mean within the ancient walls,
I walk from one epoch to another without a memory
to guide me. The prophets over there are sharing
the history of the holy… ascending to heaven
and returning less discouraged and melancholy, because love
and peace are holy and are coming to town.
I was walking down a slope and thinking to myself: How
do the narrators disagree over what light said about a stone?
Is it from a dimly lit stone that wars flare up?
I walk in my sleep. I stare in my sleep. I see
no one behind me. I see no one ahead of me.
All this light is for me. I walk. I become lighter. I fly
then I become another. Transfigured. Words
sprout like grass from Isaiah's messenger
mouth: "If you don't believe you won't be safe."
I walk as if I were another. And my wound a white
biblical rose. And my hands like two doves

on the cross hovering and carrying the earth.
I don't walk, I fly, I become another,
transfigured. No place and no time. So who am I?
I am no I in ascension's presence. But I
think to myself: Alone, the prophet Muhammad
spoke classical Arabic. "And then what?"
Then what? A woman soldier shouted:
Is that you again? Didn't I kill you?
I said: You killed me... and I forgot, like you, to die.

Mahmoud Darwish

IN APRIL OF 1984, Karim earned his medical degree. Cairo had been his home now for some time, so it was with mixed emotions that he packed to leave. Hoping to create lasting images in his mind, Karim walked to the banks of the Nile one last time and took in the sights, smells and sounds of the great river. It had been a source of fascination and awe for him since he was a child, and now it took on an even greater significance. It was in Egypt that his dreams had become a reality.

His student residence permit in Egypt had expired so he could not stay any longer. It did not really matter, though, because Karim wanted to return to Gaza. Wherever life would lead him eventually, his path needed to begin in Palestine.

When he arrived in Gaza, Karim was given a warm welcome by his parents, extended family, neighbors and friends. They threw a party in his honor. A young man returning from university in Egypt as a physician uplifted the entire refugee community; it was an event to be celebrated.

While he was honored and happy by his enthusiastic reception, he was still hurt over losing Sara. He wanted her to be here with him, celebrating his academic success and also their forthcoming marriage. There was a hole in his heart now, an emptiness inside. He wondered if this void would ever be filled.

For years they had planned on being together, perhaps working side by side as physicians, starting a family, building a life—and in one harsh and capricious edict from her parents all of that was cast aside, as if the love they shared and the happiness they pursued was meaningless.

When he was alone and his mind drifted, he thought about the sadness that his father must have felt three decades earlier. Saeed too had lost a betrothed. Yet if this had not happened, Karim would not be alive and neither would his brothers and sister. Their family would never have existed. In the end, he decided, it was God's will that governed such matters. While we are hurt when we lose someone we love, we must remember that everything is in God's hands.

Sadly, although Karim had grown and changed, conditions at the Beach Camp were very much like they were when he left many years earlier. Saeed and Miriam were still living in the same two room "house" they had been in for over two decades. When it rained, water still leaked in through the shake roof. The floors were still made of sand. They had few municipal services.

His agenda upon returning to Al Shati was simple—improve his family's living conditions. Before he could change the way his family was living, Karim had to find a residency position. He had an outstanding academic pedigree—he had graduated with honors from medical school—but there were no true hospitals in Gaza in 1984, only a variety of medical clinics and aid centers. To complete his residency, he had to find a position in a full service hospital.

In 1956, the Islamic Charitable Association was formed by a group of concerned Palestinian citizens. The goal of the Association was to provide medical services to all citizens regardless of race, religion, social or political affiliation. In 1968, the Association opened AlMakassed Hospital in East Jerusalem, which was dedicated to serving the Palestinian people and served as a training facility for new Palestinian physicians. Residencies at AlMakassed were highly sought-after prizes. Karim applied to become a resident at AlMakassed as soon as he reached Gaza, and he was quickly accepted.

In May, he took a taxi from Gaza City to East Jerusalem. After a nearly two-hour, 90-kilometer ride, the cab dropped him off in the heart of the city. AlMakassed Hospital sits atop the famous Mount of Olives, the place where Christians believe Christ ascended into heaven. From the Mount of Olives, one can look down on the Holy City and see the Al-Aqsa Mosque, the third holiest place for Muslims all over the world. It is believed to be the second mosque ever built on earth, only after the one built by Prophet Abraham in Makkah.

Karim began his residency in pediatrics and immediately immersed himself in his work. He and his fellow residents had a dorm at the hospital where they slept, ten to a room. He was free to return to Gaza on his days off.

The Dome of the Rock

During the periods when he was not working or sleeping, he enjoyed exploring the streets of the great city. He prayed at the Dome of the Rock and spent time at the Church of the Holy Sepulcher, the place where Christian tradition says Christ was laid to rest and then rose from the dead. He loved everything about Jerusalem—the aroma of Mediterranean spices wafting from the cafes, the beautiful little shops, the narrow passageways. He imagined himself being in the Old City 14 centuries earlier when the Prophet walked the stone streets or 20 centuries ago when the Jews and the Romans planned to execute Jesus Christ.

As he walked, Karim thought about where he was and what this Holy City meant to billions around the globe. For Christians, it was the place where Jesus was crucified, rose again and then ascended into heaven. For Muslims, it is the place where Mohammed ascended into heaven and back again, on the Dome of the Rock. For Jews, Jerusalem is the City of David, the capital of their homeland that was given to them by God.

More than anything else, Jerusalem for Karim was a symbol of the tragic fate of the Palestinian people who are comprised of all three Abrahamic faiths. Since the end of the 1967 Six-Day War, Jerusalem was completely under Israeli control. The Palestinians have always believed that East Jerusalem—Al Quds—is the capital of the State of Palestine, but this was a hope yet to come true. Israel was in charge here, and the Zionists were determined that an "undivided Jerusalem" belonged to them and no one else.

For centuries, Jerusalem was part of the Ottoman Empire. Then the holy sites were open to all. Now, in the late 20th century, this beautiful city was the nexus of hatred between the sons and daughters of Abraham. Where was the God of peace and love in this volatile mix? It was hard to see God amidst all the violence and strife. Would God approve of his creation constantly being at odds with each other in His Holy City? Surely not, Karim believed.

When he got his first monthly paycheck, he thought he was a rich man. Never before had he held 750 U.S. dollars in his hands. He cashed his check, took the money with him to Gaza and gave all the money to his father. After some discussion, Saeed took his son's suggestion and purchased building materials with the funds. After that, every weekend was devoted to adding two rooms to the family home and completing the required repairs to the existing structure. Asbestos sheets were added to the roof as a barrier between the shingles and the boards to keep out the wind and the rain. By July, the additional two rooms were done, as were all of the other renovations.

Also in July, Karim got word through the UNRWA, The United Nations Relief and Works Agency, that his application to travel to Saudi Arabia for a job and perhaps to complete his residency had been granted. Now Karim and his family had another decision to make—should he stay in East Jerusalem and complete his residency at AlMakassed Hospital or move to Saudi Arabia where the pay and the facilities were much better? This was not an easy decision, so he went home to discuss it with his parents.

For many years he had been in Egypt and away from his family, so for him living away from Gaza was not an unfamiliar condition. But the plan had always been that he would get his medical degree and return home to help his people. By living and working in Jerusalem during the week, he could be home on most weekends. After he completed his residency at AlMakassed, he could choose from a number of different possible medical appointments in Palestine.

In the end, Karim and his parents decided that the best thing to do was for him to go to Saudi Arabia to make a living and develop his career there. The pay was better, and so was the training. From the viewpoint of enhancing his long term career opportunities, the choice was easy. But now he would be leaving Palestine, perhaps for an extended period of time. Would he come back and practice medicine in Gaza? That was by no means a certainty.

When he returned to AlMakassed to tender his resignation, his superiors did all they could to persuade him to stay. Their arguments were to no avail. Karim finished out the month at AlMakassed and then set out for Saudi Arabia through Jordan.

But nothing in his life had ever come easy, and the trip to Saudi Arabia was no exception.

Israeli checkpoint in Palestinian territory

Chapter 17

A DIFFICULT JOURNEY
AUGUST 1984

I dream of white lilies, streets of song, a house of light.
I need a kind heart, not a bullet.
I need a bright day, not a mad, fascist moment of triumph.
I need a child to cherish a day of laughter, not a weapon of war.
I came to live for rising suns, not to witness their setting.
He said goodbye and went looking for white lilies,
a bird welcoming the dawn on an olive branch.
He understands things only as he senses and smells them.
Homeland for him, he said, is to drink my mother's coffee,
to return safely, at nightfall.

Mahmoud Darwish

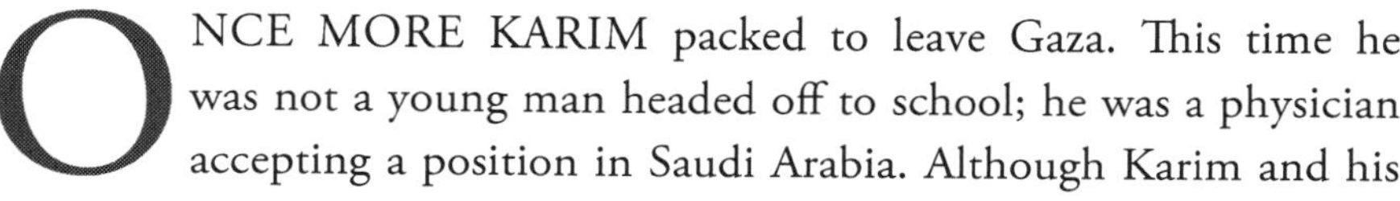

ONCE MORE KARIM packed to leave Gaza. This time he was not a young man headed off to school; he was a physician accepting a position in Saudi Arabia. Although Karim and his parents were comfortable with his decision, it was always bittersweet to leave Al Shati. There were many uncertainties. No one could be sure when they left Gaza if they would be allowed to return or what they might find when they came back.

At 3 a.m. Karim made his way to the place in Gaza City where he could find a taxi to take him to the Jordanian border. It was August, so the temperature was already warm before sunrise. The taxi was waiting for him just as he had arranged. He checked his bag and travel documents one last time. Everything had to be in order—permission to travel from the Israeli authorities, permission from Jordan to enter that country and the UNRWA documentation on his new position. Since he had no national passport, traveling across borders was a complicated process. If even the smallest detail of his paperwork was out of order, Karim knew that he might not be allowed to pass.

The cab ride was pleasant. They drove north through Gaza and then turned east towards Jerusalem. From Jerusalem, they drove further east until they reached the ancient city of Jericho. Located on the West Bank of the Jordan River, Jericho is a major point of entry into Jordan. It is an ancient city, believed by scholars to be one of the oldest continuously occupied cities in the world.

The taxi took Karim to the Israeli border control station. It was midday now and miserably hot. The temperature was over 35 degrees Celsius with high humidity. He got out of the cab and walked toward the checkpoint.

There were two lines, each leading to a different border control officer. Karim waited patiently in the queue. Jericho is famous for its large and aggressive summer mosquitos, so as he waited he occasionally set his bag down and used his free hand to swat the attacking insects. Almost an hour after he first stood in line, he finally reached the officer's station. He presented his papers, expecting that soon he would move through the checkpoint and take a cab to Amman.

The Israeli officer reviewed the paperwork. Then he looked at a clipboard and ran his finger down some list. Karim assumed that the officer was cross checking his credentials to ensure that he was authorized to leave occupied Palestine.

"You are not allowed to leave," the officer said. "Please return to Gaza immediately."

Karim was stunned. Over the past few weeks, he had diligently shepherded his travel approvals through the UNRWA and the Israeli authorities. He was sure that everything was in order.

"Can you check again, please?" Karim asked, his heart racing.

"There is no need for me to check again. You are denied leaving." The officer rudely threw the paperwork back at him.

There was no other choice; Karim had to step out of the line. For a few seconds, he was too stunned to think, much less move. What could possibly be wrong with his papers? The sweat rolling in his eyes brought him back to the present. He could not just stand off to the side; he had to do something.

Perhaps the officer had made a mistake. Maybe his name was misspelled either on the confirming list or on one his documents so there was not an exact match. So Karim decided that the best thing to do was to ease his way into the second line and present his paperwork to the other official. Perhaps the second man would see the simple error, correct it and let him pass.

So without saying a word to anyone, he picked up his bag and slowly moved toward the second line. Once in line, Karim braced himself for the hand of a soldier grabbing his arm and instructing him to leave the area immediately. When this did not happen after a few minutes and more travelers filed in behind him in line, he was mildly relieved.

It was incredibly hot and getting hotter by the minute. Karim's anxiety rose along with the temperature. Reality hit him like a thunderbolt—he had no job, little money and a huge potential problem on his hands. Why was he being denied entry into Jordan? Had he been misidentified as a security risk? Did something else happen? Had his job offer been rescinded without his knowledge? A hundred horrible scenarios passed through his mind, one after another.

After an agonizing hour waiting in the queue, Karim reached the desk of the second border control officer.

"Leaving the country is denied. You must return to Gaza."

"Why? Everything is in or—"

"Report to the Intelligence Office in Gaza. They can tell you why you are not allowed to travel."

Karim's anxiety had now become a terror. The Intelligence Office? He stood there motionless, mouth open for a moment. He did not know what to say or do.

"Go back to Gaza!" the officer shouted and tossed his papers at him.

There was no other choice. Hoping that it was not too late, Karim looked for a taxi that was headed back to Gaza. He was fortunate at least in this respect; there was a taxi available to take him back. It was midafternoon. Rather than getting processed by Jordanian customs, he headed back to Al Shati.

It was early evening when he arrived back home. He had no idea what to say to his parents. He felt like he had done something wrong, made some horrible mistake. Had he somehow ruined his life without knowing it? Why would he be on a security watch list?

When he walked through the front door, his parents sat at the table, looking towards the two new rooms of the house they had finished constructing just ten days earlier. They were shocked to see him standing in the doorway; they looked at him as if they had seen a ghost.

"Karim, what are you doing here? What went wrong?" Saeed asked.

"They would not… they sent me back…" He could not talk anymore. The tears he had been holding back for hours now came pouring out. He was deeply ashamed, but he was not sure why. He felt that he had done something wrong, but he had no idea what that could be.

Karim ran into one of the new rooms of the house, locked the door and started sobbing. A few minutes later Saeed knocked on the door.

"Karim, please. Open the door."

Taking a deep breath and wiping the tears from his face, he opened the door.

"Son, what happened?"

"I tried to pass into Jordan, and the Israeli border guards denied me entry. They said that I need to speak with the Intelligence Office about it."

His father's expression now switched from empathy to fear. Every Palestinian in Gaza knew exactly where the Intelligence Office was and what went on there. If Moshi, the despised Israeli Chief of Intelligence, called someone into his office, most often he disappeared into a Zionist jail cell, perhaps for years. Moshi's power in Gaza was near absolute.

"I must ask you this, Karim. For your own sake, please be honest with me. Have you done anything to become a security risk?"

He had asked himself this same question over and over again ever since he left the border guard's station. "No. I can think of nothing. I truly have no idea why they did not let me pass."

"Then I will speak with Mustapha about this. Stay here. I'll be back shortly." With that, he left, and Karim went back into the front room to sit with his mother. Mustapha was a family friend with solid contacts in the Israeli army and intelligence apparatus. Half an hour later, his father returned.

"The best thing for you to do is go and see Moshi," Saeed said. "Mustapha is confident that you will be allowed to leave."

"No one can make me a guarantee."

"That is true, son. But unless you go and see Moshi you cannot leave. You are expected in Saudi Arabia soon. Mustapha says there might still be time to see Moshi tonight if you leave right now."

An immediate decision was required. Karim knew very well that the Zionists did not need a valid reason to detain or imprison anyone—they did as they chose. That said, the Israelis were normally not capricious. Unless they had what was, in their minds at least, a valid reason to detain someone they usually did not do so.

"I will go," Karim said. "I would rather be in jail than sitting here thinking about my failure."

"I will go with you."

"No, Dad, I will go alone. They would not allow you to go inside anyway. You know that. I have business with Moshi, not you."

"Of course. It will be alright, Karim. Trust God. Go now, and you might be able to leave in the morning."

It was already late. Would they allow him entry into the Intelligence Office in the early evening? Karim had to try. His future was at stake.

The Intelligence Office was in an old building in Gaza City that dated back to the British occupation of Palestine. Surrounded by a large wall and guarded by soldiers, it was the most hated place in all of Gaza. Over the years, countless numbers of Palestinians had been ushered into this building and ended up in Israeli prisons—or worse. He was walking into hell.

There was only one entryway in the fence that surrounded the building. A guard stood on either side of the door. Karim told them his name and that he needed to see Moshi because he had been denied leaving the country earlier in the day. He was careful to tell them he was "Dr. Karim from Gaza."

Part of him hoped that he would be told go away and never come back. That would save him from the nightmare of having to venture into the labyrinth.

Seconds after one of the guards talked to someone on the phone, the guard barked, "Step inside this door and wait for your escort."

The door opened. Karim was committed now; there was no turning back.

After being led into another room attached to the building, he was strip searched. He had expected this. After this humiliation, he was led inside the building and put in a windowless room. He heard the door to the room lock as he sat down on one of the steel chairs.

Half an hour later the door to the room opened.

"Come with me," the guard instructed.

With a gun at his back, Karim was led through a series of doors. He was told to stop in front of an office. Seconds later Moshi emerged from this office shouting, "What is the matter? Why are you trying to get into Jordan?"

Moshi was short, bald and fat. He had wild, wide blue eyes. It seemed like he never blinked. His angry look and body screamed that he was ready and willing to fight anytime, anywhere. He smelled like an ash can, was never without a cigarette dangling from his mouth and always had a gun strapped to his side.

"I was given permission by the UNRWA to travel to Saudi Arabia and work as a physician. That is why I need to pass through Jordan." Karim tried his best not to appear totally petrified.

Moshi looked at him for a minute without saying anything. Perhaps he is sizing me up, Karim thought to himself. Who does Moshi think I am? Some type of militia fighter or a saboteur?

"Come in here." He gestured. Karim and his guard walked into the office.

Karim stood a few feet away from the desk as Moshi sat down and began typing on his computer. Tortuous seconds passed. Karim imagined what Moshi was looking at on his screen. Had someone passed false information to the Israelis accusing him of being a spy or a rebel fighter? That seemed incomprehensible.

The guard handed Moshi all the paperwork—the same paperwork the Israeli border guard had used to deny him entry into Jordan earlier in the day. He looked it over. "You may travel to Jordan tomorrow."

Karim was so on edge that he did not know what to say. "Are you sure?"

"Am I sure? Are you questioning me? Just go!" Moshi slammed his fist on the desk.

He took his paperwork, turned and walked out exactly the way he had come in—with a guard right behind him, sticking the business end of his rifle in his back. In a flash, Karim was standing in the street. He went straight to his house.

The smile on his face, indeed the fact that he was back at all, told the story before he uttered a word. After relating the entire episode to his parents, he looked at his watch. It was 11 p.m. The bus for Jericho left at 3 a.m. There was not much time for sleep.

Doing his best to both think positive and get some rest, Karim passed the next few hours in a semi-comfortable stupor. He believed Moshi because there was no reason for him to lie. If Israeli Intelligence wanted to seize him, they had him in their lair. Still, Moshi could change his mind, or perhaps his message to the border guards could be lost or mishandled…

At 3 a.m. Karim began the entire process again, just as he had done the day before. The weather was the same—not a cloud in the sky and stiflingly hot. After the taxi dropped him off in Jericho, once more he stood in line waiting to be cleared by the Israeli border guard.

Thankfully, this guard was not on duty the previous day. With his heart in his throat, he watched as the officer looked at his papers and then checked him against the list of those approved to travel. This time the guard said nothing as he stamped the papers with the red exit stamp and told him to move on.

Now Karim was in Jordan. He was forced to wait in line again for his bag to be searched and his papers to be checked once more, but he did not care. He was away from the Zionist occupiers. He felt much the same as he did at the border crossing in the Sinai years before when he was on his way to medical school. Leaving Palestine was in many ways like getting released from prison. Once more he was free, or as free as he could be for a man traveling without a passport.

After he had been processed, he took another taxi to Amman. It was time for him to make his mark on the world.

Riyadh, Saudi Arabia

Chapter 18

A NEW LIFE BEGINS

Lesson from the Kama-Sutra (Wait for her)

Wait for her with an azure cup.
Wait for her in the evening at the spring, among perfumed roses.
Wait for her with the patience of a horse trained for mountains.
Wait for her with the distinctive, aesthetic taste of a prince.
Wait for her with the seven pillows of cloud.
Wait for her with strands of womanly incense wafting.
Wait for her with the manly scent of sandalwood on horseback.
Wait for her and do not rush.
If she arrives late, wait for her.
If she arrives early, wait for her.
Do not frighten the birds in her braided hair.
Take her to the balcony to watch the moon drowning in milk.
Wait for her and offer her water before wine.
Do not glance at the twin partridges sleeping on her chest.
Wait and gently touch her hand as she sets a cup on marble.
As if you are carrying the dew for her, wait.
Speak to her as a flute would to a frightened violin string,

As if you knew what tomorrow would bring.
Wait, and polish the night for her ring by ring.
Wait for her until the night speaks to you thus:
There is no one alive but the two of you.
So take her gently to the death you so desire,
and wait.

Mahmoud Darwish

WHEN KARIM ARRIVED in Amman he was exhausted, both emotionally and physically spent. He found an inexpensive hotel, checked in and promptly passed out, fully clothed, on the bed. When hunger woke him up hours later, he washed his face and went out hoping to find something to eat. Although the hour was late, he found a small restaurant in downtown Amman that was still open and ate two falafels and some hummus. The food and the walk briefly energized him, but by the time he returned to his hotel he was again tired and immediately fell asleep.

The next morning Karim asked the man at the front desk for the address of the Saudi Arabian embassy. He had to go to there to get a visa. Unlike his recent experience in Palestine, he was certain there would be no problem with getting the required documentation and permission to travel to Saudi Arabia because everything had been prearranged.

After eating breakfast, he went straight to the embassy and spoke with a staff member. All was in order. He was told to return in two days and his visa would be waiting for him. Now all he had to do was wait.

He decided to explore Amman. Karim had never been to Amman before, but he knew that many Palestinian refugees called Amman home. During the 1948 calamity, Palestinians fled south to Gaza, north to Lebanon and Syria and east to Jordan. While life was difficult for the refugees no matter where they went, for the most part Palestinians who fled to Jordan fared better than their counterparts in other countries.

Sara was from Jordan. As he walked the streets of Amman, drifting in and out of shops and cafes, Karim thought of her. He missed her, and although it had about a year since he had seen her, she was never far from his heart. He thought about trying to find her and speak with her, but he was not sure if she was in Jordan. She could be in Egypt or possibly somewhere else. Besides, her family had spoken. Their relationship was over. He had to find a way to move on.

Rather than dwelling on the loss of his love, his spirits rose as he strolled around Amman. This was a prosperous Arab city. There were no Zionist soldiers here and no overt political or military oppression. Jordan reminded him of Egypt. Once again, he felt alive and free. He allowed himself to imagine what life would be like in Riyadh. Yes, in many ways he would miss Gaza. He would certainly miss his parents and family, but to live as a free man in the Arab world—that notion had a great appeal.

After two days had passed, Karim went back to the Saudi embassy and collected his visa. His next stop was the airport, where he booked a flight later that same day to Riyadh. He had never flown before and had only seen commercial airliners from a distance. Flying from place to place was something rich people did, not him. But now his time had come. Despite having to work through a bit of initial anxiety when he boarded the aircraft, he enjoyed every minute of his flight to Saudi Arabia.

From the Riyadh airport, he took a taxi to his Uncle Hassan's home. Hassan was Saeed's cousin. Although they knew that he was coming, Hassan's family was astounded and overwhelmed with joy to see him when he arrived. Saeed's son was a physician! He was all grown up, and he had made it out of Gaza alive and was doing quite well for himself. They showered him with affection, which made him happy and even more thankful. The plan was for him to live with Hassan and his family for a short time until he got established as a physician.

The next day Hassan took him to the Ministry of Health. The Kingdom of Saudi Arabia provided comprehensive health care free of charge to all of its citizens. Karim had been hired by the Saudis to work as a physician in one of their many health care centers. After filling out the required forms and sitting through an orientation interview, he was given a check for 4,000 U.S. dollars to cover his traveling expenses and an initial housing allowance.

This was more money than he had ever seen before at one time in his life. When he left the Ministry with his money and went to open a bank account, he thought about how, only a few years before, he had mixed soap in an Israeli factory for far less than a living wage. Going back even a little further in time, he remembered picking fruit in the hot sun for what amounted to pocket change. Now his family's assistance and sacrifices and all of his hard work and dedication were finally paying dividends.

Fortunately, Karim was assigned as a primary care physician to a health center not far from Hassan's home. While the commute was a bit onerous, he had to take a taxi to and from work; it was manageable for the short term. Initially he was given two work shifts per day—from 8 a.m. to noon and then from 4 to 8 in the evening, six days per week. During his off hours he looked for a place to live, but it was tough to find an apartment or a home nearby. Bachelors were not allowed to live in the same neighborhoods as married families, so the supply of rental properties was limited.

After a few weeks, he was told about a house that he could possibly rent. It was too expensive for him to rent on his own, but Errol, a Pilipino male nurse who worked at the health care center, also needed a place to live, so they decided to share the house. Karim bought some basic furniture—a bed, TV, couch, etc.—and soon he was living independently.

A couple of months passed. He received regular paychecks now. For the first time in his life, he lived without any financial assistance from his family. Now it was his turn to give back. In addition to sending money to his father every month, he set aside 20 percent of his salary to help support his younger brother, Yasin, who was studying medicine in France.

Karim was a young professional living in Saudi Arabia. There was no refugee camp that he had to return to on the weekends and no occupying force watching his every move. In early 1985 he bought an eight-year-old Toyota Cressida. Now he held a steady position, had a nice place to live, and no longer had to rely on public transportation. He settled into a pleasant routine of seeing patients and relaxing during his free time.

It was not long before patients came to the clinic and asked to be treated by the young Dr. Karim. Why? He had inherited his father's natural affinity for people. He showed genuine concern for his patients' physical health, but he also took an interest in their family life and in how they were doing overall. People responded to his empathic nature. Word spread quickly that this new doctor was a good physician and also a kind man.

His superiors noticed his outstanding people skills and appointed him to the position of Director of New Physician Orientation. The health care center where he worked was a regional hub of sorts for the Saudi Ministry of Health—they sent all their new family practice doctors in the area to this clinic for training before they were permanently assigned elsewhere. So, in addition to his regular medical duties, Karim was now conducting workshops for groups of new doctors educating them in effective family medicine practice techniques.

In May of '85, the center director asked him to drive to Riyadh to pick up two new Palestinian physicians arriving from Jordan who were coming to work in the Kingdom. These physicians were different than the ones he had trained over the past few months—not only were they were both Palestinians from Jordan, they were also both female. A female cannot drive a car in Saudi Arabia, and unmarried women must usually be escorted from place to place. Someone had to go to the ministry and get them. Because Karim was the Director of New Physician Orientation, the duty fell upon him.

The morning came, and he drove to the Ministry in Riyadh to pick his new colleagues. He parked his Toyota and went inside. He knew where to go; he had been there many times before. He waited outside the Human Resources Office as the two new physicians completed their initial interviews.

After a while, two women emerged and approached him. At first, he did not notice anything unusual. But the closer they got to him, the more excited Karim became. He blinked twice to be sure that he was not hallucinating.

Sara was walking straight toward him.

There was no doubt in his mind that it was her. He would recognize her eyes, her face and her walk anywhere. His heart nearly leaped out of his chest. For a minute or two, he just watched her and said nothing, but when she got closer, she looked up and recognized him.

"Karim!" she said excitedly.

Sara was happy to see him too! What did this mean? He wanted to hug her, but he knew that he could not do that in public. So he simply exchanged formal but pleasant greetings with her and the other physician. They walked outside and got into his car.

On the way back to the health center, his head was spinning. Was he dreaming this? Was Sara really in the back seat of his Toyota? He stole looks at her as often as he could without being too obvious. When they made eye contact, his pulse raced.

No matter how hard he tried, Karim could not stop thinking about the unpleasant possibilities. Was Sara engaged to another man? She was a beautiful and intelligent young doctor so this was a possibility—almost a likelihood. What if Sara was getting married soon? Was her betrothed moving to Saudi as well? Would Karim have to work side by side with her, day after day, knowing that she was married to another man?

Even if Sara still loved him and she was free, would her parents now approve of a marriage they had disapproved of only a year and a half earlier? What would be worse, watching her marrying another man or watching other men try to court her right under his nose?

But all of these panicked thoughts dissipated when they arrived at the health center. Sara looked at him the same way she always had, with love in her eyes. Without having spoken a word to her, Karim somehow knew that no one had replaced him in her heart.

The workday passed slowly. All he could think about was talking with Sara that evening. The health center had living accommodations for unmarried female doctors and nurses, so she would be staying there.

Finally, after his shift ended at 8, she was waiting for him in the clinic hallway. They found a quiet place to talk.

"Sara," Karim said, "I can't believe you're here. It is wonderful to see you again."

"Today has been like a dream come true for me. You look well." Tears now flowed down her cheeks.

Unable to hold back any longer, he blurted out, "Are you engaged?"

"No. There is no room in my heart for anyone but you, Karim."

These words were music to his ears. They felt the same way about each other as they had a year earlier; at least that much had not changed. They hugged and held hands, but they knew they could not stay in their hiding place for long. Sara left first, and then Karim followed a minute or so later.

Now the only question seemed to be, would her parents approve of the marriage now that circumstances had changed? They were both working in Saudi Arabia, so her immediate physical safety was not a factor. But he was still from Gaza. If they married, she would no doubt accompany him there on occasion, and the possibility existed that at some point in the future they might return to Gaza permanently. It might be difficult for her family to visit her in Gaza because of the restrictions and regulations imposed by the Israeli military governor.

As it turned out, his worries had no substance. It was not long before her parents gave their permission for her to wed, and in July 1985 Karim and Sara began their life together as husband and wife.

Was it fate or faith that brought them back together? They believed that God was in control and that He was blessing them abundantly. They set up a household. Surely children would soon arrive. They were blissfully happy and looking forward to a long and prosperous life together.

Ameer AlShaikh

Chapter 19

A MOST WELCOME ADDITION 1987

When the sky appears gray
and I see a rose suddenly grew
From the cracks of a wall,
I do not say:
"The sky is gray"
but contemplate the rose
and say to it:
"What a beautiful day!"

Mahmoud Darwish

EARLY IN 1987, Karim and Sara were preparing for the arrival of their first child, a baby boy. They greeted the news of her pregnancy with joy. This child was a blessing from God, an answer to their prayers. Their son, whom they intended to call Ameer, would inherit two devoted, loving parents and a rich cultural and national heritage.

While he would be born on Saudi soil, Ameer would be a Palestinian. Both Karim and Sara had mixed emotions about this. They were thankful that their son would not be raised in a refugee camp but rather by prosperous, well-educated parents living in a modern Arab country. But they were unhappy that their unborn child's birthright had been stolen from him decades earlier. They knew that Ameer should be growing up in Beit Daras, Jerusalem or Jericho, not Riyadh.

Despite their mourning over the fate of Palestine, there was no denying that life for the young family was good. They had a nice apartment and steady incomes, and they were now integrated into Saudi society, at least as much as that was possible. As ex-pats, Karim and Sara enjoyed most of the freedoms and benefits of Saudi citizens, but they were denied some privileges. One of those was the ability to receive medical care in a public Saudi hospital. While there were private hospitals in the Kingdom, they were not conveniently located to where they lived and worked. Private hospitals also often lacked a full range of treatment options and specialized care facilities.

In Sara's seventh month of pregnancy, she began to experience some pain. As a precaution, her OBGYN ordered her to rest at home for the remainder of her term. This made life tougher because at this same time, due to the sudden illness of another physician, Karim was reassigned from the clinic where he had worked for two years to another health center that was 40 kilometers away. Despite his request not to be reassigned, there was simply no other alternative. He had to take the place of the ailing physician because there was no one else qualified who was available to step in.

So he began a new, more arduous daily grind. He still worked six split shifts a week—from 8 a.m. to noon and then from 4 p.m. to 8 p.m. Only now, he drove back to his home after his first shift and tended to the household chores of shopping, cooking and cleaning and saw to his wife's needs. At 3:15 he drove back to work. When he returned at 8:45, there were more tasks to complete before retiring. Although his immediate circumstances were trying, Karim was happy. More than anything else, both he and Sara wanted to start a family. Any short term sacrifice that was required to bring a child into the world was well worth it.

At night when Karim had finished with his job and domestic chores, he and Sara would lie in bed and talk about how wonderful it would be when their son arrived. They wanted more than one child, so this was the beginning of their happiness, not an end point. She felt bad that she was forced to do nothing but relax, but she knew that her husband's only concern was for her and the baby's health and wellbeing.

Early in the eighth month of Sara's pregnancy, Karim came home during his midday break and found his wife lying down and crying. She was also bleeding some from her uterus. He rushed her to the clinic only to be told what he already assumed to be true, that she needed to be hospitalized. The problem was there was no private hospital in the immediate area that had the proper neonatal facilities that she required.

For the next 48 hours, he made dozens of phone calls and went from hospital to hospital trying to find a suitable place for his wife to receive care. It was incredibly frustrating for him. Here he was, a physician in the Saudi Health Service, and yet he was forced to beg like a pauper for his wife and unborn child to get the medical treatment they required. As he struggled to solve the problem, Karim was not angry with the Saudis but with the Zionist occupiers of Palestine. Why was it that he and his wife were forced to live as guests in a foreign land? He knew how incredibly blessed they were to be living in Saudi Arabia, but they were still outsiders.

Finally, after two full days of searching, Karim found a facility with a proper neonatal intensive care unit that agreed to take her as a patient. It was a university hospital, a short drive from work and home. Karim was grateful that Sara and the baby would now be well looked after.

Now he had a new routine. After his first shift ended at noon, Karim stopped by the hospital to spend time with Sara. Usually when he came she was sleeping or resting comfortably, but one day when he arrived, a number people were in her room. Something was wrong. The attending physician was surrounded by three nurses. When the attending saw Karim, he motioned for him to accompany him into the hallway.

"Your wife's bleeding has increased. Both her life and the baby's life are in danger," the attending physician said.

"What do you recommend?"

"We must perform a C-Section as soon as possible. The baby will be born prematurely, but there is no other alternative."

"What have you been waiting for?" Karim asked, not in an angry tone, but one of concern. "You do not need me to—"

"Sara would not allow us to take her into surgery unless you first approved it. I'm glad you arrived when you did, Doctor. You're right; she should already be undergoing the procedure."

He nodded. Upon reflection, he was not surprised. Sara did not want to take any steps without consulting with him first. He and the attending doctor went back into her room.

Karim held his wife's hand and then gently kissed her on the forehead.

"Sara, it is time. We have given the baby every possible opportunity to develop, but he must be born now. To continue this present course would be unwise."

"I agree." She was so exhausted she could barely speak.

With that, the nurses prepared her for transport and then the orderlies wheeled her out. Karim made his way to the waiting area and found a comfortable place to sit. Now all he could do was wait and pray.

More than anything else, he would have loved to have been able to call his parents. They were only 2400 kilometers away—two days drive, less than three hours by plane—but they might as well have been on Mars. There was still no phone service from the Arab world into Gaza because of the Israeli occupation. Again, he grieved about his status as a man without a country. If he had been born in Saudi Arabia or Jordan, his parents would be with him right now, waiting for the arrival of his baby boy. But because he was a Palestinian, his family was forced to live on the outskirts of normal national life.

Less than half an hour after he had sat down, the attending physician reappeared. His heart raced. What was he doing here so quickly? Did something go terribly wrong?

"Dr. Karim, I have good news for you," the doctor said with a smile. "When we got your wife into the operating theater she gave birth naturally. A C-Section was unnecessary. Your son is premature, so we've taken him to the neonatal unit and placed him in an incubator. Sara will be fine, after the proper rest and treatment, of course."

"My son. Is he in any danger?" Karim asked hesitantly.

"He's stable but critical. We'll know more in 72 hours. Tell me, do you have to go back to the clinic?"

"Yes, I'll be a bit late as it is, but I must return."

"When you come back to the hospital after work, Sara will be awake and ready to see you."

When he made it back to the clinic, he was barely able to keep his mind on his work. He hoped that Sara was okay, and he was even more concerned about his young son. The staff at the health center knew that his wife was in the hospital waiting to give birth, so they asked him about her and the baby. When he shared the good news with them, they brought out desserts and snacks. Karim realized that he had not eaten a thing since breakfast, and then it was only biscuits and tea. The celebration at the clinic lifted his spirits a bit, but he could not escape the fact that he desperately wanted to be at the hospital with his wife and son and not at work.

When 8 o'clock finally rolled around, he left as quickly as his duties would allow. While he was working the afternoon shift, a winter storm had blown in and settled over Riyadh. It was unseasonably cold and wet, and the wind was howling. Braving the elements, Karim stopped at a flower shop and bought Sara a bouquet of carnations and a box of chocolates.

Despite the brief diversion, he made it to the hospital in record time and rushed into his wife's room. Sara was awake and filled with joy when she saw her husband walk through the door. They embraced, and she thanked him for the flowers. The same concern was on both of their minds.

"Have you seen our son?" she asked.

"Not yet. I was waiting to go with you."

An orderly brought in a wheelchair. Karim lifted his wife into the wheelchair and then rolled her into the hallway towards the elevator. They were headed to the neonatal section a couple of floors above them.

They both knew roughly what to expect. Their son had a low birth weight, so he was tiny and vulnerable. Ameer was having difficulty breathing. Preemies are subject to a whole host of risks, any one of which could potentially be fatal. Such babies did not always make it, and if they did, complications could arise that might disable them for life.

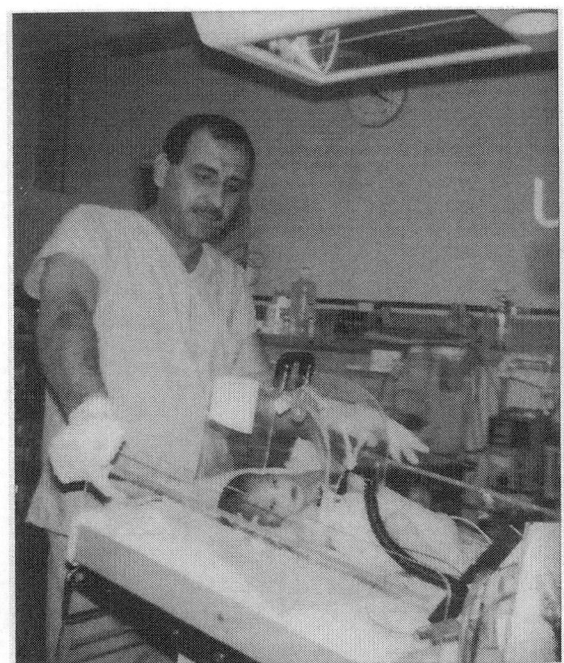

Karim and young Ameer

Karim and Sara went inside the neonatal unit and approached their son's incubator. Ameer was incredibly small but beautiful. They fell in love with their baby immediately. Sara reached in and held Ameer's hand. It was warm and comforting. They stayed there and talked to their son for almost an hour, until the nurse on duty told them it was time to go.

A couple of days later Ameer was out of immediate danger. A few days after that, Sara was released from the hospital. As often as they could, Karim and Sara came to the hospital and spent time with their baby boy. They could see the progress he was making—Ameer was gaining weight, breathing better and generally getting stronger. For more than two weeks, Sara provided the nurses with bags of her breastmilk to feed her son. When Ameer was three weeks old, Karim and Sara were allowed to bring him home.

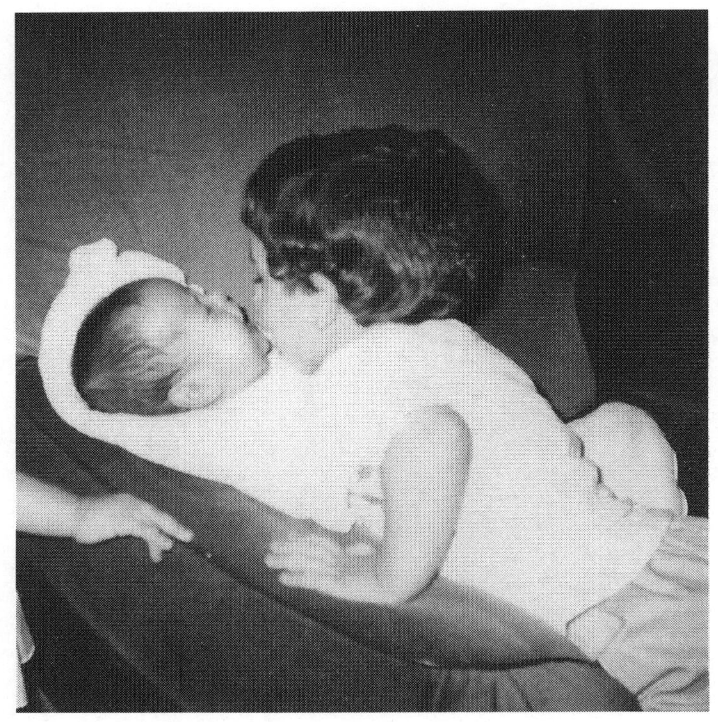

Ameer and his baby brother Saeed

Chapter 20

THE UNTHINKABLE HAPPENS

Intensive Care Unit

I whirl with the wind as the earth narrows before me.
I would fly off and rein in the wind,
but I am human… I felt a million flutes tear at my breast.
Coated with ice I saw my grave carried on my palms.
I disintegrated over the bed. Threw up.
Lost consciousness for a while. Died.
Cried out before that short-lived death occurred:
I love you, shall I enter into death through your feet?
And I died… I was completely extinguished.
How serene death is except for your weeping!
And how tranquil if it wasn't for your hands
pounding my breasts to have me return.
I loved you before and after death,
and between the two I saw only my mother's face.
It was the heart that strayed for a while,
and then returned. I ask my love:
In which heart was I struck?

She bent over me and covered my question with a tear.
O heart... heart, how is it you lied to me and disrupted my climax?
We have plenty of time, heart,
stabilize So that a hoopoe bird may fly
to you from the land of Balqis (Yemen).
We have sent letters.
We have crossed thirty seas and sixty coast lines
and still there is time in life for greater wanderings.
And O heart, how is it that you lied to a mare
that never tires of the winds. Hold on
so we can complete this final embrace and kneel
in worship. Hold on... hold on.
Let me find out if you are my heart or her voice crying: Take me.

Mahmoud Darwish

IN THE SUMMER of 1988, Karim and Sara welcomed another son into the world. Her second pregnancy was much easier than her first. While Ameer was born prematurely and his delivery was a difficult and risky process, baby Saeed came into the world easily and without complications.

Karim and Sara chose to name their new son after Karim's father. While Saeed Sr. could not be there to see his namesake being born, he looked forward to the day when Karim would be able to bring his grandson to see him in Gaza.

As 1988 became 1989, Karim was busy completing his residency in pediatric medicine. Young Saeed was thriving, and Karim's family spent every moment they could together. Ameer loved his younger brother and spent hours sitting with him and entertaining him by his mother's side. Saeed had a loud laugh, especially when Ameer played with him.

Right after they celebrated Saeed's first birthday, Karim noticed some things about his son that made him worry. For one, when he stood, he was not steady on his feet. When Saeed heard or saw something around him he turned his head abruptly, in an unnatural jerking motion, to see what it was. Everything about him seemed a bit off, although he remained a happy baby and showed no outward signs of physical distress.

A couple more months passed. Saeed was getting worse, not better. He was less focused at times, and now he could not even stand, much less try to walk. His head appeared to be larger than normal. Sara was anxious, and Karim could no longer live in denial. Something was wrong with their son.

Karim decided to take Saeed to the hospital where he worked to be examined by Dr. Zain, a senior pediatrician on staff. On the way to the hospital, all of the fears that he had chosen to suppress over the past few months rose to the surface. Young Saeed was exhibiting symptoms indicative of a serious illness, something related to the brain or nervous system. A number of horrible possible diagnoses ran through his head as he picked his son up and took him inside.

After half an hour, Dr. Zain came out of the examination room.

"What are you waiting for, Karim?"

"I'm not sure what you mean."

"Saeed needs a CT scan immediately. There is clearly swelling of the brain. Something is causing that. We need to find out what's going on."

"Yes, you're right. I just did not want to face it. Saeed needs help."

A few days later the CT scan was complete. Karim dreaded the call he knew he would receive from Dr. Zain. There were many possible reasons for Saeed to have swelling within the brain, but none of them was pleasant to contemplate.

"Karim," Dr. Zain said, "Saeed has a large mass within his brain. It's a tumor. Of course, we must relieve the pressure on his brain from the swelling before we can make any other decisions about the proper course of treatment. You know what we have to do for hydrocephalus; we must insert a shunt and remove the excess fluid."

"Yes, of course." Karim tried his best to fake being a detached physician. "We need to bring in a neurosurgeon."

"I've already done that. We will schedule the procedure for as soon as possible."

"Yes. Let me know when it is arranged."

Karim took the call from Dr. Zain in the middle of his work day. The rest of the afternoon went by in a fog. He was happy that he was not required to make any medical decisions for patients during this time because he would have been unable to do so.

His beautiful baby boy had a brain tumor. Whether it was cancerous or not, any brain tumor was potentially lethal, especially in someone so young. From experience, Karim knew that removing such tumors did not guarantee that another one would not quickly return in its place. Also, brain surgery in infants could cause disastrous side effects, leaving the patient disabled in any number of ways.

What was he going to tell Sara? She was a physician, so there was no way he could completely sugar coat it. Their son had a brain tumor. What could be more devastating? As he drove home, he thought of just how he should phrase his comments and how optimistic he could be with his wife without lying to her.

As soon as he walked in the door, the expression on Karim's face gave his emotions away. Sara began to cry. Saeed looked at his parents with his dark, penetrating eyes as if he was asking them what was wrong. When he smiled at them, it nearly broke their hearts.

"Saeed has a brain tumor. The tumor is causing swelling within the brain. They must drain the fluid before they can address the tumor." Karim's words sounded clinical, matter of fact. He was trying to sound detached, but this was their child, not a patient. He could not express himself in any other way and maintain his composure. Sara and Saeed needed him to be strong.

She nodded between her tears. All they could do was stand there in the fading light of the early evening and look at their son. Both of them knew that, at best, Saeed would have to endure painful and difficult procedures, beginning with the operation required to drain the excess fluid that had built up within his brain.

Two days later Karim, Sara and Ameer bundled up young Saeed and took him to the hospital. Karim tried his best to reassure his wife that removing excess fluid from around the brain was not a complicated or especially dangerous surgery. This was a half-truth, but it was a half-truth they both needed to believe in.

When Dr. Zain and the neurosurgeon came to take Saeed away for surgery, neither Karim nor Sara were immediately willing to let him go. For a few minutes, the physicians had to wait while the parents held their child and did their best to reassure Saeed that everything was going to be okay. Although he was too young to understand their words, they told him how much he was loved.

Less than a year and a half ago they had brought a healthy baby boy home from the hospital. Now they were sending their son off to endure something no baby should ever have to go through.

One hour passed and then another as Karim, Sara and Ameer sat nervously in the surgical waiting room. Karim went over the operation in his mind. He had been present when this procedure had been performed on his patients. After making an incision, the surgeon would carefully place the shunt and then the catheter in a space where it could effectively drain the excess fluid. In theory, this was not a difficult thing to do. But in practice, especially with a patient so young and depending on the type of the tumor, some things could go wrong. While he wanted to avoid thinking about the grim possibilities, his trained physician mind would not allow him to remain in denial any longer.

The doors opened to the surgical theater. Then the nurse and orderlies wheeled out a baby covered by a shroud. They were headed to the ICU. A moment later, Dr. Zain and the neurosurgeon emerged and spoke to Karim and Sara.

"We are very sorry," Dr. Zain said, "but when we inserted the catheter we inadvertently grazed the tumor, and there was serious bleeding. I'm afraid bleeding from a tumor, as you both know, is very difficult to control. Saeed is on a ventilator, and he is being taken to the ICU."

Karim did not respond. He was too stunned. Sara began to cry and immediately reached for Ameer, taking comfort in the touch of her healthy, young son. It would not be possible to see Saeed for a few hours.

There was no denying it now; their baby was in desperate trouble. Both Karim and Sara knew this; they did not have to be told more. The odds were stacked against their son; severe bleeding in an infant's brain can easily be a death sentence.

They had been through so much in their lives. Each of them, Karim especially, had lived through war, violence and extreme poverty. They had made it to a place of refuge, Saudi Arabia, miraculously found each other and had begun to live normal lives. Now this? They both begged God for a reprieve, relief from this trial. Everything they had endured before paled in comparison to this nightmare. No one should ever have to watch their child die. That is the greatest tragedy any human being can suffer.

Saeed remained in the ICU for a couple of days. Karim and Sara visited him, but they were not allowed to stay for long. They wanted to be there all the time. The only thing worse, they thought, than their son having to go through this was for him to go through it alone. Every day he looked worse, if that was possible. The tubes running into kept him breathing and fed him, but his eyes were closed, and he was completely unresponsive.

On the third day after surgery, Karim was called into a conference room by Dr. Zain and some other consulting physicians. Once again, Karim was filled with dread. He knew what they were going to tell him.

"Karim," Dr. Zain said, "Saeed is brain dead. There is no higher brain activity and no brain stem function. We conducted the same test twice; there is no doubt. The bleeding simply caused too much damage. We must ask you now—do you wish to disconnect Saeed from the ventilator?"

It took Karim a moment to compose himself. He knew this was coming; it was inevitable, but it still hit him as if it was a shock, something unexpected. To get through the situation, he responded in the only way possible.

"Please do not treat me like I am a fellow physician. I'm a father; I'm grieving and in tremendous anguish. You consult with each other and whatever you think is best to do, I will support it."

The physicians nodded and then asked him to step outside for a few minutes. He did so, all the time thinking how he was going to tell Sara that they had to let Saeed go, that all hope was gone. Then the physicians called him back into the conference room.

"Saeed should be taken off the ventilator. There is simply no rational hope of recovery. We are very sorry, Karim."

Karim nodded. He sat there in silence for a moment and then spoke. "Give us a day or so to say goodbye. Then remove him from the machines."

The physicians agreed. Karim stood up and walked out to his car. How was he ever going to be able to tell Sara this, to prepare her heart for such a terrible burden?

"Sara," Karim said as they sat down in their living room. "We must let Saeed go. There is nothing else they can do. All brain function has ceased. He's already gone."

They said nothing for the next hour. They held each other and wept. It was almost too much to bear. They looked across the living room at Saeed's crib, where he would never play in again. In their minds, they both saw their baby boy laughing as his big brother tickled him. All they could do was let the pain wash over them and pray that God would see them through what was to come next.

A day later Karim, Sara and Ameer went to the hospital to do the unthinkable—to say goodbye to Saeed. It was a bright, sunny day, pleasant outside. What they were doing seemed surreal; it could not be happening, yet it was. Ameer was far too young to understand, which was a tremendous blessing. Karim and Sara took comfort in the good health of their older boy and in the fact that he would be spared the tragedy they were about to endure.

Saeed was waiting for them. He was technically alive, but that was more illusion than reality. His eyes were shut, never to open again. His skin was cool, but not cold. His little chest rose up and down as the ventilator filled his lungs with air.

They prayed by Saeed's side, asking Allah to have mercy on his soul. Sara held her son's hand one last time. Ameer asked if he could kiss his brother and he was allowed to do it.

"Saeed is going to be sleeping for a long time," Sara told him. There was no other way to explain death to someone so young, to tell him that his little brother would soon be gone forever.

As they had planned, Sara and Ameer went home. Karim was left alone with Saeed, the attending nurse and Dr. Zain. On Dr. Zain's signal, the nurse shut off the ventilator. Karim held on to his son's hand tightly. It was a last act of defiance against the inevitable and a father's attempt to be there for his son when he needed him most.

Minutes past. The EKG meter showed a slowing heartbeat. Then, too suddenly for Karim, it went flat. Saeed was gone.

Karim sat alone for a while with Saeed's small, lifeless body. Even though he knew where he was and what had just happened, it did not seem real. How could something so horrible, so unexpected, so cruel, be true? Was there no justice in the world, no sanctuary for his family? Alone in the room, he let his tears flow freely. Until this moment he had been forced to control his emotions for the sake of others, but now he allowed himself to wail with grief. After a time, he composed himself. There were some things he needed to say before they took his son away forever.

"I will never forget you. I know that you are in a better place now where there is no suffering, only peace. Your grandfather and grandmother both love you very much, Saeed. Someday we will all be reunited." Karim whispered a final prayer for his son's soul. Then he called the nurse back in the room to take care of his son's body.

This was not the first tragedy in his life, nor would it be the last. But it was the most painful, the toughest to endure. With life there is always hope, always possibilities, but when death comes for someone so young, there is only sorrow.

White tear gas billows up against the black smoke from burning tires during the First Intifada

Chapter 21

BATTLING A GREATER ENEMY 1993

To My Mother

I long for my mother's bread
My mother's coffee
Her touch
Childhood memories grow up in me
Day after day
I must be worth my life
At the hour of my death
Worth the tears of my mother.
And if I come back one day
Take me as a veil to your eyelashes
Cover my bones with the grass
Blessed by your footsteps
Bind us together
With a lock of your hair
With a thread that trails from the back of your dress

I might become immortal
Become a God
If I touch the depths of your heart.
If I come back
Use me as wood to feed your fire
As the clothesline on the roof of your house
Without your blessing
I am too weak to stand.
I am old
Give me back the star maps of childhood
So that I
Along with the swallows
Can chart the path
Back to your waiting nest.

Mahmoud Darwish

FROM 1948 TO 1987, the number of Palestinian refugees grew exponentially. Unlike Karim and Sara, the vast majority of children born to the original refugees who were exiled when the State of Israel was created remained in place. Whether it was in Lebanon, Syria, Jordan or Gaza, most Palestinians had little choice but to stay put.

Now two full generations had come of age, people who had no personal memory of what Palestine was like pre-1948. All they knew was that they were forced to live in refugee camps and that their homeland was occupied by a foreign power. Frustration led to militancy, and militancy led to resistance.

From the 1950s through the 1970s, the Palestinian question was largely viewed as an outside, or international, matter. Wars were fought between the Arab States and Israel with the goal from the Arab side being to send the Zionist colonizers back to their original countries and restore the state of Palestine. By the mid-1980s, factors converged to create a different dynamic. If change was to come in any form in Palestine, it had to come from the inside.

Egypt had made peace with Israel. Other Arab countries had become allies with the United States due to security concerns in the region, most notably the rise in power and influence of dangerous regimes like Saddam Hussein in Iraq and the Ayatollahs in Iran. For the Palestinian people, the never-too-realistic hope of an invading Arab army conquering the Jewish state and restoring their homeland to them had become an improbable fantasy.

Because of the stifling effect of the Israeli military occupation and a lack of economic resources, Palestinians were forced into the lowest strata of the socio-economic spectrum whether they lived in Gaza, Syria or wherever. There was seemingly no solution, no way out of this box, no escape from a cruel set of circumstances.

So, inevitably, Palestine reached a boiling point. In December 1987, spontaneous protests began and mushroomed into something far greater. While Israel blamed the Palestine Liberation Organization (PLO) for inciting the conflict, the truth was that greater forces were set in motion. Israel was dependent on cheap Palestinian labor. A series of uncoordinated work stoppages by Palestinians led to a general strike, which threatened to seriously damage the Israeli economy. Many Palestinians refused to pay taxes or drive cars with Israeli license plates. Failure to give justice to the Palestinian people had given rise to civil disobedience and outright rebellion.

For the first time, the PLO had some competition for the political hearts and minds of the Palestinian people. Hamas, a group dedicated to the liberation of Palestine "from the river to sea," rose to more prominence. On the one hand, intellectuals and professionals in Jerusalem under the broad banner of the PLO and the United National Leadership were advocating increased civil disobedience and limited physical resistance in the form of rock throwing and Molotov cocktails. Hamas was promoting a guerilla-style campaign of violence and terror with the clear intent to destroy the "Zionist invaders."

An increasingly large number of people in the West—America and

Europe—began to sympathize with the Palestinian cause. For 40 years, America and Britain had led the way in championing the Israeli state and marginalizing the Palestinian people. While Western governments' pro-Zionist policies did not change, the general mood and attitudes of the Western public did, at least to some degree. For the first time, a large number of ordinary American and European citizens became more aware and educated about what was really going on in Palestine and why.

The conflict simmered, calmed down and then boiled up again—month after month, year after year. The Palestinians declared their independence in November 1988. Israel came forward with a peace initiative in 1989 and for the first time recognized the population of the West Bank and Gaza as legitimate players in political discussions of their own future. This recognition by Israel that the Palestinian people had a right to a seat at the negotiation table eventually led to the Oslo Accords.

Karim and Sara were forced to watch the conflict at a distance from Riyadh. Despite repeated requests to be allowed into Gaza, the Israelis denied them access. Karim and Sara's concern was for their family. Karim's younger brother, Adam, had gotten caught up in the conflict; he had been arrested and imprisoned for the crime of protesting against Israeli oppression.

Al Shati refugee camp was at the heart of the uprising in Gaza. Saeed's home was on the main street of the camp and therefore central to the protests and the subsequent backlash by the Israeli forces. Phone communication from Saudi to Gaza was impossible, so postal letters through a third country were the only way to keep in touch. Letters from Gaza came infrequently, and the news was often not good.

The protestors used the tactic of lighting old automobile tires on fire in the middle of the roadway as a way to slow the Israeli army or prevent attacks. The result was that the air above Gaza City was often filled with noxious black smoke. The Israelis countered with tear gas, which they poured liberally into the crowds of young people gathered in the streets. The smoke from the tear gas grenades was white.

On any given day, Al Shati and the rest of Gaza City looked like exactly what it was—a war zone. Plumes of white smoke rose and mixed with the streams of black smoke from the burning tires. Groups of Palestinians, mostly young people, roamed the streets and engaged in impromptu clashes with the Israeli security forces. The protestors threw stones and Molotov cocktails. The Zionists responded with live rounds—especially when the Intifada began—and killed 332 Palestinians during the first 13 months of the uprising. Bowing to international pressure, the Israeli Army then switched tactics and adopted a stratagem of "might, power and beatings" namely to "break Palestinian bones."

Finally in the summer of 1992, Karim and Sara and their two surviving children, Ameer and Salam—who was born in late 1990—were given permission to return to Gaza for an extended visit. The Intifada was not over, but the daily violence was diminishing. Because Karim left Gaza in 1984 through Jordan and specifically Jericho, he, Sara and the kids had to return the same way.

They flew to Amman and then waited patiently at the Jericho checkpoint to gain admittance into Israel. After several hours, they were allowed to pass. They found a taxi and climbed in for the long ride to Gaza City.

Saeed and Miriam were expecting Karim and his family, but there was no way to know for sure exactly when they would arrive. So when Karim and Sara walked through the front door, Miriam was both excited to see them and mildly surprised. She rushed toward her son and covered him with kisses. Then Miriam turned her attention to Sara and the children, whom she had never seen. Saeed and his son exchanged hugs and greetings.

They talked for a few hours about the trip, work, the children and the general state of affairs in Gaza. While they were talking, Miriam was having difficulty breathing. She labored to take in air. As they continued to talk and share stories, Karim increasingly focused on his mother. During a break in the conversation, he approached her and whispered in her ear, "Mom, let's go in the bedroom. I bought a new stethoscope. I need to listen to your heart and lungs, please."

Miriam nodded but did not say anything. They went into the bedroom, and Karim briefly examined her. The look on his face told Miriam what she did not want to hear.

"You know that the smoke bothers me, Karim, especially the black smoke from the tires."

"Yes, so you have said. Mom, I..." Karim was searching for the right words and could not immediately finish his thought.

"Well, is there a problem?"

"I cannot be sure, but we need to get your chest X-rayed. It's probably just an infection or an allergy, perhaps."

"I do not suffer from allergies, Karim," Miriam explained.

"We should not worry about this. I'm a doctor; it's my job to be concerned. You should be enjoying your grandchildren. Let's go back and join the others."

"I'm making you a traditional Palestinian meal tonight. I hope you still enjoy my cooking."

"Mom," Karim said, as he somehow managed to smile, "You have no rival in the kitchen, but don't tell Sara that I said that."

They went back to the front room, and the evening progressed. Karim was happy to see his parents, but the entire night was now clouded by what he had heard through his stethoscope. His mother had a serious problem in her lungs. There was no way to be sure exactly what the problem was until he looked at the X-rays, but his intuition was telling him that she was in trouble.

That night he could not sleep. He had told his mother it was likely a minor matter that could be addressed by a prescription of some sort. But he knew better; or rather, he knew worse. All of the smoke in the air in Gaza City for the past four years was toxic, and it affected some people more than others. His fear was that the smoky environment had caused a real problem for his mom—a serious medical condition, not a routine allergy or simple infection.

Getting an X-ray done in Gaza City was not an easy task. Karim spent the better part of the next two days going from place to place trying to find a machine that was capable of taking a clean chest X-ray. He found a suitable private clinic and scheduled his mother for an appointment the next day.

After the X-ray was taken and the film was processed, Karim looked at the pictures of his mother's chest. Just as he suspected, she had a large mass in one of her lungs. Unfortunately, he had seen this condition before. Almost always in such cases the mass on the lungs was malignant. He scheduled a biopsy, but he was afraid the biopsy would only confirm what he somehow knew from the moment he listened to his mom breathe as they were talking at her house—that Miriam had lung cancer.

Karim was faced with an enormous challenge. Before the Intifada, medical facilities in Gaza were limited, but since the uprising began hospitals were forced to make do with little in the way of medicine and even less in terms of diagnostic equipment. Miriam needed a CT scan and a biopsy, and she needed them immediately.

There were three possible choices. Karim could take his mother to Egypt, and there she could receive proper care, but it was doubtful that Miriam would survive such an arduous journey. Jordan was closer, but the trip there was difficult, and the paperwork required to get permission to cross the border was onerous. The only viable alternative was to seek medical care in Israel.

Because of his personal history and his employment in Saudi Arabia, Karim had good connections with the UNRWA. A contact at the UNRWA told him that it was possible for patients to travel from Gaza to Israel to receive treatment if they were very sick and their medical status was documented by the UNRWA. Miriam certainly qualified under those rules, but for Karim to accompany her he was told that he had to submit his own paperwork and wait for approval from Israeli authorities.

Through his United Nations contacts, Karim found an Israeli physician in Tel Aviv who worked at the Tel Hashomer Hospital complex. Dr. Debra had an outstanding reputation for diagnosing and treating diseases of the lungs. After Karim had spoken with her, Dr. Debra agreed to see Miriam immediately. Now the only question for Karim was, "How do I get Mom to Tel Aviv, and how can I get permission to go with her?"

The security situation in Israel remained tense, despite the fact that the Intifada was winding down as a peace accord drew near. Regardless, it was still forbidden for non-Israeli citizens to cross the border into Israel proper unless there were special circumstances, such as the urgent need for medical care under the UNRWA umbrella. If someone did not have permission and tried to cross into Israel, he was subject to immediate arrest and possible imprisonment.

There was no way that Karim was going to put his mother in a vehicle, ask the driver to take her to Tel Aviv, drop her off at the hospital and let her fend for herself. So he chose to take the risk and go with her.

Miriam and Karim were going to Tel Aviv with a small group of other patients who had been receiving medical treatment in Israel. All of this was done under the general banner of the UNRWA and was a humanitarian effort. Regardless of the fact that he was a physician and he was accompanying his mother, Karim had no paperwork to show to the soldiers at the checkpoint. All he could do was hope and pray that they would let him through with the others.

The checkpoint between Northern Gaza and Israel was called Checkpoint Aries. As their vehicle approached this checkpoint the only person in the car more nervous than Karim was his mother. Miriam and the other patients took out their paperwork to show the soldiers. Karim had his credentials as a physician but nothing else.

Miriam was not doing well. The stress of the situation, both the car ride and the fear of Karim possibly being arrested, was taking its toll on her. Karim wondered if his mother would make it to Tel Aviv without the assistance of an ambulance.

One of the guards looked at everyone in the vehicle while the others circled around the car. Miriam did her best to remain calm and smile, but it was apparent that she was in distress. For a moment, the guard said nothing. He looked at Karim and then back Miriam.

"Proceed," the guard said in Hebrew. Then he motioned to the driver, urging him to get moving.

Karim said a silent prayer of relief. Miriam's prayers were audible as she thanked God for His mercy. An hour later they made it to Tel Aviv and then to Tel Hashomer Hospital.

The directions to find Dr. Debra were easy to follow. In short order, they were inside the clinic.

"Dr. Karim." Dr. Debra extended her hand.

"Karim, please," Karim said as he shook hands. "We are very sorry to be a little late. It is not easy to get here from Gaza City."

"No apologies necessary. You must be Miriam." Dr. Debra touched his mother's arm.

"Yes. Thank you for your kindness."

"Let's go into my office and talk for a moment."

Karim and Dr. Debra reviewed the X-rays and Dr. Debra gave Miriam a cursory examination. There was no doubt what needed to be done next—Miriam needed a CT scan and a biopsy of the mass in her lung. He paid in cash for these procedures, as he had agreed to do before he came. Seven hours later, they and the other patients were headed back to Gaza City.

"We will know the results of the tests in a few days, Mom."

"I'm sure it will be all right, Karim," Miriam said. "You are not to worry."

The drive to Al Shati was less stressful than the journey to Tel Aviv because there was no threat of being stopped at the checkpoint and not allowed back into Gaza. Karim spent the entire ride home thinking about only one thing—how he could treat his mother's illness in Gaza.

It was time for Sara to take the children back to Saudi Arabia. That night as they said their goodbyes, he told his wife, "Mom has lung cancer. Test results are needed to confirm that, but I know. There is no use hiding from the truth, especially between us."

"What will you do?"

"All I can do. It is so difficult, Sara…" He was overwhelmed by the emotions he had kept bottled up all day. "Mother needs proper care. In the matter of a few hours, I could have her in a modern hospital in Egypt or Jordan. She's going to need chemotherapy, perhaps surgery… It is so unfair."

All she could do was console her husband and hope for the best. She had two children to care for and a household to manage. "Your mother will be in our prayers constantly. You are always in my heart, Karim."

A few days went by. He closely monitored his mother's condition. He was concerned about the amount of fluid building up around her lungs. As the water around her lungs increased, it became even more difficult for her to breathe.

There was only one way to relieve this pressure, and that to find a suction machine to remove the excess fluid. He went from clinic to clinic and to the hospital. Finally, he found an old suction machine gathering dust in the back room of a doctor's office. It was not the best; in fact it was barely adequate. But it would have to do.

Removing excess fluid from around a patient's lungs was a procedure that was normally done only in a hospital setting. The patient should be sedated and closely monitored for any possible complications. But Karim had no choice; the procedure had to be done at home.

So he laid his mother out on the bed. She was already in terrible pain. He stuck a large needle in her chest in between her ribs. Slowly he sucked the excess water out, and Miriam began to breathe much easier. Despite the pain from the needle, she fell fast asleep when she no longer had to labor to breathe.

Karim was using all his skills as a physician, but he could not remain emotionally detached as he could from his regular patients. This was his beloved mother. More than anything else he wanted to take her out of Gaza to Israel, Saudi Arabia or Jordan. Why should his mother have to die in agony like this? Again, the same thoughts about injustice went through his head as when Sara needed a hospital with a neonatal ward. Why must the Palestinian people suffer so much? What great offense had they committed to deserve such punishment?

Individual Jewish people were not the problem. Like Dr. Debra in Tel Aviv, most Jews were good, decent, God-fearing people. Zionism was the problem. No matter how persecuted the Jews were elsewhere, they had no right to take land and treasure from an innocent nation. Karim knew that the European Jewish Holocaust was an unimaginable human tragedy. But he had always wondered how the people who had suffered under such horrific oppression could turn a blind eye to the terrible suffering they created.

Miriam was dying. Karim did not need a phone call from Dr. Debra to tell him this, but she called nonetheless. When she told him that his mother had advanced phase lung cancer, he was momentarily stunned, but he really did not understand why. Perhaps it was hearing the words from a fellow physician. More so than he expected, getting that phone call was a bitter and difficult moment.

His father took the news especially hard. He was realistic about his wife's prognosis too, but when he told him that, basically, his wife would be dead soon, Saeed's normally stoic manner yielded to his grief. He did not shed a tear in front of Miriam—he vowed to be nothing but positive in her presence—but he could not hide his devastation from his son.

Again using his contacts in the UNRWA, Karim was able to obtain a regimen of chemotherapy for his mother. Despite knowing that it would probably be ineffective because her cancer was simply too advanced, Karim had to try to heal his mother. For a couple of weeks, he watched helplessly as his mother's hair fell out and she vomited after each treatment. Miriam was in agony.

Her most fervent wish was to see her youngest son once more before she died. Adam had been sent to prison for two years for the crime of throwing stones at Zionist soldiers. Even though her illness was documented, the Israeli authorities refused to let him come home for a final visit with his mother.

Karim could do no more. He had used all of his vacation and sick leave time with the Saudi hospital where he worked. He had asked for and received an extended unpaid leave to stay in Gaza and treat his mother. The situation could not go on forever. His employer sent him a letter in the form of an apology informing him that he must return to Saudi Arabia immediately or he would lose his job. When Miriam found out about the extent of his troubles, she insisted that he return home.

In August 1992, Karim said goodbye to his mother. When he left, he knew that he would never see her again.

In early January 1993, the Israeli authorities relented and allowed Saeed's family to visit Adam in prison. Miriam was too weak to go. Saeed and Leen delivered the terrible news to Adam that his mother was not long for this world. Overcome with grief, he broke down. After he collected himself, he wrote a letter to his mother which Leen read to Miriam when they returned to Al Shati.

The last line of the letter read, "I love you, Mother, as much as I love Palestine."

On January 23, 1993, Miriam AlShaikh died. Her life was cut short by the tragedy of the Intifada, but the real tragedy of her life was the fact that she had to live all her adult years and raise her children in Al Shati. Miriam should have spent her days tending to her husband's home in Beit Daras as Saeed managed the family farms and orchards and took his place as a village elder.

This tragedy, however, paled in comparison to her triumphs. All of Miriam's children were either physicians or professional people except Adam, who was certainly headed down that road upon his release from prison.

She and her husband had not succumbed to hatred; they had not allowed the great injustice to destroy their children's lives. She had indeed done her best for Palestine.

Since his mother's death, Karim's favorite song is "My Mother." The lyrics were taken from a Darwish poem, and the song was composed by Marsail Khaleefa:

I long for my mother's bread, my mother's coffee, her touch. Childhood memories grow up in me, day after day. It must be worth my life.

And if I come back one day, take me as a veil to your eyelashes. Cover my bones with the grass, blessed by your footsteps.

Bind us together, with a lock of your hair, with a thread that trails from the back of your dress that I might become immortal. I Become a God if I touch the depths of your heart.

Saeed and Karim AlShaikh

Chapter 22
AN INNOCENT VICTIM 2001

He Embraces His Murderer

He embraces his murderer.
May he win his heart: Do you feel angrier if I survive?
Brother… My brother!
What did I do to make you destroy me?
Two birds fly overhead.
Why don't you shoot upwards?
What do you say?
You grew tired of my embrace and my smell.
Aren't you just as tired of the fear within me?
Then throw your gun in the river! What do you say?
The enemy on the riverbank aims his machine gun at an embrace?
Shoot the enemy!
Thus we avoid the enemy's bullets and keep from falling into sin.
What do you say?
You'll kill me so the enemy can go to our home

And descend again into the law of the jungle?
What did you do with my mother's coffee; with your mother's coffee?
What crime did I commit to make you destroy me?
I will never
Cease embracing you.
And I will never
Release you.

Mahmoud Darwish

SAEED MADE HIS way to the mosque to pray his afternoon prayer called Aser. He greeted people on the way, the young before the old. He walked the same route every day. He loved his neighbors. They loved him back. Saeed was 77 years old, a fixture in Gaza, a beloved citizen of traditional Palestine and one of the remaining original Nakba refugees.

As he stepped one foot in the mosque's door, a gunshot fired by an Israeli soldier rang out from behind him. The soldier was firing at a group of children who were demonstrating in front of the mosque. At first Saeed did not know what had happened to him. He was still trying to process what was going on when he dropped to the floor.

The bullet penetrated tangentially to his vertebral column, went through his liver and then exited. The men in the mosque stopped praying and turned their attention to the old man who was lying motionless in the entryway and bleeding profusely. A few minutes later Saeed was in an ambulance racing towards the hospital.

The hospitals in Gaza were not well equipped and short on manpower, but because of the ongoing violence they were fairly proficient at dealing with gun wound emergencies. Ali, who was Saeed's oldest son and a physician, and Adam, his youngest son, were notified. Adam made it to the hospital first. When he got there, he found his father lying on a mobile bed surrounded by half a dozen doctors and nurses. A couple of men from the neighborhood who accompanied Saeed from the mosque were also there. Saeed was given attention but not a room. They were treating him in the hallway.

He was not the only gunshot victim that day. At least four other people had been shot. The Second Intifada was raging on. It began in late 2000 as a result of Israeli occupation policies that continued to violate international law and deprived Palestinians of their basic human rights.

On September 28, 2000, Ariel Sharon appeared at the Al-Aqsa Mosque compound in Jerusalem's Old City with more than a thousand Israeli police. In a blatant attempt to provoke Palestinians, he repeated a phrase that was broadcast during 1967 Six-Day war when Israeli Occupation Forces seized East Jerusalem: "The Temple Mount is in our hands." Palestinians reacted almost immediately to the threat to Al-Aqsa, the third holiest site in Islam.

The Israeli Occupation Forces launched a series of sweeping military offensives and administrative policies designed to collectively punish Palestinians for the uprising. The United Nations quickly released Resolution1322, citing Israel for the use of excessive force against the Palestinian people. The resolution came less than three weeks after the start of the violence, by which time hundreds of Palestinians had already been killed and injured.

The violence was ongoing. The Israelis answered rock-throwing with machine gun bursts and sporadic rocket fire with targeted weapons attacks that leveled buildings. Saeed was one victim among many.

His bleeding was getting worse. He was placed on his side, in the left lateral recumbent position. The doctors were nervous, unsure what to do next. Two of them were arguing loudly about which patient should go into surgery first. Saeed was moaning and looked dizzy as if he was trying to sleep. His eyes closed for a few seconds and then reopened a moment later. They were infusing him with blood in a desperate attempt to replace what he had lost.

His physician argued that he should be taken into surgery first. Adam, who had a short temper and was panicked about the condition of his father, was about ready to take matters into his own hands and wheel his father into surgery himself.

Just then Ali arrived and said, “No, let another patient into the OR, we will wait.”

Adam was outraged, but he quickly calmed down when Ali explained that he had arranged for a better surgeon to come and operate on their father. The surgeon was an old friend of his, practicing abroad. He had come back to Gaza to visit his family but then got stuck there for two months.

A few minutes later Ali’s physician friend arrived, and Saeed was taken to the OR. Although the surgery was successful, he was not stable. He was sent to the intensive care unit, where he stayed for ten days. For most of that time he was unconsciousness. Every so often he would call out, “Miriam! Miriam!”

Between other muffled words no one could understand, Saeed told his wife, “I’ll be coming soon, Miriam.”

On the tenth day, he was able to open his eyes and breathe spontaneously. He recognized his sons and doctors. Ali and Adam were overjoyed. The room was crowded with people who had prayed for Saeed. He was quickly transferred to the ward from the ICU.

Karim was in Saudi Arabia. He could only monitor the events from afar because it was impossible for him to travel to Gaza. There was no way the Israeli authorities were going to allow him in, given the current state of unrest. A few days after Saeed woke up and was transferred to the ward, he was well enough to be released.

All of Saeed’s children were relieved. Ali, a physician, was seeing to his father’s care. Adam never left his father’s side. As for Karim, Yasin had come from France to pay him a visit in Riyadh. The holy month of Ramadan had just ended. They were celebrating Eid together.

Karim was uncomfortable, but he could not explain why. He had recently been promoted, he was generally happy and his family was doing fine. Despite his father’s recovery from his gunshot wound, he remained worried. He could not get Palestine’s troubles off of his mind.

Throughout the Second Intifada, Israeli forces enforced an oppressive siege. Initially, Israel placed severe restrictions on Palestinians’ ability to move. Israeli human rights group B’Tselem reported that Israel had blocked access to Palestinian cities and villages with “concrete blocks, piles of dirt, deep trenches, or checkpoints.” Israeli authorities also enforced an early curfew that prohibited Palestinians from even being outside of their own homes at certain points throughout the day and night.

Salam was upstairs playing a computer game. The rest of Karim's kids and his nephew were also upstairs counting their Eideia money and blowing up balloons for the Eid decorations. Karim and his brother were in the living room talking medical jargon and discussing where and how Yasin should specialize. Sara had just finished lighting the bakhoor and was taking it around the house to give it a nice smell. She was headed to the kitchen to prepare food for the guests. Relatives and friends were expected without invitation, which was the custom on Eid.

His brother's wife, who was also Sara's sister, was with Sara in the kitchen dealing with her baby twin girls who were both crying, giving the young mother no break. The men were taking turns on the phone trying to reach their family in Gaza. They were used to not being able to get through because of the regular blackouts. Most of the time communication was difficult, but they were fortunate because Adam worked in telecommunication. It was easier for them to get through than it was for others. Adam always had a solution. Today, though, he did not call and also did not pick up.

"Nothing?" Karim asked.

"Not yet, no one is picking up," Yasin said. "But the phone is ringing. Maybe they are busy or visiting someone."

"Okay. Let's go out. We should take the kids somewhere fun." Every Eid, Karim took his kids to the arcades in the afternoon before the guests came over. He walked near the stairs and called out, "Kids, anyone interested in going to the arcades?"

The phone rang. He walked back from the door of the living room and picked it up. He thought it might be Gaza, but it was not. His brother-in-law was calling from Manchester.

"Happy Eid," Karim said after he and his brother each said hello. "How's family? Any news from Gaza?"

"Oh, you did not hear." He sighed. "I thought so..."

There was silence for a moment and then he replied with the traditional consolation phrase, a prayer usually offered to the family of the dead. "Great may your reward be (for whom you've lost)," he said, "Your father passed away this morning."

Karim had spoken with his father while he was in the hospital ward and once after he was discharged. He had also talked to him just yesterday, during the last day of Ramadan, and asked him to pray for his family. He was fine. He was getting better and healing well from his injuries.

However, a few hours ago he had insisted on standing up to greet his grandchildren, who came to wish him a happy Eid, Adam explained later when he finally got through to Karim. "We were all happy to see him on his feet again, even though he was leaning heavily on his crutch. Our happiness lasted only a few minutes, before he clenched his chest and fell down. He gasped for breath." He had still smiled as he stretched out his hand to his grandchildren and said, "Take care of each other and don't forget Beit Daras."

The doctors later explained that Saeed had developed respiratory complications and went into distress. The official cause of death was a pulmonary embolism, caused by the long immobilization during his recent morbidity.

Karim could not explain to the kids what happened, except to say, "We are not going anywhere today." He knew they were disappointed, but there was strangely no protest. They realized something was wrong. Maybe it was the tears in their father's eyes.

Muslim families everywhere were preparing to receive their guests, but now Karim's family was getting ready to receive guests not for rejoicing, but rather for mourning. They opened their house for three days and nights, as is the tradition called Azaa, for people to come and support their family. People came and left not too long after as to not burden the family. They served Arabic coffee and dates. In such circumstances, nothing fancy is served. The neighbors usually prepare coffee and help the wife. The relatives usually do the hosting and welcome the guests.

The first night Karim, Yasin and their guests prayed the Janaza prayer. This prayer is usually prayed for the deceased before his burial and in the presence of his body after it is washed and wrapped in clean white sheets, the Kaffan. Since they were not in Gaza, they prayed their own prayer for their father at home.

Tomorrow Saeed's funeral service would be held in Gaza, so there was only one thing on Karim's mind—how could he get into Gaza, even with the closed borders? He asked his guests this question.

"You can talk to the embassy and make some arrangement with the Egyptians," a friend suggested.

Another guest added, "My brother-in-law tried to go in last week. I am telling you, there is no way to get there now. The Israeli soldiers have closed all access to the Strip for two weeks and counting."

"Why don't you arrange for a diplomatic departure?" offered an older man, a hospital administrator. "If you have any connections here or there, if you know any of your patients who could help, you could probably, say, arrange for a royal order?"

This idea interested Karim. He excused himself, stepped outside and made a phone call.

Karim never liked to ask for anybody's help, but today was an exception. He called a Saudi Princess, the king's niece. She had given him her private home phone number because she brought her children to his clinic for treatment. The princess was impressed by his work and his demeanor. He did not want to ask for anything in return, but now he had no other choice. He dialed her number.

"This is the princess's residence," replied a gentleman.

Karim introduced himself and requested to talk to her Royal Highness. The gentleman replied that he would pass the message on to her.

A few minutes later, she called Karim back. He explained to her that his father's burial was tomorrow and that he needed to be in Gaza to attend the ceremony. The princess was compassionate. She pulled a lot of strings for Karim that night, for which he was thankful, but under no circumstance was he to enter Palestine; the politics were too complicated.

After he had received the bad news, Karim needed some time alone to calm himself. He had now been forced to miss the burial of both his mother and his father. To deny someone the chance to say goodbye to a deceased parent is not only cruel—it is inhuman. He hated the fact that his people were in such a weak position, that they had no rights, no voice, no power at all.

On the third and final day of Saeed's Azaa, Sara's aunt—who was about the same age as Saeed—visited and not just to offer her consolations. The old woman asked to talk to Karim in private. They went in the study and closed the door.

"Your father was a most elegant person, always well dressed," she said. "He only dressed in Jokh." The wool was imported from the United Kingdom and tailored by the best tailors in the country.

"Oh, but he was handsome, tall, and most of the girls would fancy being married to him," the old woman said with a wave. "Yes, they would talk about him!"

Karim was not sure what she was getting at, but her eyes were determined, focused and moving as if she was following a distant shadow.

"Saeed was a modest man. He probably told you that he had a house. It was big and your family was rich. But there is something I'm sure he never told you. He lost most of his money not in the invasion, but to people. He always gave and never asked for anything in return. There were many loans too, to people in the village and people outside. He always made more money by trading and continued to give. Your father left Beit Daras in a carriage, not on foot. He made sure that all his extended family had left safely—cousins, second cousins, in-laws, everyone. We all wrapped our cloths and left.

"He wrapped his gold and left. I thought he would talk to the businessmen in Gaza and make money again. It should've been easy for him! He had anticipated a disaster and people did not listen to him. He thought that one day we might lose our village to the Zionists. When he arrived in Gaza, instead of securing a place for himself, and get a house, for example, he spent every last penny he had to gather up the big family. He made sure they got the better shelters in the camps."

She sighed deeply. "Son, the camps were not a charity. They abused people. Most of the families had to pay for a good shelter. They weren't all bad, don't get me wrong, but the poorer families… my God, they were put in the most rotten of places deep in the camp. God only knows how they pulled through."

Karim was speechless. He had not heard this before, although he knew that his father was a generous man. The extent of his generosity truly amazed him.

"People did not feel the difference in class around him in the village. But it was always different when he visited other towns. Your aunt told me that they knew who he was and welcomed him accordingly. I also heard things from friends outside the village. He was to be married to the daughter of the Mokhtar, the leader in Deir Yasin, before the massacre, but she was killed.

"He always helped the poor and needy. He always stressed on education, didn't he?" she asked Karim.

"Yes," Karim answered.

"Before you were born, and before he was married, he made the effort to encourage people to be educated," she explained. "Most of all, he tried to keep the peace between the families. He even paid the Deyah for one of the families when their son was accidently killed by one of the farm tools by another young man. He took care of it. He was only 23, but like your grandfather, he was wise. Despite the fact that your grandfather died when he was a small child, he took after him in many ways.

"Son, I can see that you are sad, but you should be proud. Your father was a great man. I hope that he is in a better place."

She tapped Karim on the shoulder and then slowly pulled herself up, pressing hard on the chair arms. She left the room in small steps.

Karim remained seated behind his desk. No one had spoken about this in decades. He wondered, how many lives did his father save? Counting future generations the number could be in the thousands.

It was staggering to think what Saeed did and for nothing in return. But that was not true, he quickly reminded himself. His father had indeed earned a great reward. His family loved him without measure, and Karim had no doubt that Saeed was in Paradise enjoying eternal bliss.

During the Second Intifada a few brave people from across the globe – journalists, peace activists and ordinary citizens - risked, and sometimes gave, their lives to provide the world with a firsthand account of the humanitarian tragedy in Gaza. One of them was a young American woman, Rachel Corrie.

> *"I got a number of very thoughtful responses to the email I sent out last night, most of which I don't have time to respond to right now. Thanks everyone for the encouragement, questions, criticism. Daniel's response was particularly inspiring to me and deserves to be shared. The resistance of Israeli Jewish people to the occupation and the enormous risk taken by those refusing to serve in the Israeli military offers an example, especially for those of us living in the United States, of how to behave when you discover that atrocities are being committed in your name. Thank you."*
>
> Rachel Corrie

From Wikipedia (Edited):

Rachel Corrie *(April 10, 1979—March 16, 2003) was an American peace activist and diarist. She was killed by an Israeli Defense Forces armored bulldozer in Rafah, in the southern part of the Gaza Strip during the height of the Second Intifada. She came to Gaza from America as part of her senior-year college assignment to connect her home town with Rafah in a sister cities project. While there, she engaged with other activists in efforts to prevent the Israeli Army's demolition of Palestinian houses. On March 16, 2003, Corrie was killed during an Israeli military operation after a three-hour confrontation between Israeli soldiers operating two bulldozers.*

Karim and his family enjoying the day at Niagara Falls

Chapter 23

O' CANADA JULY 2000

I dream of white lilies, streets of song, a house of light.
I need a kind heart, not a bullet.
I need a bright day, not a mad, fascist moment of triumph.
I need a child to cherish a day of laughter, not a weapon of war.
I came to live for rising suns, not to witness their setting.
He said goodbye and went looking for white lilies,
a bird welcoming the dawn on an olive branch.
He understands things only as he senses and smells them.
Homeland for him, he said, is to drink my mother's coffee, to return safely, at nightfall.

Mahmoud Darwish

WHEN KARIM'S MOTHER died in 1993 during the First Intifada, he could not attend her funeral. As a Palestinian he did not have the right to visit his homeland, even if that "homeland" was limited in definition to Gaza. However, if he had been a citizen of a North American or European country, he could have returned to Palestine with little difficulty by applying for an Israeli visa.

For a while, Karim had been considering applying for citizenship in North America, either in Canada or the United States. He would not abandon Palestine, that was not the issue. The hard truth was that he had no nation to abandon. He was simply tired of being a man without a country. He could stay and work in Saudi Arabia indefinitely, but he could not become a Saudi citizen.

A couple of years earlier he had met a Palestinian physician who had become a Canadian citizen. He had said that Canada was a nice place, peaceful and less involved in world controversies than England or America. Karim thought about this and did some research. Indeed, it was possible for his family to become Canadian citizens. More than anything else, it was his goal for his children to rise to the top. He wanted to give them every chance in the world to succeed.

So he visited the Canadian Embassy in Riyadh. He applied for citizenship and paid the required fees. He retained an attorney to deal with all of the paperwork. The amount of documentation required was onerous, but there seemed to be no hurry, so Karim did not rush the process. Then his father was shot and died during the Second Intifada. As with his mother, he was not allowed into Gaza to attend his funeral. If he had been a Canadian citizen, he could have easily traveled to Tel Aviv, signed the required waivers, rented a car and driven directly to Gaza.

After Saeed's death, he accelerated the process of immigrating to Canada. He completed his application packet by acquiring all of the needed documentation—birth certificates, school transcripts, medical records and so on.

The summer rolled by. One day at the hospital, the mailman delivered a package with the return address of "Canadian Immigration" on the top left corner. Karim opened the package and examined the paperwork inside. He and his family were approved. All they had to do now was complete cursory medical examinations, send in their Palestinian refugee documentation, wait for their visas to arrive and schedule their flights to Canada.

It was indeed a dream come true, but it was not yet real. He had to tell his family about this before it would really sink in.

On the ride home from work, Karim was both excited and a bit sanguine. He was becoming a citizen of the First World. Intellectually, he knew that this was a great benefit to himself and his kids. The opportunities, the freedom, the lifestyle—these possibilities excited him. But then he thought about his father. For all of his life, Saeed kept the keys to the house in Beit Daras in his pocket, hoping against all hope that by some miracle he could return home someday. Was he giving up on his father's dream by immigrating to Canada? Was he disloyal to Palestine?

Most of Saeed's other children had already moved on. Leen was a British citizen, Yasin lived in France and Omar lived in the UAE. Now Karim would be joining them as ex-pats. What other choice was there? Live as a stateless nomad? Saudi Arabia was wonderful, but it was not home. Karim knew that he could always return to Saudi Arabia and work; that was no problem.

The more he thought about it, he was sure that Saeed would agree with his decision. Like his father before him, Karim's first priority was his children. There was simply no doubt in his mind that immigrating to Canada was the right thing to do for them.

Walking through the front door with a big smile on his face, Karim went into the kitchen and hugged and kissed his wife. She started to call for the kids, but he interrupted her and asked her to speak with him alone for a minute. Then he told her that Canada had approved their application for citizenship. Sara asked all the questions Karim knew that she would ask. "Will you get a job in Canada? Do you have to re-take your medical exams? Will we have friends there? How cold is it in Canada?"

Then Sara added, "We received some important mail at home today too. Ameer has been accepted into three Canadian universities." They were proud of Ameer and pleased that he would be able to complete his undergraduate studies in Canada before attending medical school. They thought this might give him some much-needed perspective on life in general and on becoming a physician specifically.

After their visas arrived, Karim and Sara scheduled the trip, but then an unexpected complication arose. Sara got sick. Her condition was serious enough to require immediate abdominal surgery. Their trip was booked, and to unravel all their arrangements would be a serious burden to the family.

"You look much better today, Sara," the doctor said, addressing his patient with a smile.

"Yes." She was still breathing heavily; it had only been two days since her operation. "But I still feel the abdominal cramps. They are quite painful."

Karim held his wife's hand. "You're being weaned off of your morphine drip. From today on you'll be given only pills. You will have to start drinking water and try eating some soups. The pain will lessen every day, my dear."

"Well said, Dr. Karim. I guess I don't have anything left to explain to your wife," the doctor replied with a grin. "If everything continues to go well, Madame Sara, you will be discharged tomorrow. I'll follow up with you in my office in one week."

She smiled, and then looked at her husband. "Karim, take him outside and ask him about our traveling."

Sara turned her head on the pillow and closed her eyes. Karim and the doctor walked out into the hall.

"Dr. Karim, your wife would be better off staying at home for a week. Do you really plan on traveling in six days?"

"Would it harm her if we traveled? Was there too much damage done during the surgery?"

"The surgery went well, but there are still risks."

"I contacted my travel agent and managed to delay our flight from England to North America," Karim said, "but I couldn't find any other flight from here to England within the next month. They are all booked. We will stay at my sister's home in England, which will give Sara some time to rest. I was going to cancel the trip altogether, but the visas arrived the day before she went into the surgery. Sara asked me not to change our plans unless it was absolutely necessary."

"It is not absolutely necessary to cancel your trip. You're a physician, you know enough," the doctor said. "If Sara travels in a few days, there could be some issues."

"Yes, I understand. She pretends that everything is okay in front of the kids. She knows how much they want to go, and she does not want to disappoint them."

Karim was unsure about Sara's fitness to travel. He needed her doctor's honest opinion because his own judgment might be clouded by personal concerns. The worry was not the plane ride, per se, but possible complications such as severe in air turbulence. If she were tossed around, it could cause internal bleeding or something worse. What if they got in a car accident in England from the airport to Leen's house?

After their brief discussion in the hall, Karim asked the doctor to speak with Sara and advise her not to travel.

While Karim waited in the hallway, the doctor went back into Sara's room. He emerged a couple of minutes later. He and Karim exchanged nods, and then Karim went in to discuss the situation with his wife.

"You told him to talk me out of traveling, Karim?" Sara said, with a hint of sarcasm in her voice. "He was less concerned about me traveling than you are, dear!" After Karim kissed her tenderly on the forehead, she added, "We went through so much to get those visas. You shouldn't worry about me; let me worry about myself, okay?"

Then they discussed the matter as two physicians, not as husband and wife, and agreed to wait until two days before their travel date to determine if Sara felt well enough to go.

"Get better quickly!" Karim teased. "The children miss your cooking! I can only make the same simple meals so many times." He tried to change the subject to ease the tension.

"Did Ameer's transcript arrive yet?"

Karim looked out the window at the burning sun and the clear summer sky. Heat waves were shimmering off of the hospital's parking lot. "Yes, it did, and he did just fine."

Ameer had just finished high school and earned near the top marks in his class. Two weeks earlier, right before Sara became ill, Karim and Ameer had another lengthy discussion about Ameer's future.

"Son, are you sure you want to become a physician? It's hard work, and you have many other talents. You are excellent with people and gradually becoming more proficient in English. You have outstanding leadership qualities as well." Karim's concern was that Ameer's skills and abilities might be better suited to another profession.

"Dad, I can use all my skills in medicine," Ameer answered. "I've grown up watching you and Mom. I'm sure this is what I want to do with my life."

"The academic requirements are very tough... and then there is the internship and residency to consider. I know that most of your friends want to be doctors or engineers, but there are more choices than medicine or engineering. I just want you to fully consider all the options."

Karim saw Ameer's skills as being better suited for the arts or in media and public relations. Medicine was attractive because it offered a guaranteed future of money and status, but despite these benefits, if medicine was not right for Ameer, he would not be happy.

"I'm doing this for the right reasons, Dad. I want to become an otolaryngologist." There was no equivocation in Ameer's tone. He was certain, or as certain as a teenager can be about his future profession.

Although Ameer was an Arab, because he was Palestinian he was not accepted into the public universities of Arab countries, despite the fact that his marks and test scores were superior. He had applied to private universities in Egypt and Jordan—schools that would accept Palestinian students. But he really wanted to go to school in North America.

A week after Sara was discharged from the hospital, she was feeling well. She could not carry heavy objects and had to avoid getting jostled as much as possible, but she was okay. So they made the decision to leave. Then Karim and Sara gathered their kids and explained that it might be difficult for a while and that they were going to a place with people they did not know. There might be some discrimination. There would be some communication problems because English was not their native language. Cultural differences existed in terms of clothes, family relationships, drinking, praying, marriage, etc. Karim told his children that they would respect those differences, but they would not compromise their principals.

He knew that his younger kids did not understand what he told them. They would discover on their own what life was all about in North America. With a degree of sadness, he knew that his kids would now be subject to all of the temptations of modern Western society, but he was confident that he had raised them properly and that they would make good decisions.

So in August 2000 Karim's family began their big adventure. First, they spent a marvelous week in England with Leen and her family. Karim had not seen his beloved sister in almost ten years. They talked for hours—in many ways it was as if they had never been apart.

Then it was on to Canada.

The flight from London to Toronto was smooth. Thankfully, Sara had not been required to lift anything, and there was no turbulence to speak of on the flight. Karim spent most of the time looking out the window at the vast Atlantic Ocean below him. His anxiety rose a bit as they got closer to Toronto. He was not worried about the decision to immigrate; he just hoped that all of his paperwork was in order. Too many times before in his life, he had difficulty crossing national borders. While he knew this time things were different, old memories haunted him.

After retrieving their baggage, they passed through the customs line smoothly. They made their way to the Immigration Office at the airport. This was a new land for them—new faces, new people, new rules. Karim and Sara both wondered, what would the immigration officers be like? They hoped they would be fortunate enough to deal with a nice person or at least someone efficient who would process them quickly and send them on their way.

Any worries they had were soon forgotten. A nice immigration official reviewed their paperwork, and in less than two hours they were processed and sent on their way. Everything was in order, and there were no complications. This came as a mild surprise to Karim because he simply was not accustomed to uniformed customs officers treating him well. He asked the officer where he could go to find transportation, and they left the airport and took a cab to Toronto.

The city fascinated the children. The tall buildings were a sight to behold. Toronto was neat and organized—cars were carefully parked in driveways, lawns were closely mown, garbage and recycling trash cans were in front of every house and large trees were everywhere. Unlike Saudi Arabia, Canada was very green.

They were headed for Mississauga. A friend of Karim's had helped him find a place to stay for a short amount of time until he figured out where he and his family would like to settle. Their apartment was well furnished and overlooked a park. From their balcony there was a terrific view of a lake and the downtown Toronto skyline.

Karim and Sara were pleased to see so many diverse people all going about their business in peace. It felt like the world had converged in one place. Karim remembered his father telling him about the other nations that lived beyond the Mediterranean Sea. Now he was here, in a country far away from Palestine. While he had no illusions that Canada was a perfect, Karim felt content. He had no doubt that he had taken his family to the right place.

A few days later, the family took a trip to Niagara Falls. It was an amazing experience for everyone. The dull roaring sound of the falls was soothing and reassuring. The kids loved playing in the mist and looking up at the water spilling over the edge and down into the river below. They rode the Maid of the Mist and got thoroughly soaked as the boat got close to the gigantic waterfall.

A couple of weeks later, Karim found his way to Peterborough, a suburb of Toronto. Through connections, he reached out to a Libyan urologist and an Egyptian engineer who had been living in the area for decades. They helped him get acquainted with Trent University. He also met an Ethiopian who was the Head of the Mathematics Department at Trent.

Peterborough was a small town that was conveniently located in the greater Toronto metropolitan area. There were friends here, and the city was both safe and serene, so they decided to make it their new home. Ameer had chosen to attend college at Trent. The family found a nice little house to rent in a quiet part of the city near a golf course, grocery store and public transportation stops.

Sara met Dr. Afaf, a biochemist who was married to an Egyptian man, and they quickly became good friends. Dr. Afaf helped Karim's family get assimilated in the area and especially helped Sara adjust to life in her new home.

Most of Karim and Sara's neighbors were native Canadians. They were skeptical at first, not sure what to make of their new Arab neighbors, but Sara's warm and open nature quickly won them over.

Their next door neighbor Wally was an older man who lived with his wife, Selma. Sara loved to garden and take care of the yard. Nothing made Sara happier than when she had her hands in the soil and was planting or trimming something. Wally loved to work in his yard too, so he and Sara saw each other on a daily basis. They developed a ritual.

As soon as the kids left for school, she would appear dressed in her all-purpose trousers, a long-sleeved denim jacket, gardening gloves and one of her colored head scarfs. Wally would then pop out, and they would exchange greetings. Soon they were exchanging plants and gardening tips. He showed her which plants and shrubs were most appropriate for the area, the ones that could endure the cold winter weather and some that did not lose their color all year round. It was not long before they became good friends with their neighbors.

Karim and Sara were worried about the schools their children would attend. The culture was a concern because the kids were not accustomed to Western mores and ways. A bigger issue was the need for the kids to be enrolled in an English as a Second Language program. It took a bit of searching and homework, but in short order they found a nearby school that could accommodate their children's special needs.

Canada provided a nurturing environment for growth and self-actualization for every member of the family. The ethnic, cultural, and religious diversity exposed the kids to different worldviews and expanded their horizons. Community events kept them busy and introduced them to new experiences.

Karim registered his family at a local YMCA sports center. The kids learned to play musical instruments and took drama lessons at school. The local mosque co-organized an annual interfaith event called Abraham's Day where Muslims, Christians and Jews came together for interfaith dialogue. Karim and Sara loved this event and enjoyed meeting their Christian and Jewish neighbors.

An eighth-grade teacher at Prince of Wales School named Mrs. Holland played an important role in their young daughter's life. Mrs. Holland took an interest in Leen and went above and beyond her duties; she contacted the Individual Educational Plan coordinator at the school and arranged for Leen to take the Otis-Lennon School Aptitude test.

A couple of months later Karim and Sara were told that Leen was a gifted student. They were asked if they would like to move her to a local school for gifted children. Leen politely declined the offer since she loved her school and friends and did not want to move again. However, the school made an Individual Educational Plan for her and offered her means to enrich her learning as she continued to be part of Mrs. Holland's class.

Salam was given guidance and special attention with a group of students from multiethnic backgrounds. His group took frequent field trips and engaged in regular cultural exchanges. One of his teachers, Mrs. Cristall, took a special interest in Salam and helped him integrate into Canadian society. One result of Mrs. Cristall's efforts was that Salam became highly motivated to learn English.

The years passed quickly and peacefully. After the required waiting period ended, Karim's family was invited to receive Canadian citizenship and officially swear allegiance to Canada and the Queen. Karim was pleased. Canada had wholeheartedly embraced him and his family. They now felt part of the country.

Citizenship also meant receiving a recognized passport that would allow him to travel with freedom and dignity. Now he could fly to international medical conferences without any problems. No longer would airport customs officials have to struggle to determine what to do with his inadequate travel document for Palestinian refugees every time.

The citizenship ceremony was held in Oshawa. The entire family was excited and picked out nice clothes for the occasion. They bought Canadian flags to display their patriotism as they walked in the courthouse. Karim's children put temporary tattoos of the Canadian flag on their faces.

The proceedings were short but remarkable. The courtroom was full of a diverse group of people with one thing in common—in a moment they would all be Canadians. The judge walked in, gave a short speech and asked everyone to rise. He then asked all the new citizens to repeat the oath:

> I swear that I will be faithful and bear true allegiance to Her Majesty Queen Elizabeth II, Queen of Canada, Her Heirs and Successors, and that I will faithfully observe the laws of Canada and fulfil my duties as a Canadian citizen.

All present swore the oath in unity and then they sang the national anthem for the first time as citizens.

جمهورية مصر العربية
وثيقة سفر
للاجئين الفلسطينيين
CANADA
PASSPORT
PASSEPORT

Chapter 24

THE PASSPORT

Passport

They did not recognize me in the shadows
That suck away my color in this Passport
And to them my wound was an exhibit
For a tourist who loves to collect photographs
They did not recognize me,
Ah… Don't leave
The palm of my hand without the sun
Because the trees recognize me
All the songs of the rain recognize me
Dont' leave me pale like the moon!
All the birds that followed my palm
To the door of the distant airport
All the wheat fields
All the prisons
All the white tombstones
All the barbed boundaries
All the waving handkerchiefs

All the eyes
were with me,
But they dropped them from my passport
Stripped of my name and identity?
On a soil I nourished with my own hands?
Today Job cried out
Filling the sky:
Don't make an example of me again!
Oh, gentlemen, Prophets,
Don't ask the trees for their names
Don't ask the valleys who their mother is
From my forehead bursts the sword of light
And from my hand springs the water of the river
All the hearts of the people are my identity
So take away my passport!

Mahmoud Darwish

FOR THE FIRST 15 years of his life as a physician, Karim lived and worked in Riyadh, but he was not a citizen of the Kingdom. He had permission to live and practice medicine in Saudi Arabia, but he remained a Palestinian refugee in terms of national identity.

The only travel document Karim had was his Egyptian-issued Palestinian Refugee paperwork. This was not an Egyptian passport and did not even allow Karim to travel to Egypt without obtaining a visa.

When the British ruled Palestine from 1924 through1948, they issued British passports to the people there. The official documents were entitled "British Passport—Palestine," but they were valid forms of identification and they allowed Palestinians to travel freely to most countries of the world. When the British left Palestine in May 1948, these passports became invalid. The new State of Israel issued passports to its citizens, and Jordan issued passports to the Palestinians who were living in the West Bank, then under Jordanian control.

As for the Palestinian refugees living in camps in Gaza, Syria or Lebanon, they were people without a homeland. They were not issued passports; in most instances they could not get any official identification, vote in elections or buy homes or land. Even getting permission to work was sometimes a problem.

Jordan allowed hundreds of thousands of Palestinian refugees to resettle there and become citizens. Most of these refugees came from the West Bank area. But after 1988, Jordan stopped allowing Palestinians to freely immigrate there.

Egypt, Saudi Arabia, Lebanon and other Arab countries refused to create a standardized and convenient method that would allow Palestinians to become citizens of their country. The answer as to why was complex, but it revolved around two main issues.

First, the Arab countries did not want to take any political steps that might be seen as acknowledging Israel's right to exist. If they absorbed Palestinians into their society, allowed them to become citizens and fully integrated them, they would no longer be refugees, and therefore, their claim to Palestine would be greatly diminished. Second, Arab countries did not desire to take in these refugees because of the tremendous burden required to integrate such a large and economically challenged population. Also the hard truth was that many in the Arab world viewed Palestinian refugees with prejudice and disdain.

This ugly and messy situation left people like Karim in a perpetual state of limbo. Some—very few but some—Palestinians managed to escape Gaza or Lebanon, etc. and make their way into another country and apply for citizenship. After the Six-Day War in 1967, the October 1973 War and the signing of the Camp David Peace Accords in the late 1970s, it became abundantly clear that Israel was here to stay. Yet the problem of what to do with the Palestinian people not only remained, it had been amplified; there were far more refugees now than there were in 1948.

In many ways, the creation of the State of Israel can be viewed as the crux of all of the turmoil in the Middle East over the past 60 plus years. The massive displacement of people caused by the creation of Israel has never been addressed. There has been no justice or compensation for the refugees, and the refugees have not been offered a new home of their own.

Many, or perhaps the vast majority, of Palestinians in the refugee camps are not interested in relocating to anywhere but Palestine. By becoming citizens of another country, they believe that they would be giving up their birthright, homeland and very identity. Although the refugees are now two or three generations removed from those originally displaced, the feelings of loss and the desire for a national identity burn just as strong in the Palestinian refugees of today.

The Palestinian issue can be compared to other historical displacements. For example, those suffering religious persecution in Europe fled to America and established a new home there in the 16th and 17th centuries. Australia is a country established by those seeking a better life overseas. The Jews lived for centuries in other nations after being dispersed by the Romans in 70 A.D. National borders are regularly redrawn.

Some say accept reality and move on. But there is really nowhere for the Palestinian people to go. The states they are living in will not allow them to integrate, Jordan being the partial exception. Other Arab countries will not accept them en masse. The poverty and turmoil in the camps breeds a simmering discontent. Radicalism is bred in the hopelessness. It is a self-perpetuating cycle of hate.

Karim was faced with a difficult choice. He could remain stateless and raise his family in Saudi Arabia. Against all odds and even common sense, he could refuse to become a citizen of another country and steadfastly maintain that his country was Palestine, a nation that simply does not exist. Or he could try to immigrate to another country that would accept him as a citizen and raise his family there in peace.

Almost immediately after being sworn in as a new citizen, he went to the Canadian passport office in Whitby. After doing all that was required of him, he left the office after being told that passports for him, his wife and children would be sent to him by mail in six weeks or so.

A month and a half later, the postman delivered a registered package. With a sense of wonder, Karim opened the large envelope. There were passports inside, proof that he was indeed a citizen of Canada, and as such, free to move around the globe with relative ease. Just as important, he now had a permanent home in a stable, peaceful and prosperous country. His wife and children were safe, and their future was secure.

He thought about how far he had come since those tough days of his childhood growing up in Al Shati. Back then, he could not have imagined that he and his family would be able to settle down and live normal lives thousands of miles from Gaza. It still did not seem totally real.

The weekend after Karim and his family got their passports, Karim and Sara drove to New York City. While they both wanted to visit New York, the real purpose of the trip was to test the validity of their passports. Intellectually, he knew this exercise was silly. Of course, his passport was genuine. However, knowing that and experiencing that were two different things.

As they pulled up to the United States border checkpoint, a flurry of thoughts competed for his attention. He had been to border checkpoints many times before crossing from Gaza into Israel, from Israel into Jordan or from Gaza into Egypt. Each of these times there had been fences and military vehicles and soldiers with guns manning the border. Crossing the border had always been a time when he considered the possibility of being arrested or turned away or at least being seriously inconvenienced and detained.

As he pulled into the checkpoint, Karim did not notice any outward display of force. He drove into a pull-up kiosk, much like a toll booth on an expressway.

"Good morning, sir. Welcome to the United States. May I see your passports please?" the U.S. Border Patrol agent politely asked him.

Karim handed the officer his and Sara's passport. When he did, Karim looked around anxiously. He was nervous as if by some bizarre set of circumstances his passport was invalid, or it was all a cruel hoax or…

"Enjoy your trip to the United States," the officer said as he handed the passports back. For a second Karim just sat there and smiled at the officer.

Then Sara nudged him. "Darling, the officer wants you to drive on."

"Yes, of course." He put the car in gear and moved off.

Now he knew it was real. He allowed himself to relax and enjoy the moment. For the first time in his life, he truly felt free. They continued on to New York City.

The next morning after breakfast Sara asked, "Karim, what shall we see first in New York?"

"There is so much," Karim said. "Times Square, Central Park, the U.N. But I want to start by visiting the National September 11 memorial and museum."

"Why?"

"I want to pay my respects to the 3,000 people who were murdered by terrorists on that day. They were innocent victims. As a Muslim, I should deny and condemn such criminal acts."

They spent all morning and most of the afternoon at the September 11th memorial. Karim stood at the base of the towers, which are now gigantic fountains, and tried to imagine what it was like on that awful day. As he looked around, Karim recalled the images he had seen on television of commercial jets slamming into the sides of buildings.

Whether it happened in New York City or Gaza City, terror was terror; death was death. Violence answered nothing and solved less. He said a silent prayer for all the victims of this massacre and thanked Allah that he was alive and well and living in freedom.

The next day they visited the United Nations Headquarters in New York. This was the source of all of the help he and his family had received over the decades. Without the UNRWA, Saeed's family and many others may have starved to death. Looking at the United Nations Headquarters building, Karim said a silent prayer of thanks and asked God to hasten the day when the UNRWA would no longer be needed, when the people of Palestine could fully integrate into their nation and become economically self-sufficient.

Chapter 25

DREAM HOUSE 2010

I Come From There

I come from there and I have memories
Born as mortals are, I have a mother
and a house with many windows,
I have brothers, friends,
And a prison cell with a cold window.
Mine is the wave, snatched by sea-gulls,
I have my own view,
and an extra blade of grass.
Mine is the moon at the far edge of the words,
and the bounty of birds,
and the immortal olive tree.
I walked this land before the swords
turned its living body into a laden table.
I come from there. I render the sky unto her mother
when the sky weeps for her mother.

And I weep to make myself known
to a returning cloud.
I learnt all the words worthy of the court of blood
So that I could break the rule.
I learnt all the words and broke them up
To make a single word: Homeland…

Mahmoud Darwish

IT WAS TIME for Saeed's family to gather. A joyous event was planned. Hana, Omar's daughter, wanted to be married in Palestine. While she and the groom lived in the United Arab Emirates, her fiancé was from Gaza. This was the opportunity Karim and his siblings had anticipated; it was the right moment to make many dreams come true.

The desire for freedom and the yearning for a better life had scattered Saeed's children. Once, long ago, they huddled together precariously in a makeshift shelter in Al Shati. Back then, Saeed and Miriam struggled just to keep everyone alive and well. More than three decades later, Karim was settled in Canada. Leen was living in England and Omar in the United Arab Emirates. Yasin was now a French citizen. Ali, the eldest of the siblings and the youngest brother, Adam, had remained in Gaza, and both of them were prosperous.

None of them had forgotten their father's desire to someday return to the family home in Beit Daras. This was Saeed's most fervent wish, a flame of hope he kept burning for his entire life, despite the fact that Beit Daras was no more and his house had long since been razed by Zionist occupiers.

The time had come to realize Saeed's dream, at least as much as it could be realized given the realities of the 21st century. The wedding was to take place in the house Saeed and Miriam's children built for the family in Gaza. While it was not on the land the family had owned for generations in Western Palestine, it was on land they owned in Gaza. Beit Daras was a memory, but it was still very much alive in the minds and hearts of a family that had survived decades of persecution and triumphed over great adversity.

A wedding ceremony in the Palestinian tradition is not just the marriage of a couple; it is an announcement of the union of two families. But this wedding was much more than the union of two families. In a very real way it was a life-affirming statement in the midst of an ongoing national tragedy. It was the family's way of saying they had not forgotten their roots; they were Palestinians no matter where they may live. It was their way of affirming that the beauty of Palestine was still alive. Traditions endure. People endure. Foreign armies can take land, force can be used to expel innocents from their homes and steal their treasure, but no soldier can destroy what love has written on the soul.

Karim and his family boarded a plane in Toronto, bound for Egypt. From there they would make their way to Gaza. He had flown to all parts of the globe for humanitarian purposes, medical conferences or to see relatives, but this was the first time in many years that he and his siblings would be together in Gaza.

On the long flight to London, his thoughts wandered. As he watched the flight attendants see to the passenger's needs, he looked at his kids and said a silent prayer thanking God for His mercy. His children were not raised in a refugee camp. His kids had never known poverty or war. They had not been forced to live under the yoke of oppression. They were still Palestinian in many ways but also Western. Karim was happy about this. His goal had been to make a good life for his family, and he had succeeded.

But despite their freedom and prosperity, something would always be missing. His children were now two generations removed from the great injustice that had been done to their grandparents. As they got older, would they remember where they came from? Would their children remember? Their children's children?

Regardless of the struggles, compromises and triumphs of the AlShaikh family, one fact remained inescapable—this wonderful celebration of life should be happening at the family home in Beit Daras. The entire community should be participating. Muslims, Jews and Christians should be living together in peace, respecting each other's right to worship God and live as they choose in the Holy Land, the nation of Palestine.

While in many ways it still seemed like yesterday, it was in fact decades ago when Karim was a boy living in the Beach Camp. He recalled the countless hours he had spent talking with his father about life, God, honor and what it meant to be a good human being. He had done his best to pass Saeed's wisdom on to his children, to teach them the life lessons he had learned from his strong but gentle father. Had he succeeded? He thought he had. All of his kids were well-adjusted young adults with budding careers and bright prospects for the future.

As the North American coastline disappeared behind the wing of the plane, he closed his eyes. When he did, he saw Al Shati as it once was and in many ways still is—a miserable place filled with people who only wanted to leave, to live a better life and to give their children a chance at happiness. He saw the soldiers marching through the streets, heard the fighter planes roaring through the sky and saw the bombs exploding. He heard the Egyptian radio station playing and the announcer telling him the lie that the Arabs were winning the Six-Day War. Karim remembered the curfews, the beatings, the constant harassments and the endless insults. He remembered his young friends being hauled off to prison. He remembered the night the Zionists came for Omar and how they almost lost him forever. He remembered his baby sister dying in the primitive shelter they were forced to call home.

Karim's mind was flooded with questions. Why were they, young children, stopped in the streets and searched by soldiers on the way to school? Why did they have to see bloodshed? Why was he not able to come back to Gaza whenever he wished to see his family? Why was he not allowed to stand by his father when he was injured by that damned bullet? Why was he not even able to attend his funeral, just like he was not able to attend his mother's funeral a few years before?

There were simply no valid reasons why all of this had happened. Well, Karim reminded himself, there was a reason—simple human cruelty, the desire to dominate and subjugate rather than to live in peace.

How often had he seen this over the years? This disease was not particular to Palestine; it existed throughout the world in Somalia, in Iraq, in the United States, in Europe—it was sadly universal.

What happened to Karim and his family was inexcusable, yet the chain of violence, the cycle of hate had to be broken.

When Karim looked again at his children and his wife, he said to himself that the cycle had been broken, at least in his family. Omar, Leen, Yasin and their children had broken it. Ali and Adam were still in Gaza, still caught up in the unending search for peace and justice, but they had not succumbed to the temptation of retribution and revenge. Was this enough? Was the answer to what happened to the Palestinians in 1948 simply to relocate, to move on? Was the solution to abandon their homeland forever, to forget about the idea of making what once was come alive again?

Then Karim's thoughts turned to his parents. They were not here to celebrate their family's joy. This left a sour taste in his mouth, but then he thought about everything his parents stood for, how they had lived their lives. Would they want him to dwell on the negative, on everything that still was not right? Or would they want him, his brothers and sister to celebrate life and be happy? Karim knew the answer, and he smiled.

The larger questions of Palestine would have to wait. For now there was a wedding to be celebrated. He vowed as he flew towards London that he would choose to be happy and not become lost in sadness.

Everything from his childhood was not grim. While they had little money and their circumstances were difficult, there was an abundance of love in Saeed and Miriam's home. He recalled how his family used to talk and laugh with only candlelight to see their food on dark nights. During one of those nights Saeed had told his children, his eyes glowing with the reflection of the orange oil lanterns, "My sons, and my dear daughter. Love and knowledge are the two weapons that are unbeatable in this life."

Miriam had added, "As long as you love each other, you will never go astray. And remember that God said, 'Indeed, their eyes are not sightless. Rather, what is blind are their hearts within their chests.'"

The love Karim shared with his brothers and sisters had not faded over time. Despite being separated by long distances, they had managed to stay close and connected. Each of them had risen above the poverty of their youth and soared to great heights. Ali was the director of the United Nations Relief and Works Agency's Health Division in Gaza. Omar was an engineer for a multinational oil company. Leen was the principal of Manchester, England's most famous high school. Yasin was a physician, a consultant in anesthesia and chronic pain management and the head of the ICU unit in his hospital. The youngest brother, Adam, was the owner of a successful telecommunication company, providing telephone and Internet services to Gaza.

After landing in London and switching planes, Karim and his family arrived in Cairo. There they met up with Omar and Yasin and their families and together they traveled to Rafah. As Karim enjoyed the ride, talking with his brothers, nieces and nephews, he recalled crossing the Sinai many years earlier on his way to Tanta to start university. Now under Egyptian control for many years, the Sinai was no longer littered with the rusting shells of burned out tanks or other refuse of war. He was not traveling in a bus that was more of a rolling jail than a transport vehicle. Now he was passing the time talking with his loved ones and catching up on what everyone was doing.

Waiting for them in Rafah were Ali and Adam. After a brief delay at the crossing point, the brothers were reunited.

"Welcome and thank God for your safety!" Ali said as he saw Karim, Omar and Yasin. They exchanged hugs and then the entourage climbed into three cars.

The cars made their way north along the coast. It was not long before the brothers passed by Al Shati. Sadly, the camp was still there, housing refugees with no other place to go. Karim looked at the camp and let out a heavy sigh. He looked at his brothers, but no one said a word for a moment.

Then Omar offered, "That is the past. We are driving towards the present."

"You are starting to have a few white hairs, my brother," Karim teased.

"Perhaps it's better to have white hair than none at all!" he teased back.

"The both of you," Adam said, pointing at Karim and Ali, "are rapidly becoming bald guys."

Yasin laughed. Then all the brothers laughed.

"Is Leen at the house?" Karim asked.

"She is," Ali answered. "She arrived two days ago."

"Wonderful," Karim said. "How about you, Omar? Still swimming out to the oil platform rather than taking a perfectly good boat?"

"Have to do something to stay in shape," Omar said.

Ali said, "We finally finished the health survey for the U.N."

"What will come of that effort?" Karim asked.

"Perhaps more funding, better clinics. We must keep the pressure on them for more resources."

Now they were close to the shoreline. Karim looked at Yasin. "Do you remember what we used to do around here?"

"Yes, of course," he said. "You loved to build sand castles. You got so angry when the tide came in and destroyed them. You always said the same thing when that happened, 'One day I'll build a house the tide cannot destroy.'"

"We did it, Karim," Adam said. "No tide will ever come near this house."

They pulled into the driveway, and there is it was, right before Karim's eyes. Of course, he had known what it looked like before he arrived. He had spent countless hours going over the blueprints and looking at pictures from various stages of the construction process.

Saeed's family house had taken ten years to construct. A large portion of each sibling's savings had been used to construct the residence. They called it simply "the house," but it was more of an apartment building than a house. On the ground floor was a large, open reception room, and on the roof was a sitting area. Each of the six floors in between was a separate residence, one floor for each of the brothers and sister. An elevator in the middle of the building serviced each floor.

The building was white with blue accents that stretched in a bowed fashion to cover the balconies on each floor. Each balcony was protected from the elements by a glass sliding door so the space could be used year round. The house was covered with Jerusalem mountain stones in keeping with Palestinian heritage.

Karim was overwhelmed. It was indeed a dream come true. Although Saeed shared in its planning, he was not on Earth to see its completion. Karim could feel his father's presence as he walked in the front door and into the reception hall. This was Saeed's house. His dream had been realized, as far it was possible.

Many thoughts were competing for Karim's attention as he took his time walking through the ground level. He was truly happy, full of joy. He felt the satisfaction of having done a great thing for his mother and father, while at the same time creating a place where his family could gather for years to come.

Was this house a metaphor for all of Palestine? He pondered this thought as he watched his children bring in his family's baggage from the cars. This house should be in Beit Daras, but it was in Gaza. Did this make the house any less beautiful or any less precious? No, he answered himself. Perhaps this was the way of things in Palestine now—no one could get exactly what he wanted or felt that he was entitled to by justice, but somehow God would see that all was made right in the end. He considered the idea that the solution was perhaps not what they envisioned because they did not see Palestine through God's eyes; they saw it through their own.

Karim sighed, took a deep breath and was the last to ride the elevator to the first floor, which was Ali's apartment. The door to the apartment was a meter in front of the elevator. He could hear the wonderful sound of many people laughing and talking behind the door.

When he opened the door, Ali was there to greet him. "Enter with your right leg, my brother! May it be a blessed home!"

Karim did as he was asked. He heard Leen's and his wife's voices coming from the kitchen, so he immediately went there.

"Welcome home!" his sister shouted as soon as she saw him.

They embraced. Karim loved his sister in a special way. They had always been close since they were young children. No matter how long it was between visits, Karim and Leen seemed to pick up right where they left off as if time and distance had no bearing on the fullness of their relationship.

After he greeted Ali's wife, he turned and faced a mirror that was hung behind a door leading into the kitchen. He was completely unaware of it until he saw his reflection, but a single tear was running down his cheek.

Adam noticed this and smiled at him. "May God send blessings and mercy on their souls."

Karim listened to what his brother said. Then he understood why he was crying. Saeed and Miriam should have been here to share in this happiness. This was their celebration.

He nodded. Before he and Adam could continue their conversation, they heard Leen announce, "Dinner is served!"

The dining room in Ali's apartment was jammed beyond capacity. The smaller children went to the living room to eat because there was simply not enough room to accommodate everyone.

"I prepared maglooba," his sister announced. Miriam was famous for Maglooba; it was one of her specialty dishes. Leen served it with a green salad, yogurt, and plates of olives and pickles, in the proper traditional fashion. The whole family ate and laughed. The clicking of the plates and spoons gave a rhythm to the conversations of the family.

The food was delicious. But what Saeed's family ate was not just food; it was a symbol of their gathering, a signpost of their origin. They ate Miriam's cooking, a traditional Palestinian plate their mother prepared like no other. Maglooba means "flipped" in Arabic. The yellow-brown Egyptian rice and meat with potatoes, eggplants, onion and garlic was cooked in a pot and flipped outside-down when it was served so it looked like a cylindrical cake.

As the meal concluded, Karim noticed how each of his nieces and nephews had a different accent when they spoke the Palestinian dialect. The family was united today, but their speech patterns testified to the distances between them. All of the young people looked strong, healthy and happy.

His mind was full of thoughts of his parents, of meals past, of the many times he wanted to be in Gaza with his parents and brothers but was prevented from doing so. He knew that his life was full of strange events; twists and turns that simply could not be expected, much less predicted.

The brothers retired to the glass-enclosed balcony in Ali's apartment. There were orange sofas on the balcony and a large table in front of the sofas. Arabic coffee was served.

Karim stood and walked toward the glass sliding door. He opened it and looked at the Mediterranean Sea that was only 500 meters away. The smell of the sea was comforting and familiar to him—this smell was his most vivid and enduring memory from Gaza. He stood there, lost in his thoughts, looking at the ocean and sipping his coffee for a minute or two. Yasin and Adam then joined him.

"I love that sea," Karim said.

"This portion of the Med is unlike any other," Omar said as he approached his brothers from behind.

"By God, I miss it," Yasin added.

Now all the brothers stood on the balcony watching the waves splash against the sand. Karim saw himself and his father standing on the beach in the fading light of day. Saeed often brought his sons to the seashore to watch the sunset together.

"Mother used to say that her wish was to see us all together under one roof," Adam said, breaking the silence.

"She said to me," Ali added, "'I entrust to you, dear, that all of you will take care of each other and never let anything in this life tear you apart.'"

They all nodded in agreement. They knew their mother's words and wishes because they were imprinted on their hearts.

"Well, Ali, where are the keys to my apartment?" Karim asked his older brother.

"Just a minute. I'll get them for you." Ali went inside and then reappeared a moment later on the balcony. "Here are the keys. I suggest you get some sleep, my brother. You look really tired."

"Yes," Karim said. "I am exhausted."

When his brother handed him the key, Karim's thoughts immediately flashbacked to his father.

Many times while growing up in Gaza, Saeed shared his Beit Daras house key with Karim and his brothers. Despite everything, their father never gave up his precious key to the family home. It was an old-fashioned bronze skeleton key with pins on both sides. No one was allowed to hold the key unsupervised. The key Ali gave him was modern, but when Karim looked it, at all he saw was his father's old key.

The apartment was not yet fully furnished, but an inviting bed waited for him. As Sara and his children continued to enjoy the company of the family downstairs, he fell into a deep sleep.

He was awakened a few hours later by the sound of the call to Magrib prayer at sunset. Tonight was the "Night of Henna," the first night of the wedding festivity. The close family of the bride and the close family of the groom would get together soon. This celebration was not formal, yet it was a crucial step leading to the wedding ceremony. The bride and groom would see each other one last time today before they left hand in hand as husband and wife tomorrow.

Chapter 26

WEDDING DAY

The New Testament

Love is patient and kind. Love is not jealous or boastful or proud or rude. It does not demand its own way. It is not irritable, and it keeps no record of being wronged. It does not rejoice about injustice but rejoices whenever the truth wins out. Love never gives up, never loses faith, is always hopeful, and endures through every circumstance.

Three things will last forever—faith, hope, and love—and the greatest of these is love.

1 Corinthians, Chapter 13

BY EARLY EVENING, the bride and her family had begun to apply the henna tattoos that are a part of the Palestinian wedding tradition. They were settled in Ali's apartment. The bride chose floral henna tattoo patterns that matched her dress. The tattoos were temporary and would fade away after a few days.

The groom's family and friends were gathered on the ground floor, in the reception room. The groom himself had not yet arrived—he would make a more dramatic entrance a little later. Karim's and his brother's eldest sons greeted all the guests, male and female, and directed the women upstairs.

Just before the groom arrived, Karim went up to see how his niece was doing. She was wearing a modern version of the traditional Palestinian dress, or Jallabia. The dress was pink and made her look like a beautiful spring rose. She was nervous but smiling. He gave her a kiss on the forehead and wished her well.

As he was walking downstairs, he heard a commotion. The groom's car had arrived. All the men walked outside and stood in two lines forming a human entryway into the building. The women went to the outside balcony and watched as the groom stepped out of the car and was greeted by applause and roars of approval.

Before settling into his own party, the groom went upstairs to spend a few minutes with his future wife and her friends and family. All of the ladies wanted the chance to see the groom, who was dressed elegantly.

Karim soaked it all in. He wanted to stop time, to freeze the house and everyone in it and extend the celebration forever. He cherished every cheerful face, every broad smile and every second of this blessed event. People were happy, and no one was discussing anything other than how wonderful it was to be alive. The sorrow that all too often permeated life in Gaza was completely absent this night. For one special moment, there was nothing even remotely bittersweet—it was as if everything was right with the world.

On the ground floor, the chairs were arranged in a large square around an open middle area. Each chair was covered with a red cloth to make them uniform. Tables were set up with coffee and tea and sweets on them. The groom made the rounds, being sure to greet and spend some time with everyone. Then music started playing.

The younger men stood and danced the Dabka. Upstairs the women had their own music and dancing going. A magnificent symphony of loud voices, music and feet stomping continued in the AlShaikh home until almost 11 p.m.

After the groom's family had left, Karim, his brothers and their families each retired to their own apartments. Yasin, who like Karim was making his first visit to the family home, had not yet even modestly furnished his apartment so he and his family stayed with Karim.

The children were restless. Karim could hear them scurrying about and chattering as he and Sara got ready for bed. It was an exciting time, and with so many new relatives to meet and wonderful sweets to eat, it would be a while before all the young ones settled down.

All of this made Karim profoundly happy. He went to bed that night ignoring the dull roar from the younger kids in the main room. How many times before had he gone to sleep in Gaza while other members of his family were still awake and active? Hundreds of times, only the last time he did so, he lived in Al Shati and was a teenager.

Seven hours later, as the sun rose from beyond the city to the east, Karim woke to pleasant aromas. The smell of the sea was the first thing he noticed. The light salty breeze was unique to Gaza. Karim had lived around and visited oceans in many parts of the planet—in North America, Africa and the Middle East—but there was nothing quite like the smell of the Gaza Sea. The other scents were coming from the kitchen where a traditional Palestinian breakfast was being prepared.

Lying in his bed half asleep, Karim could easily distinguish the smells of the three separate dishes. Dogga, a traditional Arabic recipe of ground spices with sesame was eaten with olive oil and bread; fool, or beans, was cooked with tomato sauce and a number of spices until it became a thick liquid that was topped with diced tomatoes, olive oil and parsley; and falafel, the meal that is now served around the world. In Palestine, falafel is made like in no other place, with green, leafy vegetables integrated into the dough. It is stuffed with onions and spices.

Now everyone was up and ready to eat. Karim, Yasin and their families filled their plates and carried them down to Ali's apartment where everyone was gathered. As they sat at the table eating their breakfast, Adam said, "Don't fill your stomachs. There is going to be plenty of food around this evening."

"I'll fill my stomach twice then," Yasin joked.

Dipping his bread into a bowl of olive oil, Karim asked his brothers, "Do you remember how many different ways our father used this?"

"Olive oil was a lotion, even a tonic. He used to drink it in the morning!" Yasin answered.

Everyone laughed. There was nothing more Palestinian than olive oil. At times back in Al Shati, olive oil was all the family had to work with. It had to fulfill multiple roles in the household; looking back on it now, that seemed silly to the physicians sitting at the table.

"How did we ever survive?" Ali asked.

"Because we had two parents who loved us more than they loved themselves," Adam answered.

"Indeed we did," Karim agreed. No one said a word for a moment—they were lost in their thoughts.

Adam broke the silence. "I need at least three young men to help me in the backyard."

After breakfast, Karim's two sons and the bride's brother went with their youngest uncle to prepare the backyard for the day's celebration. They were not really preparing the space—six workers had spent many hours there the day before, setting up chairs, installing temporary water fountains and putting up tents—but they did need to apply the finishing touches.

In the center of the backyard was a large olive tree, which was encircled by six smaller olive trees, one for each of Saeed's children. Saeed himself planted all of the olive trees one year before his death after the first floor was finished. They were not hundreds of years old like the olive trees were back in Beit Daras, but they were trees of a more than respectable size.

Walking into the backyard, Karim watched his sons and Adam tidy up so that the grounds were as close to perfect as possible.

Ali came up from behind him and squeezed his arm. "Father used to say to me that olive trees were sacred. He believed that their outstretched limbs offered continual prayers to Allah."

"He said to me once that when we lost our home in Beit Daras, the olive trees cried," Karim said. "I never really understood what that meant, how a tree could cry."

"We have wept a thousand tears for Beit Daras. Our father wept a million more, but today is a day for nothing but happiness."

"Yes, nothing but happiness." He did not sound convincing, even to himself.

One of Ali's daughters ran up to her father. "The weather forecast is good today. Light winds and no rain."

"We are blessed," Ali said.

"Very much so," Karim agreed.

A locally famous cook had been hired to prepare the wedding feast. As planned, the cook and his crew arrived early. A temporary kitchen had been set up behind the center olive tree. No sooner than the cook arrived, the local butcher appeared. He brought with him three fine calves, slaughtered earlier that morning just for this occasion. It was not long before the smells of cooking meat and rice being prepared with traditional spices and chickpeas filled the air.

Upstairs the women were busy readying themselves for the wedding and helping the bride perfect her appearance. A hairdresser had arrived early, and she would be busy fixing the women's hairdos until right before the ceremony began.

In keeping with the Palestinian tradition, the bride and groom had been legally married a week earlier by the Ma'athoon. Even though their union was already official, the bride would not go home with her husband until after the wedding ceremony. This gave everyone a few days to adjust to the new arrangement. For the bride's mother, in particular, this was an important time. It allowed her to say goodbye to her daughter and adjust to the idea that her child was now a woman with a home of her own.

The wedding celebration included a drum and flute band and a group of professional Dabka dancers. A poet was standing on stage to greet the guests as they arrived with traditional verses. This same poet was also a singer; he switched between reading verse and serenading the guests in song.

Everyone from the neighborhood was there, along with the groom and bride's extended families. No one was excluded—this was a community event. When the 200 or so guests were all gathered in the backyard, the music changed, and people stopped talking and paid close attention to the entrance. The bride and groom came in, hand in hand, and took their large, red seats under the center olive tree. The groom wore a traditional Palestinian wedding outfit that sparkled under the lights, with white pants and a black rope tied in the back. He wore a black and white Kuffiya on his head. The bride wore a white dress decorated with a silk hood.

As is the custom, the men sat on one side of the backyard, the women on the other. Soon the band played, and the dancers performed.

In the West, a wedding ceremony usually ends when the bride and groom exchange vows. At that point, everyone files out of the church or hall and goes to a separate location for a reception. In Palestine, the wedding and reception are united into one event. So the party began and continued for hours as the Dabka dancers and young children danced and the band played on.

After a time, Karim saw his brothers all standing to the side and watching the ongoing party. He joined them. No one said a word for a moment. The same thought was on all of their minds. Adam spoke for all of them when he broke the silence and said, "If only they were here."

Karim nodded, as did his brothers. With this wedding, the house Saeed's sons built in Gaza had now officially become the AlShaikh family home. Karim's silent prayer was that his sons, nieces and nephews would continue to gather here—not only for weddings but for all important family occasions.

Who could know the mind of God? This was unknowable, yet standing there watching 200 Palestinians dancing and celebrating Karim allowed himself to speculate.

A third of the people he was looking at lived in different countries, yet all of them had roots in Palestine. For their children and their children's children, Palestine would only be a place their family was from, not their home. For Karim AlShaikh, no matter where he lived, Palestine would always be home. But did this unjust and unfortunate circumstance perhaps serve a higher purpose?

What greater good might come from all these wonderful and blessed people sharing themselves and their lives with the rest of the world? Would some genius who was destined to discover a cure for the next virulent plague that threatened mankind be born from one of the women in this room who now lived Canada, the UAE or Europe? Perhaps in some way the diaspora of the Palestinian people served a higher purpose.

This was a pleasant thought, but it was interrupted by seeing in his mind's eye the tragic pictures of his father and the residents of Beit Daras being forced to flee their homes in 1948, to abandon their heritage. What possible greater good could ever atone for that injustice? Right now, not 40 kilometers from where he standing, the land that was his family's heritage by birthright was owned by some Zionist who "legally" expropriated it by fiat. How was that in any way just?

Karim wondered how his father would feel today. After a moment's reflection, he knew that the answer to this question was simple—he would be enormously happy. Saeed would still have the key to his home in Beit Daras in his pocket, but he would not allow that key, that memory, that injustice, to diminish the love and joy he would feel watching his granddaughter get married.

ArcMed Hotel AlMashtal
Gaza 2011

Chapter 27

2011
A NEW FRIEND

Promises of the storm

So be it
I can assure you that I will refuse death
And burn the tears of the bleeding songs
And strip the olive trees
Of ill their counterfeit branches
If I have been serenading happiness
Somewhere beyond the eyelids of frightened eyes
That is because the storm
Promised me wine and new toasts
And rainbows
Because the storm
Swept away the voices of idiotic, obedient birds
And swept away the counterfeit branches
From the trunks of standing trees
So be it

I must be proud of you
Oh wounded city
You are lightning in our sad night
When the street frowns at me
You protect me from the shadows
And the looks of hatred
I will go on serenading happiness
Somewhere beyond the eyelids of frightened eyes
For from the time the storm began to rage in my country
It has promised me wine and rainbows

Mahmoud Darwish

SHORTLY AFTER KARIM returned from Somalia in 2011, he attended a medical conference in Seattle, Washington. The conference was about the practice of adolescent medicine in general, not the plight of refugees in Africa or the Middle East. Nevertheless, his philanthropic work was no secret to his colleagues.

One of these colleagues was an American physician named Lee Walker. Lee had met Karim before and expressed an interest in the general subject of the plight of the Palestinian people. After reuniting in the hallway during a morning break in one of the sessions, they decided to go to lunch later that day so they could talk.

"As I recall, you're from Gaza, Dr. Karim."

"Yes. I was born and raised in the Al Shati refugee camp, the Beach Camp as it's called in English," Karim responded.

"That must have been rough, Doctor."

"Please, call me Karim. Have you done any research on Al Shati or on Palestine in general?"

"I have many Jewish friends. They've told me in great detail about the tragedy of the ongoing violence over there."

"I see," Karim said. "Perhaps then you already have enough information on the subject."

"You are the first person I've ever met from the area… Palestine… who is not Jewish," Lee admitted.

"What would you like to know?" Karim asked as he took a bite of his pasta.

"Why do the Arabs hate the Jews so much? Is it all about Islam and Judaism, a religious conflict?"

"First of all, I'm a Palestinian. Some Palestinians are Muslims, some are Christians and some are Jewish. Palestine was a nation for centuries before the State of Israel was formed in 1948. Where do you think all the people in refugee camps in Gaza, Lebanon and Syria came from?"

"I'm not really sure," Lee admitted. "I've always wondered about that."

"My father, who was a young man in his twenties at the time, was driven off of his land in 1948. We had a family farm in a village called Beit Daras in Palestine. Today our village is gone. Israel expropriated my father's land, his house and exiled him to a refugee camp."

"I know some people were displaced when Israel was formed."

"An entire nation was displaced. About one million people. Those that remained are slowly being choked out of existence or put behind walls and segregated. Palestine was destroyed when Israel was formed."

"So the people in the camps are direct descendants of those original refugees?"

"Yes, just like me," Karim confirmed.

"Israel has not compensated you? Given you land somewhere else? Cash maybe?" Karim laughed. He really liked Lee and believed that he was a good man, just ignorant of the facts. "Did I say something funny?"

"No. Lee, so many people in the West simply don't know what happened to the Palestinians. The American mainstream media to a large extent is biased. Anyway, I—"

"I want to know the truth, Karim," Lee said with conviction.

"My family has never received any money from the State of Israel. Neither have any other Palestinians. Most of my countrymen live in refugee camps and have done so for six decades."

"Why don't the Palestinians go elsewhere, like to Egypt or Saudi Arabia?"

"Short answer? They don't want us, and the refugees want to go back to Palestine. I was very fortunate. I went to medical school in Egypt and was employed as a physician in Saudi Arabia. From there I made my way to Canada."

"Can't the Palestinians and the Jews make peace? Share the land?"

"The problem is intractable. Many have tried and failed to make peace," Karim explained.

"The Oslo Accords and all that." Lee took a bite from his sandwich.

"The Oslo Accords made promises neither side could keep. The Palestinians want their land back—their land is now the State of Israel. The Israelis want to take the rest of Palestinian land that they don't already control. Men and women of goodwill try to seek compromise, but more often than not, hatred prevails."

"I cannot imagine living under such conditions."

"Many have died, are dying and will die in the future suffering under such conditions. It is a human tragedy wrapped in a political nightmare."

"Do you visit Gaza often?" Lee asked.

"I still have family and friends there. It will always be home, where I am from, where my heart lives. My brothers and sister built a house there, a place where we can all gather."

"I would like to go with you and see Gaza for myself."

"That's a noble idea, Lee. As a physician, you would have a unique perspective."

"I've seen all the violence on TV. Gaza has been a war zone." Lee paused, sipped his iced tea and then repeated, "I would like to go to Gaza with you."

"If you clear some time on your schedule, call me. I promise I'll take you there."

"Don't be surprised when your phone rings, Karim."

Laughing, he said, "Okay, Lee."

They continued their lunch and talked more about Palestine. Karim sensed that Lee was sincere in his desire to learn more about his homeland. It was by no means his fault that he was born and raised in North America and that he had many Jewish friends. Karim had many Jewish friends; that was not the issue. The issue was the disastrous effect of Zionism on the Palestinian people.

Nine weeks after the conference in Seattle ended, Karim was relaxing at home in Peterborough when the phone rang.

"Hello, Karim. It's Lee. Lee Walker."

"How nice to hear from you. Glad you called."

"I'm calling you with a purpose, Karim. I'd like to go with you to Gaza. I'm not completely sure why, but I feel compelled to see it for myself."

Karim was taken aback. He recalled their conversation in Seattle, but honestly he had thought Lee's sentiments were only well-intentioned conversation. "You're serious?"

"Yes. Are you planning any trips to Gaza shortly?"

"Next month, in fact. There may not be time for you to secure all the necessary approvals to enter Gaza, but we can try."

"How do you get to Gaza?" Lee asked.

"We must fly to Cairo then take ground transportation to Rafah on the border in the Sinai desert. We enter Gaza through Rafah. There really is no other way to get there."

"I'm in."

"I'll call you tomorrow with some details," Karim said.

"You'll get the same answer tomorrow—I'm in," Lee said. "Oh, and Karim?"

"Yes?"

"I owe you an apology. Since our last meeting in Seattle, I've done some homework. I'm not as ignorant as I was before. I've looked at pictures, video… I've read a great deal of material. I'm beginning to understand."

Karim was speechless.

"Karim, are you there? I didn't lose you, did I?"

"No, I'm here. I'll call you tomorrow."

"We'll talk more then," Lee said. Karim hung up the phone.

"Karim?" Sara asked.

"Dr. Walker wants to go with me to Gaza. To see the situation for himself."

"Is he an official of some sort? Does he work for the U.N.?"

"No, he's just an American physician who wants to see Gaza. For some reason, the Palestinian issue matters to him."

"Will you take him?" Sara asked.

"Yes, of course. I'd like to take a hundred American doctors over there and then have them report back to their friends and neighbors. But I suppose one will do."

Karim called Lee the next day. He was even more eager to go to Gaza, so they made their travel plans and agreed to meet in Cairo in mid-December.

"First you must go to the American Embassy," Karim explained to Lee as they talked over tea at an outdoor café in downtown Cairo. "They can call the Egyptian authorities and arrange for you to be allowed to leave Egypt."

"I'll pay a visit to the embassy tomorrow. You went to medical school here?"

"Yes. Sara and I met here too. Cairo will always be a very special city to me."

"Egypt is on the brink of revolution, or so it would seem."

"All across the region people are rising up against oppression. Change is in the air," Karim said.

"Will what happens here have any impact on Gaza?"

"Probably not. At least not directly. It is a very good thing that people are asserting their rights, but not all change is positive. These are dangerous times."

"How long do you think it will take for me to get the paperwork done at the embassy?" Lee asked.

"Do you have an appointment?"

"Yes."

"Perhaps it can be done in a day. But Lee," Karim paused, considering his words. "Just because the American Embassy gives you the proper paperwork, that does not necessarily mean they will let you into Gaza. I'm just preparing you for complications."

"It's sound like in this part of the world there are always complications," Lee said, finishing the last of his tea.

"Count on it."

The next day Lee went to the American Embassy and met with a staff member. He emerged three hours later with the required documentation that would, in theory, allow him to leave Egypt. The travel documents came with a warning—visit Gaza at his own risk.

Early in the morning, they took a taxi to the border. They arrived at the Rafah Egyptian checkpoint at 10:30 a.m. The officer reviewed Karim's paperwork, then Lee's. He told them that Karim was allowed to enter Gaza, but Lee was not. This came as little surprise to Karim, but the denial upset Lee. They argued for an hour with the officer, explaining over and over again that they were physicians on a humanitarian fact-finding mission and that the American government had spoken with the Egyptian authorities and so on. Their pleas fell on a deaf ear.

Rather than give up, they chose to wait in a staging area, a place where people who wanted to enter Gaza could wait and see if their request would be granted. Karim was unhappy that they were denied entrance into Gaza, but he was pleased that Lee was getting a small taste of what it meant to be a Palestinian. Being detained for no valid reason, repeatedly searched and questioned, treated as if you were a lesser person—this was part of daily life for Palestinians. Lee talked on his cell phone to people back in the American Embassy in Cairo, urging them to do something, to call the right people, to make it happen. Karim also made phone calls to his friends and associates in the Palestinian Authority and the UNRWA in Gaza.

After they had made their phone calls, they approached the officer again and made their case that Lee should be allowed entry. Again they were denied. They sat back down in the waiting area, unsure what to do next.

A young man—he looked to be in his mid-twenties—approached Karim and Lee. He was not unkempt, but he looked like he had not bathed in a while.

"Speak English?" the young man asked Karim.

"We both do," Karim said, gesturing to Lee.

"Problem… not allowed to go to Gaza?" the young man said making eye contact with Karim and then Lee.

"Problem, yes," Lee answered. "Can you help?"

"I can get you into Gaza. Now, no waiting."

"You have influence with the officers here?" Lee asked hopefully.

"No, he doesn't," Karim answered. "He can get us in through a tunnel. We pay him, and they allow us to crawl underground and pop up inside Gaza. Is that right?"

The young man replied, "Yes, that's right."

"Will you be around here all day?"

"You can easily find me."

"We will keep your offer in mind. Thank you," Karim said.

The young man nodded at them in turn and walked across the crowded room.

"Perhaps we should consider his offer," Lee said.

"Do you know what he wants us to do?" Karim asked. "For a fee he—"

"I will pay the fee."

"It's not the money," Karim explained. "It's the risk. Do you have any idea what he's asking us to do?"

"I assume he has some tunnel, a way of sneaking into Gaza."

"These tunnels are very dangerous. Many of them are very small. They are called 'the tunnels of death' for a reason—they collapse regularly. People are killed making them and more people are killed using them to cross over."

Lee thought about it for a second. "If there is no other way then I'm willing to take the risk."

Karim nodded but said nothing. This was a dangerous turn of events. He was not at all sure if it was the right thing to do to allow Lee to risk his life in a tunnel. Then again, his friend had traveled a long way, and he had the right to try to get inside Gaza.

An hour passed. They made more phone calls. The young man offering entry by tunnel kept looking over at them, but Karim had not summoned him over to conclude a deal. Then the officer called them over to his station.

"Passports," the officer said.

They gave him their passports.

He stamped each passport and said, "Have a safe trip." Then he motioned for them to move on.

Once they were in Gaza, the situation was much different. The Palestinians welcomed them with open arms. In moments, Dr. Lee and Karim were walking around Rafah, looking for a cab to take them to Gaza City.

The taxi ride from Rafah to Gaza City was an eyeopening experience for Lee Walker. It was one thing to see what was happening in Gaza from the comfort of his home in North America on video but quite another to witness it firsthand.

As the taxi drove up the coast, Lee saw the bombed out buildings and the rubble created by relentless Israeli aerial and artillery attacks over the years. Most of the buildings that still stood were pockmarked with bullet holes, had broken out windows or were otherwise in a state of serious disrepair. Gaza was in a perpetual state of turmoil. Nothing was "normal" here, except for conflict and strife.

"Israel pulled out of Gaza in 2005. Is that true?" he asked, not taking his eyes off of the unpleasant scene that was passing by outside the window of his cab.

"Yes, that's true. When I was a small child, Gaza was administered by the Egyptian government and the United Nations. After the 1967 War, Israel occupied Gaza and remained here in force until 2005. But even though their troops are gone, Israel still controls everything: the utilities, the airspace, the sea. Gaza is an open air prison."

"British Prime Minister David Cameron used that term last year to describe Gaza, an 'open air prison,' and he took a lot of heat for it."

"About one and a half million people live here in extreme poverty. They cannot leave, they cannot work in Israel, and they have no access to the means to improve their plight," Karim said. "Gaza is most certainly a prison; there can be no other word for it."

"The Israelis will not allow Gaza to function as a separate country? To import goods, export products, conduct banking, etc.?

"No. The hard truth of the matter is that the Zionists simply do not care if my people live or die. What they do care about is keeping a lid on attacks against Israel."

"The rocket attacks," Lee said. "Yes, I've read about them."

"Some militant Palestinians send primitive rockets into Israel that do very little damage. Israel responds with state of the art weaponry and levels houses and public buildings, killing hundreds. As I said, the cycle of violence is seemingly endless. This is all very personal to me, Lee."

The taxi stopped at an intersection. It was almost night now, near 6 p.m. They watched a group of young boys, no more than 10 or 12, as they walked past the cab.

"That was me and my brothers in 1970. The look in their eyes—did you see that? They are not completely defeated; there is much life in them, but they are trapped. Is it any wonder that young men become violent under such conditions? It is more of a wonder that all of them are not filled with hate."

"You," Lee said, as the cab rolled on, "how did you escape the hatred?"

"My parents, my father in particular, taught me that hatred is not only contrary to God, it is counterproductive. It accomplishes nothing; it only destroys."

"I have not told you this until now, my friend, but now is the time. I have visited Israel—twice in fact. I have a good friend in Tel Aviv."

"Yes, I understand," Karim said.

"I cannot say that I believe that the Israelis I met are intent on hurting you or these people. They look on the matter as a security issue. I remember them saying to me, about the rocket attacks, 'If someone was lobbing missiles at you in the United States, how would America respond?'"

"I understand that as well. Here is the problem. There is just no escaping certain facts. Most of the people in Israel now are too young to remember the events of 1948. Those young boys that just walked by us, their grandparents were the original refugees. People can talk and debate all they want. The inescapable truth is that while millions of Palestinians live in Gaza, Lebanon, Jordan and Syria, they have no home. It is also an inescapable truth that millions of Israelis live normal lives in a prosperous country. Most of them are also too young to remember the events of 1948, and most of them are not Palestinian Jews; they are settlers, colonizers, who came to Palestine after the Nakba.

"Unless some justice—a place to live, a chance to raise their families in peace, a stable, secure home—is given to the Palestinian people, the cycle of hate will never be broken."

"What does justice look like now, Karim? Do you have any idea?"

"When I was in grade school we talked about what it would be like when we returned to Palestine. That event, Palestine being reborn, seemed inevitable to us in 1966. Then the Arab armies were crushed in the 1967 Six-Day War, or the Naksa. So what would justice be like for me today? I am a Canadian citizen. I have a prosperous life, wonderful children and the ability to help others. I am very, very blessed. But for my father? Do you know, until the day he died, he carried his house key to the old family home in Beit Daras in his pocket?"

"That's very sad, Karim. Also very telling," Lee responded.

"So what does justice look like for Saeed? I'm not sure. His generation has passed. The living must settle things, not the dead. What I am sure of, completely and totally sure of, is that this violence must end. People of goodwill, those touched by a loving God, must solve this seemingly unsolvable problem. Evil is winning here, Lee, and it's been winning for 60 years. This must stop."

As Karim said this, the cab drove by the Al Shati refugee camp.

"In there, Lee," Karim said pointing at the camp, "is Al Shati. That is where I grew up."

The cab went by too quickly for Lee to get a good look at the camp. It was also now nearly completely dark outside. "Can we go there tomorrow and see your old home?"

"I'm planning on it. Look ahead of you."

The brand new Arc Med Al-Mashtal Hotel was twinkling in the distance. This was where Karim and Lee were staying. It seemed incongruous—a five-star resort in the midst of such a war torn and challenged place.

"So that is the hotel. Quite honestly, even though I looked at pictures of the hotel online, I'm astonished that it's really here."

"As I told you," Karim said as the cab pulled up to the hotel, "many things about Gaza will surprise you."

They met for breakfast in the hotel restaurant the next morning. Lee ordered an American eggs and toast meal while Karim ate locally made bread, olive oil and cheese. They both enjoyed Sadah, a bitter tasting Palestinian coffee akin to espresso.

"I'll bet the pool is crowded in the summertime," Lee said, as they finished their breakfast. From where they were sitting, they looked out at the swimming pool. It was off season, so Lee assumed there was no one using the pool.

"Probably not. Most Gazans cannot afford to come to this hotel; they would rather go to the beach where they can swim for free. Nice decoration though," Karim said, returning the smile.

"Where is our first stop?"

"I thought you might like to visit the UNRWA—The United Nations Relief and Work Agency for Palestine Refugees in the Near East—and the Center for United Nations Aid in Gaza. You'll get a better idea there of the huge amount of food and other essentials that must be brought in constantly to care for the people here."

After they had eaten, Karim took him to the United Nations building, the Islamic and Al Azhar Universities and then the Ministry of Education. Their brief tour took most of the morning. Then Karim had an idea. He asked an official at the Education Ministry if he could visit his old high school, which was not far from the ministry building. This was not a problem, and the Education Ministry provided an escort to walk with them to the high school.

When they got to within a block of the school, Karim began to travel back in time. Everything looked the same, even the kids. They were still dressed in old clothes that had been well cared for and most likely handed down from older siblings. The school building had not changed either—there had been no additions or significant renovations in four decades.

The students were thrilled when Lee and Karim introduced themselves. As an American, Lee was an instant celebrity. While many Palestinians have negative feelings towards the United States government because of its unwavering pro-Israeli policies, they hold individual Americans in high regard. When Karim addressed the class in Arabic and told them that he was once one of them, every face lit up. Many could not believe it—someone from Gaza was now a physician who traveled the world? Karim could see the hope in their eyes as they listened to him speak. Lee soaked in every word, gesture and smile.

When they concluded their remarks, the students were allowed to address the physicians. It was no surprise to Karim when the youngsters told him that their biggest concerns were fear for their lives from the constant clashes between Palestinians and the Israeli soldiers, the extreme poverty, the lack of employment and the general lack of any real resources and infrastructure. If Lee could have stepped back in time 40 years and addressed Karim's class, he would have heard these exact same complaints.

When they were about to leave a teenage boy, Karim guessed that he was around 18 or 20, rolled into the classroom in a wheelchair. The Principal wanted Lee to meet this young man. The boy was paralyzed because he had been shot by an Israeli soldier while walking his brother to school. His crime? Crossing a street where children were throwing rocks at Israeli soldiers.

Lee knew the facts; he had done his homework. Israeli jails were filled with thousands of young men. The vast majority of these children were not hardened militants, at least not yet. They were arrested for protesting the conditions they were forced to endure. Their only crime was being brave enough to look down the barrel of a gun with nothing more than a stone in their hand to defend themselves.

As they left the school, Lee wiped away a few tears. He clearly did not want to weep in front of the kids, but now that they were walking away he could no longer completely control his emotions.

"Karim, it's heartbreaking, there is no other word for it. How has this tragedy gone on for so long?"

"Because the world allows it to continue. As long as the Zionists are not restrained by the West, my people will suffer. Now you are beginning to understand."

"Yes, I am. It amazes me how we can turn a blind eye to this suffering… how I could do so for so long."

"I think perhaps lunch would do us some good," Karim suggested.

"Yes. I'd like the chance to sit for a while and collect my thoughts."

A kilometer or so away from the school, they found a small open air café and walked in. They sat down and ordered lunch—bread and fried fish. As they ate, they watched the passersby. People were going about their daily business. Life was happening here despite the horrific circumstances.

"Do you get used to it?" Lee asked.

"Get used to it?"

"The conditions, the violence, the poverty—all of it."

"Gaza was all I knew until I was 18 years old. My only other experience with the world was in Israel. Back then, it was possible to work in Israel and return to Gaza. Now no one can leave. In that sense, things are worse now. Certainly the tension has increased."

"What's the answer?" Lee asked. "I guess I'm feeling a sense of hopelessness."

"The answer is very simple but very difficult to achieve. The Zionists must be forced from power but not through violence. We must share the land. Muslims, Christians and Jews must learn to live together in peace in one country whether it's called Palestine, Israel or by some other name."

"No one can agree to anything. Every peace accord withers and dies before the ink is dry on the document. How can something like you're proposing ever be achieved?"

"They said that South Africa could never become a whole nation. Many experts said that the experiment in equality would fail. While South Africa still has many problems and is far from perfect, it is one nation now. It can be done."

"You're suggesting something akin to the United States post the Civil War, a complete reintegration of your nation based on one person, one vote? A true democracy?"

"There is no other way," Karim said. "As impossible as it is to conceive, nothing else is really possible. The door we must pass through is very narrow. Both the Palestinians and the Israelis will have to compromise."

Lee stopped talking and looked around again. He had been to Tel Aviv and Jerusalem. He had sat in cafes there too. What a different scene that was. While Jerusalem was a bit more diverse and tense, it was nothing like this. Israel was a prosperous, modern nation. Like America and Canada, daily life was all about taking care of your family, doing your best at your job and generally enjoying life.

"Gaza is incredibly beautiful. The beaches in front of the hotel—I could see them filled with tourists from all over the world."

"Yes, the potential is here," Karim agreed. "We can thrive together, but first the hatred must stop. The idea that God promised this land to one ethnic group and one only—that mindset must no longer rule the central government. The definition of justice cannot simply be the descendants of the original refugees taking back all of their lost land and property. Compensation must be given in different forms."

"How far is Al Shati from here?"

"About a 20-minute walk. I will take you to the house where I grew up."

Adam, Karim's youngest brother, was waiting for them at the old house. Saeed's kids had maintained the home and allowed people to visit there after Saeed's death.

"Here is the main room of the house," Karim explained as they walked in the front door. "When I was growing up here, this main room and the small room behind it were all that existed. We added the two additional rooms after I finished medical school."

"Six children and two adults lived here?"

"Yes," Karim said, and Adam nodded. "For most of the time while I was growing up, there was no running water, no sewage system, no electricity, no garbage pickup, nothing."

"Why haven't these people been integrated into Gaza City or into other established neighborhoods?"

"The biggest problem is the lack of employment opportunities. If you cannot earn an income, you cannot pay rent or buy a home. My people might as well be living on a desert island."

"Everything required to sustain this and the other camps must be brought in from the outside?"

"Not everything, but without a constant flow of aid, these people would starve. They are starving in many ways, as you have seen. They hunger for freedom, dignity, respect and the chance to live in peace," Karim answered.

"Not everything is bleak, my brother," Adam said.

"Oh?" Lee said, clearly looking for even the slightest glimmer of light in the darkness.

"We must show him our dream house," Karim said.

"How far away is that?"

"A half hour walk at most," Adam said.

So Karim, Lee and Adam made their way out of the Beach Camp. The narrow streets were full of children playing one game or another. The game of choice was soccer. The ball was a makeshift sphere that consisted of old rags and other soft items wrapped into something resembling a proper ball.

While Lee looked at this and was sad, Karim's heart was filled with joy. The children were happy and playing. He remembered doing the same thing, playing soccer in these dusty streets and laughing and joking with Zohair and other children. This is what Karim needed to see—the future. Perhaps these children would break the cycle and not have to spend their entire lives living here.

Watching the children play strengthened his conviction that if he took these kids and put them with the same number of kids from Tel Aviv in some neutral location, say in Canada or the United States, they would immediately start playing together. Soon they would be friends. Children naturally like each other; they must be taught to hate.

How wonderful it would be if all the kids in Palestine—Christians, Muslims and Jews—could go to school together and develop a natural affinity for one another. Karim knew that this was the only way the problem would ever be solved. There must be no more "us and them" there must only be "we."

"You seem lost in thought, my friend," Lee said as they walked towards the new dream home.

"I… I apologize, Lee. When I come here, I often think too much."

"He always thinks too much," Adam said, jokingly. "That is Karim's problem—too much thinking."

"Someone in the family must think. Since you chose not do it, I had to pick up the slack."

They laughed. Lee noticed their laughter, and the joy all around him. Despite everything, most Gazans were cheerful. For a second he considered the possibility that everyone here was quite mad. How could people be happy amidst such miserable conditions? But they were. People greeted them as they walked. Clearly Adam was well known because he lived in Gaza, but no one knew who Lee was, and Karim had not lived here for decades.

Where does happiness come from? Lee asked himself silently. In the West too often joy comes from material objects or leisure or idle pursuits. Here it seems to come from somewhere else—an unconquerable spirit perhaps. Gazans were not simply enduring; in their own way, they were thriving saying to the world, "You will not completely rob our joy from us."

"There it is," Karim said, pointing up the street. "That is home now."

The house had somehow survived the conflicts in Gaza virtually unscathed. Lee thought it was beautiful, and he understood how important it was to the AlShaikh family. They built it as a statement as much as a residence—they had overcome with love, they had built and not destroyed and their family lives on.

"This is the house Saeed always wanted for his family. It's not in Beit Daras, but it is here in Gaza. Each of his children has a floor of their own. No matter where we may be in the world, this will always be home," Karim explained.

"I take it you've been working on this for a while," Lee said.

"Years," Adam answered.

"The olive trees?" Lee asked, pointing to the seven olive trees planted in the main floor courtyard.

"One for each of us, plus a big tree in the middle for our parents," Karim explained.

"Like the olive tree back in the house at Al Shati," Lee said.

"My father loved olive trees," Karim said. "He looked at them as something almost divine, as a symbol of something greater."

"Olive trees can live for centuries," Lee added. "They can endure droughts, fires, floods, any number of problems, and they will continue to bear fruit."

"You have just described Palestine," Adam said.

The next day, they left Gaza and returned to Cairo. Lee was pleased to have taken the time to see Gaza for himself, up close and personal. "There is nothing better to defeat propaganda than experience."

"I wish I could take more U.S. citizens here. They would leave feeling the same way you do."

"The world is learning; the tide is turning, my friend," Lee said. "The Palestinian people can no longer be ignored or this great injustice forgotten."

A Palestinian makes coffee next to the ruins of his house, which was destroyed during the Israeli offensive, in Gaza City, August 2014.

Chapter 28

GAZA 2014

Silence for Gaza

With dynamite she raps her waist...
She explodes...
It is neither death... nor suicide...
Its Gaza's style to announce her worthiness of life...
For four years and Gaza's flesh burst around... bomb's shrapnel...
Neither magic nor miracle...
It is Gaza's weapons and arms for her continued existence...
And the enemy's detritions it is...
For four years the enemy with its dreams rejoicing it had been...
For flirting with time it was fascinated...
Except for in Gaza...
For Gaza far away it is from her relatives...
And with the enemy it is stuck...
For Gaza is a bomb...
Whenever it explodes...

Never has she stopped from exploding…
The enemy's face she scared…
And from satisfaction with time she repelled them…
Another thing is time in Gaza…
For time in Gaza not a neutral factor it is…
The people it doesn't drive to cold contemplation…
But to the freedom of explosion…
And to collusion with truth… Time there children it doesn't take from babyhood to old age…
But men it makes of them…
With their first confrontation with the enemy…
In Gaza time is not relaxation…
But storming into the blazing noon…
Values in Gaza differ…
Differ
And differ…

Mahmoud Darwish

IN JULY 2014 Karim AlShaikh sat in front of his television with his iPad on his lap. He and Salam were monitoring the news every moment they were not working. Gaza had erupted in violence again. Hamas and its allies lobbed primitive rockets into Israel, and the Zionists responded as they always did—with brutal and overwhelming force.

As often as he could, Karim called Ali and Adam to get updates. How many people had died? Anyone they knew? Friends? Family? It was agonizing for both of them to watch the relentless shelling and bombing of Gaza. It was a nightmare that simply would not end, could not end until the world made the decision that enough was enough. Unfortunately, Karim knew that time had not yet arrived.

Then one day he saw a news report of a bombardment near their Dream House. When he told Salam, they both gasped.

Salam said, "Could the Israelis have destroyed in 60 seconds what it took 60 years to build?"

Fortunately, the answer was no, at least for the moment. Ali and Adam reported that the northern façade of their home had been damaged, but the structure was intact.

"We were lucky," Karim said. "Many homes have been demolished. Many people have been killed."

"I won't forget," Salam muttered.

"You won't forget what?"

"Palestine. Isn't that what Ben Gurion said? 'We must do everything to insure the Palestinians never do return... The old will die, and the young will forget.'"

"No son, neither of us will ever forget."

"Thank you, Father. Thank you for reminding me who I am and for providing a safe home to be raised in."

"We must tell the world our story, son," Karim said. "Palestinians are human beings, not some form of chattel to be herded and oppressed."

"You should write a book, Dad."

"A book?" Karim asked.

"Tell our story. It's easy to be prejudiced against groups; it's harder to dismiss the suffering of good people, especially men like you and Grandpa who fought so hard just to take care of their families."

"The Tears of Olive Trees," Karim said.

"What's that?" Salam asked. "The Tears of what?"

"The Tears of Olive Trees," Karim said. "That's the title of the book you want me to write."

Epilogue

UNTIL RECENTLY, MANY in the West have believed the lie that Israel was the victim—not the oppressive aggressor—in its almost 60-year campaign to destroy the Palestinian people. This is amazing since the truth is actually very simple to understand and articulate—the chief objective of Zionism is to establish and maintain an exclusively Jewish political state in Palestine.

The story of the AlShaikh family cannot be told outside the context of the tragedy that befell the Palestinian people, and the tragedy of the Palestinian people cannot be told without addressing Zionism. It is a hard fact that millions of Palestinians are forced to live in perpetual poverty as stateless refugees in miserable camps. It is also a fact that, regardless of whatever else they have done, the Zionists have built a prosperous, modern state in Palestine.

The whole idea of a "two state solution" to this problem – cordon off the Palestinians into small enclaves within a larger Jewish nation – has been fatally flawed from the beginning. Essentially, the "peace process" has been a cover for more annexation of land, the disposition of Palestinians and the expansion of settler-only zones. Such zones consistently and systematically creep into what would have been a Palestinian state under the two-state solution.

Many Palestinians, because they very keenly and deeply understand the gross injustice they have been forced to endure for many decades, see Israel only as an enemy. While this attitude is understandable, it neither reflects the reality of the situation nor does it lead anyone forward into a better tomorrow. The original Palestinian refugees, like Saeed AlShaikh, are largely gone. The founders of Israel—David Ben Gurion, Golda Meir, Menachem Begin, Moshe Dayan—and their contemporaries are all dead and buried. What is left is their legacy.

Is the idea of one Palestinian nation really so radical? It will be incredibly difficult to achieve. Extremists on both sides must be dealt with. Rule of law is the key. A political process that protects everyone's rights is essential. More than anything else, the notion that Palestine belongs to the Jews or the Muslims exclusively must simply be dismissed. Palestine belongs to all its people, not to any particular faith.

Saeed AlShaikh taught his children that respect for others, mercy and peace, are what God honors most. He fervently believed that people are basically good. He argued until his dying breath that hate does not come naturally to human beings; it must be taught. Love and forgiveness, on the other hand, Saeed believed were inherent human virtues. Many Jewish people also share these same values, these same worldviews.

Palestine cannot be an exclusively Jewish state where Jews rule all aspects of national life. There cannot be two classes of people in Palestine—Jews and Palestinians, the haves and have-nots—there must be one people with equal rights, justice and liberty for all.

If the olives would remember
Those who have planted them
Then it's oil would have become tears
Oh wisdom of the ancestors,
If from our flesh we gave you armor
But the fields of the wind doesn't give its slaves crops
We will pluck with our eyelashes
The thorns and sorrows
We will remain in the olives as their greenery
And around the earth as an armor

لو يذكرُ الزيتون غارسَهُ
لصار الزيت دمعا
يا حكمة الأجداد
لو من لحمنا نعطيك درعا
, لكن سهل الريح
لا يعطي عبيد الريح زرعا
إنَا سنقلع بالرموش
الشوكَ والأحزانَ... قلعا
سنظل في الزيتون خُضرتَه
وحولَ الأرضِ درعا

Palestinian Terms and Vocabulary

Allah: God.

Abaya: A long, black, long-sleeved robe worn by Muslim women in Arabic-speaking countries, often with a headscarf or veil.

Aqeeqah: Refers to the Moslem religious sacrifice that is offered on behalf of the newborn on the seventh day after birth.

Azaa: Condolences: expression of sympathy with a person who is suffering sorrow, misfortune or grief.

Bakhor: The name given to scented chips or bricks that are burned in incense burners to perfume the house with a rich, thick smoke. This is used specifically on special occasions like weddings or on holidays.

Dabka: It is a dance from Lebanon, Syria, Jordan, and Palestine. It is a form of both circle dance and line dancing and is widely performed at weddings and joyous occasions. The line forms from right to left. The leader of the *Dabka* heads the line, alternating between facing the audience and the other dancers.

Eid Alfetr: A holy day where the Moslems celebrate the end of Ramadan month being able to fulfill one of the Islam worshipping pillars which is fasting.

Eideya: Money or gift given mainly to the children as a celebration of the Eid.

Fajer: Dawn.

Hatta: Head wear for Arab men, usually white, black and white or red and white. Also known as Kufeyah.

Henna: The powdered leaves of a tropical shrub, used as a dye to color the hair and decorate the body.

Imam: The person who leads prayers in a mosque.

Intifada: Intifada is an Arabic word derived from a verb meaning "to shake off" and is the term used to describe the two major uprisings against Israeli military occupation of the West Bank and Gaza Strip.

Kafan: A simple, white plain cloth used to wrap a corpse in the Moslem tradition before burial.

Nakba: Arabic word meaning "catastrophe" or "disaster," which refers to the date and day of the expulsion of the Palestinians from their homeland that started on May 15, 1948.

Maftoul: Maftoul is a traditional Palestinian food, the name referring to both the grain product itself, as well as the dish prepared using it. The word *Maftoul* means "twisted," "knotted" or "twirled".

Maglooba: Inverted eaters widespread and famous in Palestine, especially in Gaza. It is rice with stir fried vegetables—eggplant, cauliflower, potatoes or green beans and placed with lamb or chicken. Maglooba literally means "upside down".

Ma'thoon: The official man who documents the marriage contract between the husband and the wife.

Ramadan: The Hijri month during which Muslims fast during the daytime.

Sherwal: A dress that covers the body from the navel to the knees or to the feet.

Tablya: It is a small handmade table, with a height of about 40 cm that allows people to sit on the floor around it.

Thobe: An ankle-length Arab garment, usually with long sleeves, similar to a robe. It is commonly worn in the Arabian Peninsula, Iraq and neighboring Arab countries.

Zatar: Thyme.

Acknowledgments

Illustrations by Rawya M. Wadi.
Special thanks to The Mahmoud Darwish Foundation.

Social Media

Website:
www.thetearsofolivetrees.com

Twitter:
@tearsoftrees
https://twitter.com/tearsoftrees

Facebook Fan Page:
thetearsofolivetrees
www.facebook.com/thetearsofolivetrees

If you are a member of the media and would like to request an interview, please contact us via e-mail at geniusmediabooks@gmail.com
Genius Media Inc.
P.O. Box 4125 Logan UT 84323 US
www.geniusmediainc.com

A Short Biography of

DR. ABDULKARIM S. AL MAKADMA

DR. ABDULKARIM S. Al Makadma is an internationally respected pediatrician and academic. Born and raised in Al Shati refugee camp in Gaza, he lived under military occupation and survived two major wars before leaving Gaza for medical school in Egypt in 1976. Dr. Al Makadma has practiced medicine in different Middle Eastern countries, rising to prominence in the fields of pediatrics and adolescent medicine. He is the author of several books in the health field and has published articles in prestigious international medical journals. As a clinician, teacher and mentor and through his humanitarian efforts, he has made friends across the globe. Dr. Al Makadma immigrated to Canada in 2000, but his heart will always remain in Palestine.

Printed in Poland
by Amazon Fulfillment
Poland Sp. z o.o., Wrocław